The Best Of Fine WoodWorking

Modern Furniture
Projects

The Taunton Press

Cover photo by David Klopfenstein

Taunton
BOOKS & VIDEOS
for fellow enthusiasts

First printing: February 1991
Second printing: July 1993
Printed in the United States of America

A FINE WOODWORKING Book

FINE WOODWORKING® is a trademark of The Taunton Press, Inc.,
registered in the U.S. Patent and Trademark Office.

The Taunton Press, Inc.
63 South Main Street
PO Box 5506
Newtown, Connecticut 06470-5506

Library of Congress Cataloging-in-Publication Data

The Best of Fine woodworking. Traditional furniture projects :
   24 articles / selected by the editors of Fine woodworking magazine
     p. cm.
    "A Fine woodworking book" — T.p. verso.
    Includes index.
    ISBN 1-942391-91-8
    1. Furniture making   I. Fine woodworking
    II. Title: Modern furniture projects.
TT197.B475   1990
684.1'.042 – dc20   90-49027
                                  CIP

Contents

Introduction

One of the nice things about being a woodworker is that you're not a slave to the whims of furniture manufacturers and retailers. Rather than just accept the samples on the showroom floor, you can make furniture that fits your home exactly and suits your particular tastes and lifestyle.

For many contemporary homes, the desired look can best be described as modern—with an emphasis on function and durability, simple, clean lines and minimal ornamentation. To help you design pieces in the modern style, this book includes 24 articles gleaned from back issues of *Fine Woodworking* magazine. Top-notch contemporary woodworkers present their techniques for building bookcases, credenzas, coffee tables and futon beds. And to reflect the demands of the computer age and leisure activities, a number of ideas are also included for computer furniture, outdoor loungers, music stands and pool tables.

—Dick Burrows, editor

The "Best of *Fine Woodworking*" series spans issues 46 through 80 of *Fine Woodworking* magazine, originally published between mid-1984 and the end of 1989. There is no duplication between these books and the popular *"Fine Woodworking* on..." series. A footnote with each article gives the date of first publication; product availability, suppliers' addresses and prices may have changed since then.

Extension Tables
Their design and construction

by Jeremiah de Rham

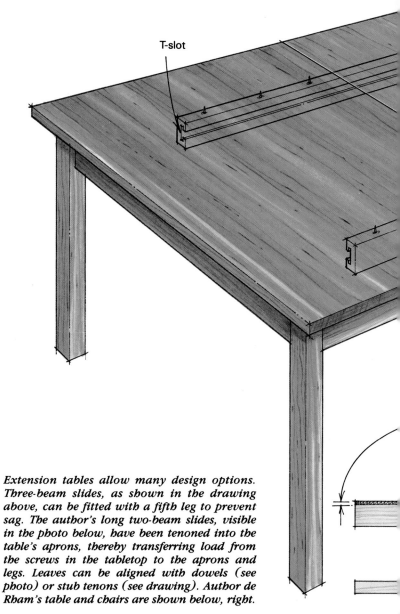

T-slot

L arge tables are wonderful for crowds of ravenous, feasting relatives. But as soon as they go home, you're stuck with a conference table for twenty—and who wants to live with that every day? Besides, where do you put such a big table? Expanding tables are the answer to filling the room and feeding the folks three times a year; adding and subtracting table leaves can transform the table into any required size. The backbone of such a useful table is a pair of table-extension slides.

Figure 1 shows the basic way any slide system operates. A single slide consists of two or more beams, sandwiched together so they can slide past each other, and held face-to-face by a coupling system. My coupling system—wooden bearing blocks screwed to the beams—works as a load-bearing mechanism that supports the weight of the table. A slide needs a small amount of play in the coupling system to work smoothly, but this play also creates some sag when the table is extended. The more beams per slide, the more pronounced the sag—especially when the table is in its fully open position. On a smaller table with just two beams per slide, sag is negligible, but a larger table with many beams can sag noticeably. There are three main ways to counteract sag and keep a big table flat: increase beam overlap, crown the slides or add a fifth leg. The table's design determines which approach to take.

Many four-legged tables are large by design—6 ft. to 8 ft. long when closed—and may not require many additional leaves. This was the case with one table I built. Closed, it measured 7 ft. 6 in. in length. The client required only two leaves, each 10 in. wide. With the table long to begin with and requiring a minimal number of leaves, the slide design was of the simplest variety: two beams per slide stretching the length of the table.

The length of the beams determines how far the table opens. Slides with two 7-ft. beams open a table 6 ft. 4 in.—allowing for an 8-in. beam overlap at the center, which I consider to be the least you can get away with. Shorter beams of 3 ft., centered under the table's midpoint, will open a table 2 ft. 4 in. (again, with an 8-in. beam overlap). Thus, either approach—7-ft. slides or 3-ft. slides—would have opened my client's 7-ft. 6-in. table wide enough to accept the two 10-in. leaves. But longer slides are superior in three ways: they effectively eliminate sag; they can be tenoned into the aprons for added strength; and they allow more leaves to be added in the future, if desired.

The farther apart the bearing blocks, the less possibility for sag. So a long table with beams from apron to apron that opens less than the full possible amount will not sag noticeably—the bearing blocks will remain 2 ft. to 3 ft. apart. When the two 10-in. leaves are in place on the table I built, the bearing blocks remain

Extension tables allow many design options. Three-beam slides, as shown in the drawing above, can be fitted with a fifth leg to prevent sag. The author's long two-beam slides, visible in the photo below, have been tenoned into the table's aprons, thereby transferring load from the screws in the tabletop to the aprons and legs. Leaves can be aligned with dowels (see photo) or stub tenons (see drawing). Author de Rham's table and chairs are shown below, right.

From *Fine Woodworking* magazine (July 1987) 65:30-36

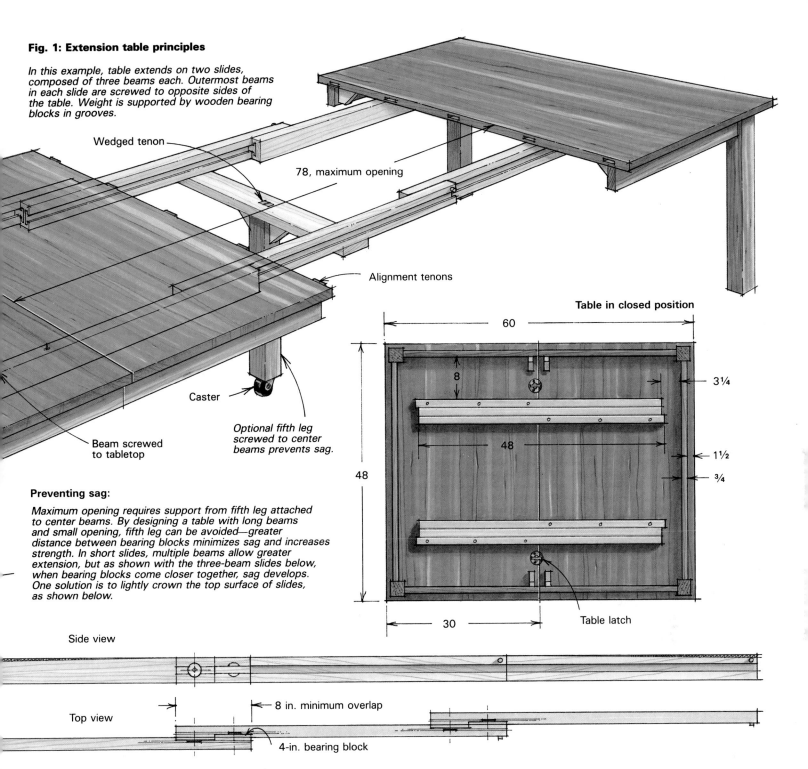

Fig. 1: Extension table principles

In this example, table extends on two slides, composed of three beams each. Outermost beams in each slide are screwed to opposite sides of the table. Weight is supported by wooden bearing blocks in grooves.

Wedged tenon

78, maximum opening

Alignment tenons

Caster

Beam screwed to tabletop

Optional fifth leg screwed to center beams prevents sag.

Preventing sag:

Maximum opening requires support from fifth leg attached to center beams. By designing a table with long beams and small opening, fifth leg can be avoided—greater distance between bearing blocks minimizes sag and increases strength. In short slides, multiple beams allow greater extension, but as shown with the three-beam slides below, when bearing blocks come closer together, sag develops. One solution is to lightly crown the top surface of slides, as shown below.

Table in closed position

60

8

3¼

48

1½

¾

48

30

Table latch

Side view

Top view

8 in. minimum overlap

4-in. bearing block

4 ft. apart. This amount of overlap makes the slides considerably straighter and stronger than if the blocks were close together. The other distinct advantage of full-length slides is that the whole table is strengthened by tenoning the secured end of each beam into the apron with a small stub tenon (figure 6). This transfers to the aprons and legs much of the weight stress otherwise carried entirely by the screws going into the tabletop.

Now suppose you want to build a four-legged table that is small to start with, say 3 ft. to 4 ft. in length, but must open up to at least 12 ft. long. With this design, you need multiple beams per slide—even with the slide beams going from apron to apron. And sag may still become a problem. Opening a 4-ft. table to 12 ft. requires four beams per slide, each 45 in. in length (this is the maximum length you can fit, assuming a ¾-in.-thick apron and ¾-in. top overhang). Allowing for beam overlap, the fully extended table will be 13 ft. 3 in. long. Adding another beam to each slide will push a little four-

Drawings: Joel Katzowitz; photos (except where noted): Lance Patterson

Fig. 2: Pedestal table

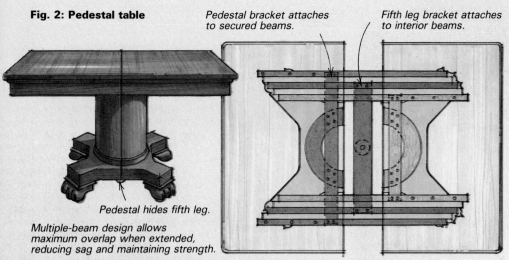

Pedestal bracket attaches to secured beams.

Fifth leg bracket attaches to interior beams.

Pedestal hides fifth leg.

Multiple-beam design allows maximum overlap when extended, reducing sag and maintaining strength.

Photo: Jonathan Wright

Photos above and below: John Michael Pierson

Jonathan Wright of Cambridge, Mass., built the ingenious three-way slider with radiating leaves shown at left. The table closes to form a three-lobed circle. John Michael Pierson of La Mesa, Calif., made an extension table (photos right) that slides on heavy-duty drawer glides (Grant #3320) concealed by the table's hollow, bent-laminated apron. Each slide assembly consists of two drawer glides screwed together, face-to-face, to allow extra extension length. When the table is extended, the glides are covered by U-shaped apron sections fastened to the underside of the wood-framed glass leaves.

footer into the big leagues at 16 ft. 4 in. Typical of any table with many beams per slide that opens a great distance, this table is ripe for sag. It's simply difficult with this design to keep the bearing blocks spread apart from each other without adding a ridiculous number of beams to each slide. If you want to avoid a fifth leg, consider crowning the slides (figure 1). This isn't difficult, just time-consuming. To tell how much the slides dip in the middle, extend the slides and stretch a string from one end of the table to the other. Theoretically, you need to plane the top of the slides so, when fully extended, the sag becomes a straight line. This often means planing up to ³⁄₁₆ in. from the ends of the beams screwed to the tabletop (planing nothing from the midpoint of the opened slides). But planing this much crown tends to crown the table itself when closed, so the idea is to strike a happy medium—planing enough crown into the slides to visually reduce the sag, but not so much that the table appears obviously hunched when closed.

Design considerations for pedestal extension tables aren't all that different. The minimal-leaf-addition/long-beam solution often works here as well. But many pedestal tables don't have aprons, and this complicates matters. Without a table apron, the slides have to be placed a little closer to the center and kept on the short side so they're not easily seen. Pedestal tables that open a great deal will almost certainly need a fifth leg, usually a turned leg hidden within the pedestal when the table is closed (see figure 2). A couple of other approaches are shown in the photos above. In one case, the three-legged "pedestal" is large enough to support the table, regardless of whether the top is in the open or the closed position. The other design uses heavy-duty drawer extensions concealed in the table's aprons as slides.

If you use a fifth leg (often two tapered legs about 18 inches apart, joined by a stretcher and riding on casters), attach it to a board screwed to the bottom of the two center beams at their midpoint (see figure 1). As the table opens, the fifth leg tends to remain centered, holding the middle beams still while the inside and outside beams travel freely. This is the surest way to prevent sag. With all the chairs in place, a fifth leg isn't that noticeable, so don't be too reluctant to use one.

Keeping all this in mind, it's easy enough to figure out the general design on paper. To find the maximum opening for leaves, draw the beams as if they were fully extended. Add the length of each beam to that of the previous one, subtracting the 8-in. minimum overlap. Then, subtract the amount of beam attached underneath the tabletop. The remainder is the available space for leaves. Those readers who are squeamish about trusting their measurements as drawn could use thin strips of scrapwood—cut to the length of the proposed beams—as models of how the various amounts of extension will add up. This provides hands-on proof that what you draw will actually work as intended.

In my search for the ultimate table slide to incorporate in a recent commission, I came across a number of designs. I settled on the one that promised versatility, strength, ease of operation and—just as important—ease of manufacture.

Factory-made table slides are available in both wood and metal, but I quickly decided against these after shopping around. The wooden slides I found were skimpy and wobbly, didn't track smoothly and were available only available in certain lengths. The metal slides worked well but, again, their prescribed length limited their use. And while metal is immune to moisture movement, I felt reluctant to incorporate metal slides into a beautiful walnut table. A custom-built dining table deserves custom-built slides.

All of the older tables I've seen utilize one of several wooden

Dovetail extension slides

by Monroe Robinson

I like the idea of all-wood, dovetail slides. The round table shown below has three sets of them. The center slide set is longer than the others, and provides that much more stability. Starting with a 3-in.-thick plank of hard maple, it takes me two or three days to complete a set.

First, rip the stock oversize. How much oversize depends on how much the stock moves and warps as it comes off the plank—$\frac{3}{16}$ in. is usually enough. I cut the parts about 3 in. over-long, then stack the pieces (with spacers) and allow them to stabilize for several days.

Next, I carefully joint and thickness the pieces. I always cut several spares—to allow for those that warp in spite of everything. I also cut several short pieces for test cuts.

I remove most of the waste on the tablesaw, flipping the stock so that both the top and bottom edges of the beams are reference surfaces against the fence. This ensures that the dovetails and their grooves are centered. The cuts are then brought to size on a router table in the same way, again centering the cuts. I aim for a tight fit, then work to the final fit using a pair of shopmade dovetail planes. I finish with a scraper, as shown in the photo at right. When final-fitting, number the slides so they will pair up again when fitted to the table.

The slide stop shown in the photo at the far right is made from $\frac{3}{8}$-in.-dia. brass tubing plugged with a short length of dowel. Epoxy holds the dowel in place, and also anchors the end of the $\frac{3}{4}$-in.-long spring. The stops engage the ends of tapered slots, which are made with a router, a $\frac{1}{2}$-in. straight bit and an angled template.

Before attaching the slides, plane down all the top surfaces that won't be screwed to the tabletop; this reduces friction. Wax is the final finish on all surfaces. ☐

Monroe Robinson is a professional wood-worker in Ft. Bragg, Calif., and an Anderson Ranch Art Center instructor.

Robinson's 58-in.-diameter table extends to a full 13 ft. 3 in., as shown below. Full-length dovetail slides require a stable wood, such as maple, and careful hand-fitting with the shopmade scraper shown in the photo, above left. The slide stops (right photo, above) engage a tapered slot about $\frac{1}{4}$ in. deep and 5 in. long.

Photo table: Hannes Krebs; other photos: Monroe Robinson

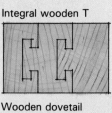

Integral wooden T

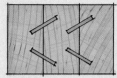

Washer dovetail

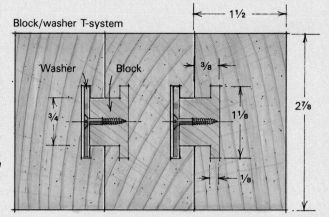

Block/washer T-system

Washer   Block

1½

⅜

2⅞

¾

1⅛

⅛

Wooden dovetail

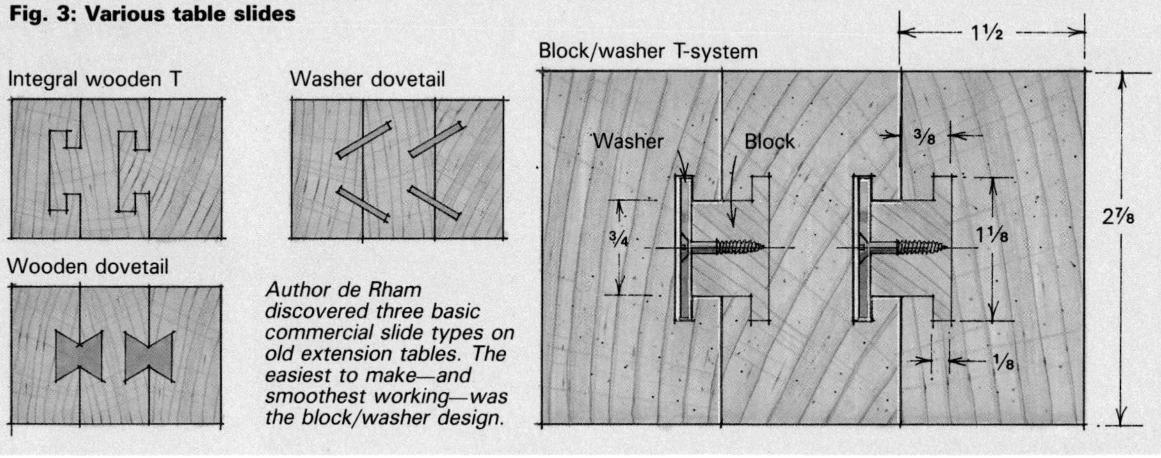

Author de Rham discovered three basic commercial slide types on old extension tables. The easiest to make—and smoothest working—was the block/washer design.

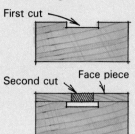

Fig. 4: Alternative method

Instead of routing, you can dado wide groove, then glue face piece and dado again.

First cut

Second cut

Face piece

slide designs (figure 3)—any of which is far more substantial than anything available commercially today. Of these, the quickest to build is what I call the block/washer system. Others include the integral wooden T, the washer dovetail and the wooden-dovetail coupling system, although I've never seen the latter on an old table. These designs all had disadvantages that I wanted to avoid. I considered using the integral wooden-T system—it appeared to be the Rolls Royce of wood slides—but it requires more stock, takes longer to build and is harder to adjust if it binds. And since wooden Ts are more easily affected by expansion and shrinkage problems, they're often greased heavily to ensure smooth operation. So on to the infinitely simple block/washer table slide.

Making slides—For the commissioned walnut table, I built two 7-ft.-long beam slides to open the table 6 ft. 4 in. But to better understand how three-beam slides open a smaller table, I'll explain how to build a pair of slides that would extend a 5-ft. table an additional 6 ft.

Selecting a straight-grained hardwood that's dry and stable is important. Maple, ash or oak all perform well. For this particular pair of slides, we'll need six beams (three per slide), measuring 4½ ft. long, 2⅞ in. wide and 1½ in. thick. Rough-mill the stock first to relieve any stress in the wood, and let it sit in your shop a couple of days. That way, it's more likely to remain straight and true when you mill it to the final dimension.

Cutting grooves for the bearing blocks is next. Each slide consists of an outside beam, a middle beam and an inside beam. The middle beam needs a groove on both faces, while the inside and outside beams are grooved only on the face that tracks against the middle beam. With dado blades on the tablesaw, cut a groove centered along the length of the beam, ¾ in. wide and ⅜ in. deep. Reference the cut from the same surface of the beams—either top or bottom—so when the slides are together, the tops of the beams will be flush with each other.

Once the grooves are cut, you must rout slots at their bases, perpendicular to the edges. The washers that hold the beams together ride along in these slots. To accommodate the washers, the slots need to be ⅛ in. wide and ⅛ in. deep. Routing out this

T-shape is a simple operation, but don't waste your time looking for an off-the-shelf bit to do it. I couldn't find one. A keyhole bit is a possible solution, but it won't cut the slots quite wide enough without widening the groove, and it'll cut too deep a slot without some alteration. Instead, I chose to alter a ⅞-in. steel rabbeting bit (shown in the top left photo, facing page) to cut the exact shape I wanted. This entailed carefully scribing the unwanted areas on the faces of the bit and then grinding them away with a high-speed hand-held grinder, using one of the variously shaped stones available. In the process, the bit's integral pilot is also ground away.

Use a router table or a router with a fence attachment. The bit will cut a full-depth washer slot on one side of the groove while, at the same time, cutting slightly into the other side of the groove. You need two fence setups to complete one T-slot. Clamp a beam to your bench and start routing. When the clamp's in the way, stop the router, leave it in place and move the clamp to the other end of the beam. Hold the router firmly, turn it on and finish the cut. Repeat this process on all beams, then change the fence setting for the opposite side of the slot. After routing is completed, the beams are ready for the wood blocks and tracking washers.

The 4-in.-long blocks serve two purposes. Primarily, they bear the weight of the table while guiding each beam along the groove of the adjoining beam. But they also serve as stop blocks to keep the beams from coming apart when fully extended (see drawing below). Place the blocks at opposite ends of adjoining beams, one block to a groove. These blocks can be T-shaped to fit the groove and slots, or they can be rectangular in cross section—the easier of the two designs to make. A tight fit holds the T-shaped blocks in place, but you'll need screws to hold the rectangular blocks.

Now, screw a 1-in.-dia. fender washer in the exact center of the bearing blocks with a flathead wood screw. (These washers don't bear any weight—they merely slide along in the T-slots, holding the beam together.) The screw's shank should be a little smaller than the washer's hole so there's a bit of slop, allowing the washer to glide along easily in the beam slots. The three beams can now be slid together. As you slide them back and forth, you may

Fig. 5: Block/washer T-system

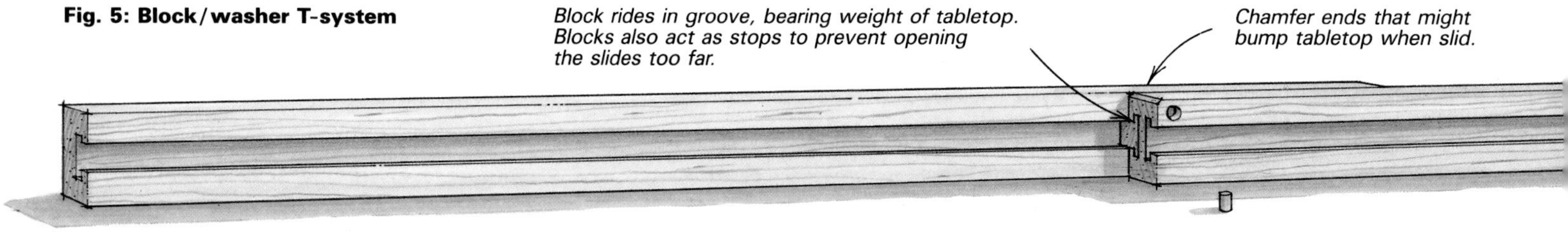

Block rides in groove, bearing weight of tabletop. Blocks also act as stops to prevent opening the slides too far.

Chamfer ends that might bump tabletop when slid.

Author de Rham demonstrates how to rout T-slots for slides. He modified a standard rabbeting bit (above, left) to enlarge the dado into a T-slot, one side at a time. The router's fence rides the side of the beam. When it reaches the clamp, de Rham turns the router off, relocates the clamp at the other side of the router and proceeds. An alternative method for machining the T-slot with glued-up stock is shown in figure 4, facing page.

notice some binding. One or two adjustments will cure these sticks. First, check to see if the washers are screwed down too tightly, clamping the beams so close that the surfaces don't want to run past each other. Loosen the screws just enough to allow the washers to run like wheels. This adjustment will also help beams that are slightly bowed. Again, slide the beams back and forth. If they still stick, one of the wood blocks probably fits too snugly in the track. To remedy this stickiness, pull the beams apart, remove the washers and take a couple of shavings from the blocks with a rabbet plane. I find that a $\frac{1}{64}$-in. to $\frac{1}{32}$-in. clearance is optimum. More than this creates too much play and sag. Smooth-planing the beams' faces and liberally applying paraffin wax will really let the slides fly.

Once the sliding action is properly tuned, put the beams together and install closure stops like those shown above right and below. Without closure stops, the beams are likely to fall apart when the table is being closed, the blocked end of one beam slipping out of the open end of another. A simple stop is a $\frac{1}{2}$-in. dowel fitted into a hole drilled $\frac{1}{2}$ in. from the open end of the outside and middle beams (see photo, top right). Drill a hole $\frac{1}{2}$ in. deep and tap in a $\frac{5}{8}$-in.-long dowel. Don't apply glue—the dowels must remain removable (with pliers) to get the beams apart. In order to stop the beams in line with each other, rout a shallow, short groove into the adjoining beam for the stop to slide into.

Now, attach the pair of slides to the table's underside. At each open, unblocked end of the inside and outside beams, drill three holes 6 in. apart, centered on the top edges, starting about two inches in from the end. Plan to use either #10 or #12 screws. Drill oversized holes, as shown in figure 6, right, and ream them further with a round rasp—to allow the screws to pivot back and forth along the length of the beam, ensuring free cross-grain movement for the tabletop. These screws are, in effect, holding the table up, so set the screws $\frac{1}{2}$ to $\frac{5}{8}$ in. into a $\frac{3}{4}$-in.-thick tabletop. For a $2\frac{1}{2}$-in. screw, countersink $\frac{7}{8}$ in. to 1 in. on the underside of the slides. To avoid dimpling the tabletop—or even cracking it—by bottoming out the screws too close to the surface, place a washer into the countersunk hole. That way, you can't tighten

The two photos above and the drawing at the bottom of the page show the geometry of a three-beam slide—the end blocks bear the weight, while the washers merely keep the beams together. As the slides extend, the center beam remains more or less in place, while the outer beams—attached to the tabletop—slide to the left and right. At the ends of the slides, press-fit dowels act as stops to prevent the beams from disengaging (top photo).

Fig. 6: Attaching slides to top

Tabletop

Tenoning the end of the beam into the apron relieves much of the stress on the screws. Taper ends of beams if apron is narrow.

$\frac{1}{2}$ to $\frac{5}{8}$

Oversize hole for slotted screw allows wood movement in top.

Apron

Washer prevents screw from coming through top.

Countersink $\frac{7}{8}$ to 1

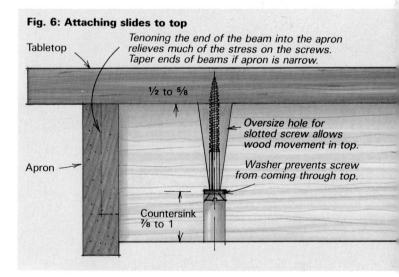

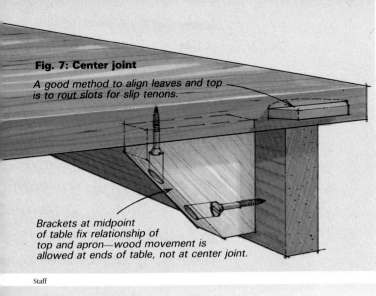

Fig. 7: Center joint

A good method to align leaves and top is to rout slots for slip tenons.

Brackets at midpoint of table fix relationship of top and apron—wood movement is allowed at ends of table, not at center joint.

Staff

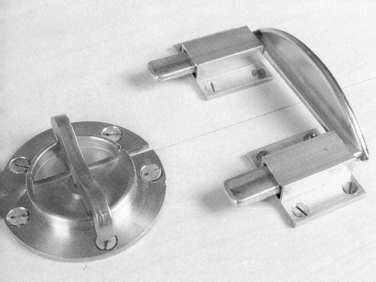

To hold an expansive table closed, round clasps, left, may be fastened to the apron or under the top. U-shaped clasps, right, are used in pairs on tables without aprons. Both clasps, Garrett Wade.

the screw heads farther into the top than planned. Use a drill press to countersink so depths are constant. And, by all means, measure carefully.

To attach the slides, place the table upside down in the closed position. Lay the closed slides down, with the midpoint of the slides at the tabletop break, pulling them open about an inch so the closure stops don't prevent the table from closing tight. Depending on the width of the table, place the slides so the outside beams are 8 in. to 12 in. in from the aprons. If there are no aprons, you may want to place the beams farther in—to ensure they'll be out of view. Mark the screw holes, remove the slides and drill for the screws. Use a wood stop block on the drill bit so you won't drill through the top. Replace the slides and screw them down, then turn the table over and push and pull until you tire of enjoying your mechanical wizardry.

Figure 7 shows how to handle the center joint of a table with an apron. At the center joint, secure the tops to the aprons with a fixed bracket; secure the rest of the top with some method that will allow the ends of the top to move (using slotted screw holes, for example). Closed, the aprons will always touch and not be held apart by a swollen top. Use table clasps (see photo, left) under the top to hold the center joint tight when the leaves are stored.

Leaf boards are usually left apronless—they're easier to store that way—but adding aprons to leaves is a nice design option. A mortised slot (made with a router and three-wing cutter) with slip tenons (figure 7) is an excellent way to join leaves. This method is very accurate to mark and easy to fit. Build a nice box to store your leaves in so they're not damaged. I've seen large hall chests that store leaves, with slots carefully lined with felt to protect the leaves as they're slid in and out. Now, invite everyone over, open up the table and enjoy. *Bon appétit!* □

Jerry de Rham is a member of Fort Point Cabinetmakers in Boston, Mass. The commissioned table and chairs shown were designed by David Handlin, an architect in Cambridge, Mass.

Another variation

by Curtis Erpelding

I built the slides for this table according to plans in Ernest Joyce's *Encyclopedia of Furniture Making* (Sterling, 1979). There are three rectangular nesting frames made of maple, each sized both horizontally and vertically to fit within the next. The slides are grooved their full length. The "bearing blocks" are full-length strips of wood glued into one of each pair of matching grooves. The frames don't need a washer system to keep them interlocked—that function is served by the short sides of each frame.

A hard-won hint to the wise: the table's diameter when closed—48 in.—turned out to be just a little too tight for comfortable dining. □

Curtis Erpelding lives in Seattle.

Photo: Curtis Erpelding

This Honduras mahogany table was chemically stained with hydrated lime.

Building Bookcases

Ideas for shelving life's clutter

by Dick Burrows

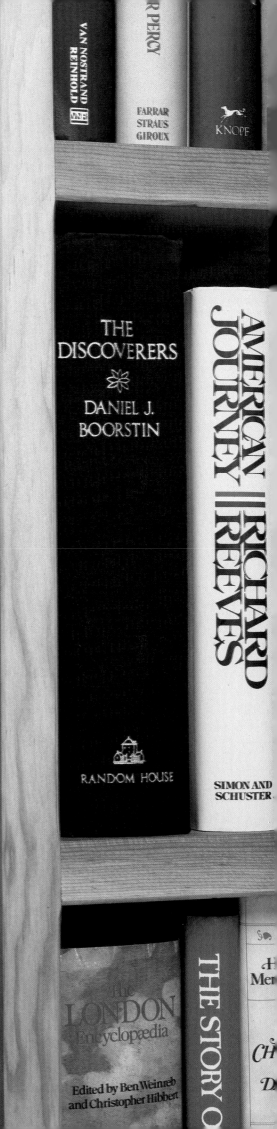

Coping with the hundreds of books, records, and assorted knick-knacks of the typical household can be a festering nuisance. Never having enough shelves, homeowners and apartment dwellers struggle many a weekend with assorted boards and nails. Even though professional woodworkers might not like to admit it, bookcases of all sorts are a major bread-and-butter item for many small shops. And, designers and interior decorators spend hundreds of dollars to make storage units into elegant and beautiful room dividers and built-ins with hand-carved moldings and leaded glass fronts.

Whether you're making a simple pine bookcase or a $2,000 room divider, the principles, and problems, are basically the same. The shelves must be spaced to accommodate specific objects; fit within the structural restrictions of a particular room; be strong enough to support the objects without sagging, racking or resembling a wooden bridge; and be attractive and blend well with the existing decor. If you're only storing old paint cans in the basement, looks aren't crucial, but in most living areas a badly designed bookcase can be a real eyesore.

If you are designing your first shelving unit, don't be intimidated by your lack of technical knowledge about spans and strengths of materials. Common sense may be the most important design factor, says David Stenstrom, shop foreman for Woodward Thomsen Co., a custom cabinetshop and millhouse in Portland, Me., that regularly builds shelving units for new and renovated homes and offices. Stenstrom outlined the basics, shown in figure 1, p. 16, as he showed me a typical custom case being built in the company shop.

Most people align their books flush with the front of the shelves and dislike having the books pushed to the rear. Generally, this means that you seldom need a bookcase that is more than 8 in. to 10 in. deep. Records fit well on a 12-in.-wide shelf, and overhang just enough for easy browsing. The span of ¾-in.-thick shelves should not exceed 2½ ft. to 3 ft., and that could be stretching it for some artbooks and records. If you want wider spans, use thicker shelves or reinforce them with hardwood edging, screw or nail the shelves to the case back or add vertical supports under the shelves. For exceptionally heavy loads, you might consider torsion-box construction. If you have any doubt about shelf strength, set different-size shelves on blocks and see how they react to a full load.

The best way to handle questions about shelf heights is to make most of the shelves adjustable. If the top, bottom and middle shelf are fixed, the case will be more than strong enough to support floating shelves in between, especially if you install a rigid back. Stenstrom supports shelves on brass pins (shown below), which are fairly unobtrusive and easy to fit in holes bored in the case sides. Short pegs made of ¼-in. dowel work, too. A section of pegboard makes a handy drilling guide for shelf pegs. Magic Wire supports (available from The Woodworkers' Store, 21801 Industrial Blvd., Rogers, Minn. 55374) also fit into holes in the carcase sides. The wire fits into a sawkerf on the shelf end, leaving no visible means of support. If you are fixing the shelves permanently, shelves for records should be spaced 12 in. or 13 in. apart. Most book-

shelves can be 8 in. or 10 in. apart, with more clearance needed for oversize books, art books or law books.

Stenstrom has developed some guidelines for shelving. Plywood is the best material. It's fairly economical, readily available and, as an added bonus, you don't have to worry about wood movement and other problems associated with solid wood. If the piece is to be painted, ¾-in. birch veneer-core plywood is ideal; for natural finishes, use cherry, mahogany or other hardwood-veneer plywood edged with solid wood. For shelves, the ¾-in. plywood can, in effect, be thickened by gluing 1¼-in. to 1½-in.-wide hardwood strips to the plywood edges. Joinery seldom need be more exotic than it has to be. In plywood, routed ⅜-in.-

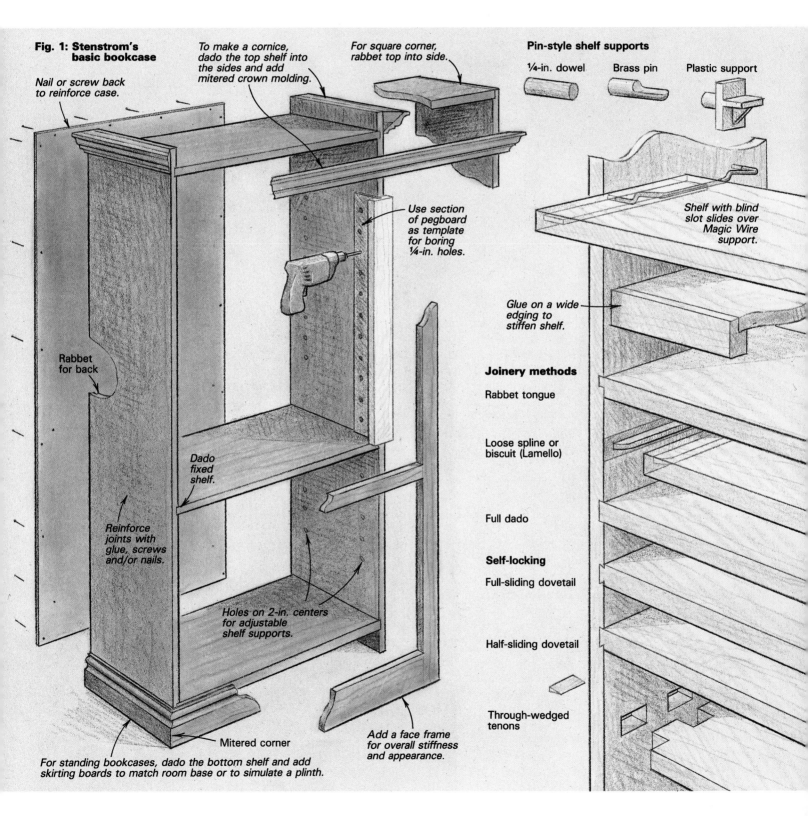

Fig. 1: Stenstrom's basic bookcase

Nail or screw back to reinforce case.

To make a cornice, dado the top shelf into the sides and add mitered crown molding.

For square corner, rabbet top into side.

Pin-style shelf supports

¼-in. dowel   Brass pin   Plastic support

Use section of pegboard as template for boring ¼-in. holes.

Shelf with blind slot slides over Magic Wire support.

Rabbet for back

Glue on a wide edging to stiffen shelf.

Joinery methods

Rabbet tongue

Dado fixed shelf.

Loose spline or biscuit (Lamello)

Reinforce joints with glue, screws and/or nails.

Full dado

Self-locking

Full-sliding dovetail

Holes on 2-in. centers for adjustable shelf supports.

Half-sliding dovetail

Through-wedged tenons

Mitered corner

Add a face frame for overall stiffness and appearance.

For standing bookcases, dado the bottom shelf and add skirting boards to match room base or to simulate a plinth.

Steve Shafer's shelves and cupboard (at left and above) are built of oak plywood, without glue. Each carcase top and bottom is nailed to the uprights, then a plywood back is nailed on to hold the case rigid. Gravity holds the shelves onto the lower cupboard, so it's easy to move and rearrange the units. A reinforcement strip is nailed beneath the lower shelf.

Exotic hardwoods can dress up a simple design. For this leaning bookcase (right), Jerry Nelson handcarved the sides of the padauk standards to accent the lines of the piece and take advantage of the wood's grain patterns.

Jerry Nelson

deep dadoes reinforced with glue and 1½-in. drywall screws hidden by plugs are more than strong enough to withstand the downward shear of the heaviest book load. Dovetails and other fancier joinery might be used on solid-wood cases (see figure 1, p. 16). A ¼-in. plywood back rabbeted and tacked to the case is perhaps the most important structural feature. It helps square up the case initially and once it's nailed or screwed in place, it keeps the piece square and resistant to racking. The rest is all decoration: a mortised-and-tenoned face frame or molding to hide the joints and improve the lines of the piece, a plinth to lift the case off the floor and help it blend in with the baseboard and other decor, crown molding for the top, doors for cabinets, decorative hardware and a carefully applied finish. These touches make the case attractive and create the impression that it is a lot more complex than it really is.

As I visited other woodworkers who frequently make shelves, I found Stenstrom's guidelines to be pretty reliable, and a good basis for all sorts of individual design interpretations. One of the most practical shelving systems I saw is by Steve Shafer, a cabinetmaker in Arlington, Va. During the past few years, he has fine-tuned his production techniques enough to be able to turn out attractive bookcases, like the one shown at left above, at prices that are competitive with commercially available, mass-produced furniture.

Shafer builds the cases of fir-core, rotary-cut oak plywood, attractive, strong and available for about $30 a sheet. The top shelf unit and the bottom cupboard are separate pieces, as shown above, center. Gravity holds them together. By sanding and finishing the panels before they're cut, standardizing part sizes so the whole case can be cut from one or two 4x8 sheets, and by building with nails and easy-to-install piano hinges, Shafer has cut construction time to eight hours, making it possible to price the finished unit as low as $200.

The first step is to cover the 4x8 plywood sheets with a coat of varnish or clear Minwax Antique Oil. When the first coat dries, the entire sheet is sanded with a belt sander and 120-grit paper. Then, another coat of finish is applied. Next, Shafer cuts

out the pieces on his tablesaw. All of his standard designs make maximum use of each sheet. The cupboard shown here, for example, is 30 in. high and 16 in. deep, so he can saw three strips of this width from a 48 in. piece of plywood. His shelves are all 8 in. deep and 32 in. wide. Odd-size cases mean higher prices because of increased waste.

To strengthen the plywood, and to make the case components look like solid wood, Shafer tongue-and-grooves solid oak edging onto the plywood. He plows the groove in the plywood edges, then mills the tongue on the ½-in. to ¾-in.-wide strips of dressed oak. Shafer finds the shaper is the fastest way to cut the joint, but it can be done on a tablesaw or with a router. He applies ⅛-in.-thick edging to the ¾-in.-thick plywood, so he doesn't have to mess around with aligning everything perfectly when he glues the banding on. After the glue dries, he uses the shaper to cut the edging flush with the plywood and to round the edges.

One reason Shafer turns out bookcases so quickly is that he avoids time-consuming cleanup problems by not using any glue to hold the case together—it's just nailed with 1½-in. (4d) finishing nails. Since the back is the case's main structural support, he says that gluing in the shelves doesn't significantly strengthen the piece. The back is nailed to a fixed shelf in the middle and in rabbets cut into the case sides and top, which makes the case rigid and keeps it from racking out of square. Hanging the doors on piano hinges also saves time because they are easier to install than butt hinges and can be quickly and invisibly shimmed with wood strips if the frame-and-panel doors need adjustment.

The bookcases by Stenstrom and Shafer are generally fairly large, elaborate constructions, but a clever idea and good workmanship can turn a small quantity of wood into a functional piece of furniture, such as the leaning bookcase shown above, right. Jerry Nelson, a furnituremaker and boat builder in Wheaton, Md., built the 48-in.-high case with padauk left over from another project. He cut the stock into seven manageable pieces, arranged them so they'd lean at a 10° to 15½° angle, then cut mortises to accept shouldered stub tenons on the shelves. The mortises are cut so the top shelf is level when the case is lean-

David Scherrer

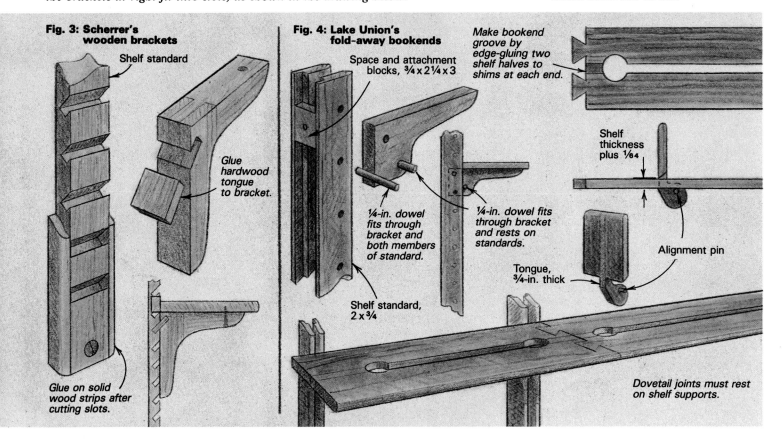

Movable oak shelf brackets by Ted Scherrer book directly onto uprights fastened to the wall. Dowel pins in the brackets on the left fit into holes in the shelf standards. Wedges on the brackets at right fit into slots, as shown in the drawing below.

Lake Union's bracket-shelving system, shown above and in fig. 4 below, incorporates sliding bookends that fold down when not in use.

Fig. 3: Scherrer's wooden brackets

Shelf standard

Glue hardwood tongue to bracket.

Glue on solid wood strips after cutting slots.

Fig. 4: Lake Union's fold-away bookends

Space and attachment blocks, ¾ x 2¼ x 3

¼-in. dowel fits through bracket and both members of standard.

¼-in. dowel fits through bracket and rests on standards.

Shelf standard, 2 x ¾

Make bookend groove by edge-gluing two shelf halves to shims at each end.

Shelf thickness plus ¹⁄₆₄

Alignment pin

Tongue, ¾-in. thick

Dovetail joints must rest on shelf supports.

Fig. 2: Hidden cables

Soss concealed hinge

Vertical cable slot

Trap door covers cable slot.

Cable to adjoining shelf or to vertical cable slot and other shelf levels.

¼-in. holes for shelf pins

Edge banding

ing against the wall. The other shelves lean slightly to the rear. Strips fixed behind the shelves keep the books from tumbling out of the case, and also help prevent racking. As a decorative touch, he bandsawed each of the upright standards in a teardrop shape and accented the lines of the piece by carving an undulating curve on the outside surfaces. He did all the carving with hand gouges, then sanded the piece smooth before finishing with several coats of clear Danish oil.

In today's age of electronics, shelves are commonly needed for personal computers, TV and VCR, and a wide range of stereo equipment. Even the best designed shelving units can be ruined by the tangle of wires that power all this equipment. Joel Katzowitz, a designer with Design South, an Atlanta, Ga., firm which designs and builds displays for exhibitions and trade shows, has a solution for hiding the clutter—movable shelves with a wire run hidden by a small trapdoor. The shelf, shown in figure 2 rests on support pins and can be moved up or down to fit the equipment. A vertical groove plowed in the case

Ron Christensen's shelves ostensibly fail the basic role of shelving, as they appear to be breaking apart, dumping books on the floor. They're actually torsion boxes fixed to the wall with metal angle brackets.

sides makes it easy to run wires from shelf to shelf.

Nelson's leaning shelves are a step away from doing away with the case altogether, and fastening the shelves directly to the wall. As the variety of commercially made bracket systems indicates, open shelving is very popular, particularly in uncluttered, modern interiors. Ted Scherrer, who operates Fairhaven Woodworks Co. in Bellingham, Wash., builds open shelving systems with all-wood brackets, shown on the facing page, that are strong and graceful. The bracket is made from two pieces of hardwood mortised and tenoned together at right angles to each other (figure 3), then shaped to a smooth, flowing radius with a drum sander. Scherrer makes two types of wall-mounted standards to go with the brackets. One has ½-in.-wide angled slots cut across the standards, which are covered with solid-wood strips glued along both edges. The other has ½-in. holes bored on 2-in. centers along its length. To fit the slots, he glues a hardwood tongue on the back of the brackets. The tongue locks into the standard with a wedging action. For the ½-in. holes, Scherrer uses a standard dowel pin.

Lake Union Woodwork in Seattle, Wash., also makes bracket shelving. The movable wooden bracket shown in figure 4 fits between vertical standards fastened to the walls. Company manager Keith McCauley said the standards are drilled on 3-in. centers for a ¼-in. dowel that reaches through the holes and the bracket as a height-adjustment pin. A second dowel, the support pin, is inserted through the front of the bracket and rests on the front edge of the standards, holding the top of the bracket perpendicular to the standards. The standards are screwed to the walls through three blocks fixed in rabbets on the back edge of each vertical member. For the system to work efficiently, the standards must be plumb and aligned on the same plane with each other. The blocks can be shimmed out with metal washers to do this.

The shelves are made up of boards joined end-to-end with jigsaw puzzle-like dovetails, which allow you to make long shelves from short, easily handled boards. Sliding bookends run in a ¾-in.-wide slot that extends nearly the length of each shelf. A tongue on the end of the bookend drops through 2-in. holes bored at each end of the slot. The bookends are fairly simple to make, but it's important that the dowel pin be located to tilt the bookend slightly toward the books it is supporting. The angle makes the bookend automatically lock itself in place with a pinching action. To move the bookend, you simply press its top toward the books, and, because the bottom edge is beveled at 45°, it will release.

Bookcases can be a challenging project for any woodworker. The case can be as elaborate as your energy and pocketbook allow, and there are numerous opportunities for you to show off your joinery and design skills. You can have a little fun, too, and throw in an unexpected twist as did Ron Christensen, a custom furnituremaker in Atlanta, Ga. His shelves are a sight gag—they appear to be broken, the books on them tumbling. The stepped shelves are actually a series of torsion boxes covered with ¼-in.-thick veneer. Despite their appearance, the shelves work fine, in addition to being a delightful eye-catcher. □

Dick Burrows is an associate editor of Fine Woodworking.

A Contemporary Trestle Table
Building with laminated mortises and tenons

by David Lloyd Murphy

Fig. 1: Trestle table construction

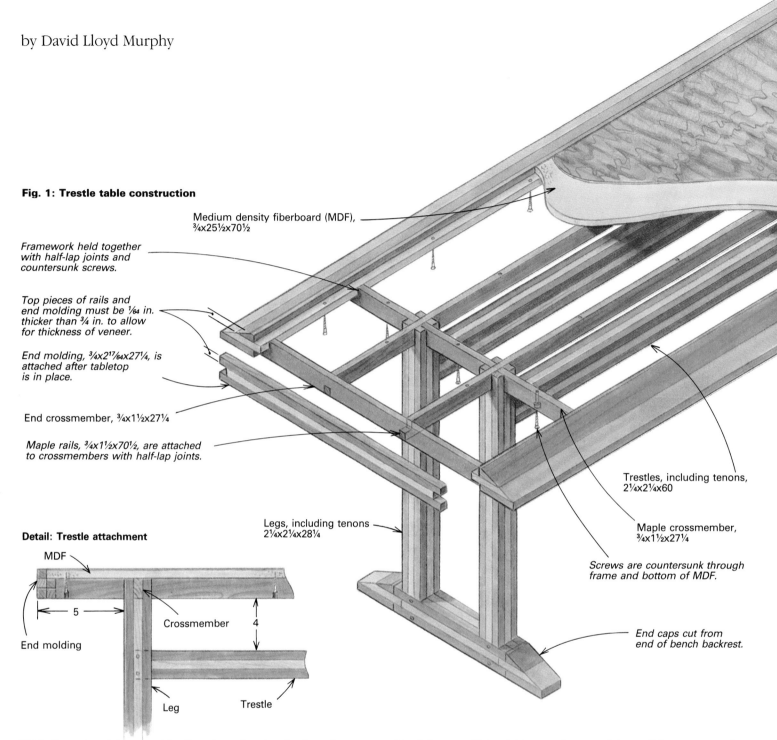

Medium density fiberboard (MDF), ¾x25½x70½

Framework held together with half-lap joints and countersunk screws.

Top pieces of rails and end molding must be ¹⁄₆₄ in. thicker than ¾ in. to allow for thickness of veneer.

End molding, ¾x2¹⁷⁄₆₄x27¼, is attached after tabletop is in place.

End crossmember, ¾x1½x27¼

Maple rails, ¾x1½x70½, are attached to crossmembers with half-lap joints.

Trestles, including tenons, 2¼x2¼x60

Maple crossmember, ¾x1½x27¼

Screws are countersunk through frame and bottom of MDF.

Legs, including tenons 2¼x2¼x28¼

End caps cut from end of bench backrest.

Detail: Trestle attachment

MDF

5

End molding

Crossmember

4

Leg

Trestle

I believe the elaborate old railroad trestles that fascinated me as a boy have substantially influenced the character of my designs. It has always amazed me how a series of posts and cross braces could withstand the great weight and vibration of a thundering steam train. And I've tried to incorporate the engineering and strength of these structures in my work.

When friends asked me to build a table for their new conference room, I jumped at the chance to do my own trestle. They wanted a simple design; I wanted something new; not rustic or traditional, but something more contemporary that would let me try my ideas for improved construction techniques. At the same time, the table had to be within the limitations of my equipment: a

6-in. jointer, a 12-in. thickness planer, a 9-in. radial-arm saw and a 12-in. disc sander.

Size limitations were also important. The table had to fit in a small room designed to serve as a combination dining area and conference room. I decided that benches would be the most efficient seating, but they would have to be durable to withstand lengthy client meetings and elaborate lunches. After numerous sketches, I felt comfortable with a design that involved a construction method I call the nine-piece joinery system. Instead of cutting mortises and tenons, you can use this system to create the joint components by strategically arranging the nine pieces that make up each leg and foot, as shown in figure 1 above. Spaces left between

From *Fine Woodworking* magazine (September 1989) 78:54-57

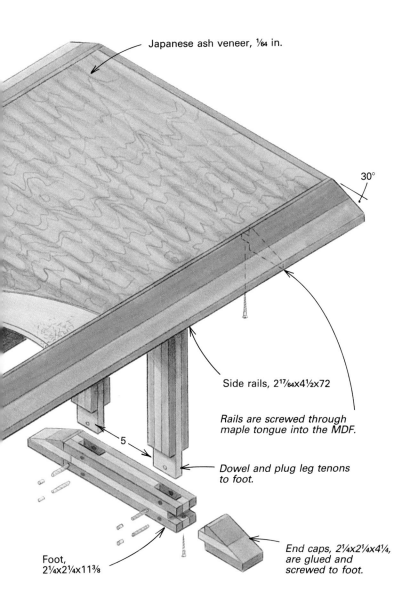

Japanese ash veneer, 1/64 in.

30°

Side rails, 2¹⁷/₆₄x4½x72

Rails are screwed through maple tongue into the MDF.

5

Dowel and plug leg tenons to foot.

Foot, 2¼x2¼x11⅜

End caps, 2¼x2¼x4¼, are glued and screwed to foot.

The author's nine-piece system results in very accurate mortise-and-tenon joints in this contemporary mahogany, maple and Japanese ash veneer trestle table.

pieces form mortises, and protruding members form tenons.

Bridle joints formed at the tops of the legs firmly hold the table surface and its supporting framework without screws. This makes it very easy to lift the top off the legs whenever the table must be moved. The double-leg design provides ample support for the wide top, and it echoes the configuration of the benches. The feet on the benches act as skids so the benches slide easily, and they visually extend the accent line of the table base. As shown in the photo above, right, the table's framework is maple and mahogany, and the contrasting colors of these woods create a pleasing, contemporary look. The removable tabletop and the benchtops are medium-density fiberboard (MDF) veneered with Japanese ash.

The nine-piece joinery system—The advantage of this system is the ease with which accurate mortises and tenons can be formed by cutting components and gluing them up in a predetermined order. It takes far less time than cutting traditional mortise-and-tenon joints, which always seem to loosen with age due to poor fit. Each of the components must be square, both for a strong joint and an accurate fit; check pieces frequently with a good try square. It's best to build one section at a time, rather than cut all the pieces at once. After completing one section, such as the table legs, you can more accurately fit adjoining pieces. Also, if you make a mistake, you won't waste a lot of expensive wood.

Gluing up the component parts from ¾-in. squares yielded the dimensions I wanted, provided versatility for laying out mortises and tenons and created visual impact by contrasting the light maple with

the darker mahogany. I've found it easiest to glue up the nine-piece legs in stages. By making three separate units of three pieces each and gluing these units together to form the leg, for example, you handle fewer pieces at one time and greatly simplify joint formation.

Figure 1 at left shows how to assemble the leg components to form the mortises for the trestles, the upper bridle joints and the tenon that fits into the foot. Careful positioning of the pieces will ensure accurate joints and eliminate much handwork later. You may want to cut scrap blocks to match the dimensions of each mortise and insert these spacers during glue-up to ensure the mortises will be the correct size. Wax the spacers to prevent them from sticking and remove them as soon as the pieces are clamped together. After clamping the three-piece units that will combine to make the legs, I immediately wipe off any glue squeeze-out with a damp rag. When the glue dries, I lightly thickness-plane the mating surfaces and glue up the leg as shown, again wiping off any glue squeeze-out. Let the glue dry and then clean up the nine-piece assembly by running it through the planer.

The feet of the table are made the same way as the legs. For through tenons, such as the leg-to-foot joint, I make the tenon slightly long, dry-assemble the joints and mark the exact tenon length. I then disc-sand the end of the tenon until it fits exactly. This is much easier than hand-sanding the rock-hard maple end-grain after the piece is assembled. Next, I glue and clamp the legs to the feet, so everything is square and perpendicular. To further reinforce the joint, I drill ¼-in. holes through the feet and tenon and then countersink fluted dowels, which I cap with plugs cut from long-grain maple. The completed leg units are now joined together with two 2¼x2¼x60 maple trestles. The trestles are secured with glue and dowels, which are covered with long-grain plugs as described earlier.

The base is topped by a ¾-in. by 1½-in. maple framework that supports the veneered MDF top. The framework is constructed with half-lap joints and later fastened to the top with countersunk screws. Rabbet the ends of the crossmembers to ¾ in. by ¾ in. to accept the tongue of the side rails when the assembled top is attached. Then, cut and fit the end crossmembers, but don't attach them until after the top is attached to the framework, which will fit neatly into the bridle joints on the legs. Although the framework drops easily into place, the bridle joints prevent any sideways

Photos: Al Ferreira, ©1987; drawings: Bob La Pointe

This simple planer jig makes it easy to bevel the backrests and rails for the benches and table. A stop keeps the rail from slipping in the jig, while the pressure from the feed rollers holds the rail down.

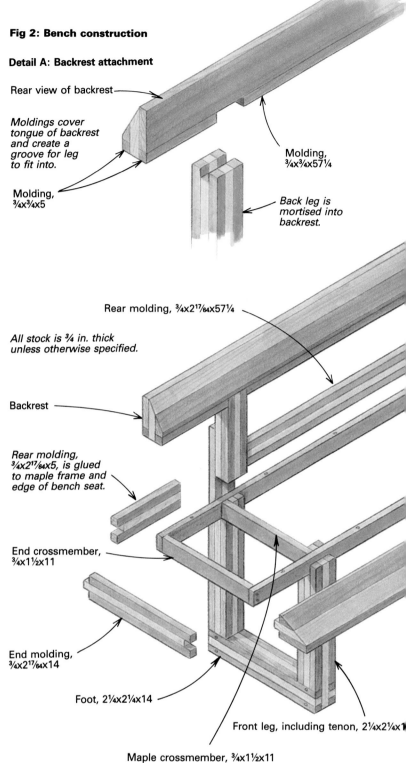

Fig 2: Bench construction

Detail A: Backrest attachment

Rear view of backrest

Moldings cover tongue of backrest and create a groove for leg to fit into.

Molding, ¾x¾x5

Molding, ¾x¾x57¼

Back leg is mortised into backrest.

Rear molding, ¾x2¹⁷⁄₆₄x57¼

All stock is ¾ in. thick unless otherwise specified.

Backrest

Rear molding, ¾x2¹⁷⁄₆₄x5, is glued to maple frame and edge of bench seat.

End crossmember, ¾x1½x11

End molding, ¾x2¹⁷⁄₆₄x14

Foot, 2¼x2¼x14

Front leg, including tenon, 2¼x2¼x1

Maple crossmember, ¾x1½x11

Using the bench assembly as an example, Murphy shows the simple but very accurate leg-and-frame joinery that is possible during glue-up with the nine-piece system.

movement of the top; weight will hold the top unit down.

The MDF top offers a dimensionally stable subsurface for the flexible foil-and-paper backed Japanese ash veneer, which I bought from Atlantic Plywood, S. Windsor, Conn. 06074; (203) 291-8020. You can also order it from Constantine's, 2050 Eastchester Road, Bronx, N.Y. 10461; (212) 792-1600. Although I had access to a vacuum press for veneering, you can veneer by hand (using a veneer hammer to fix the glue-covered veneer in place). You could also make the top with preveneered plywood. The MDF top is fairly heavy and this helps hold the top in place. If you substitute the lighter plywood, you might consider running pins through the bridle joints into the top frame.

Making the tapered rails—Because I find sharp table edges uncomfortable, I designed a 30° bevel-edged side rail to serve as an

armrest. Although their dimensions vary, as shown in the drawings, all the rails for the top, the bench seat rails and backrests are made in the same way. To make the side rails, glue a ¾-in. by 4¼-in. maple piece between two pieces of 3½-in.-wide mahogany, as shown in figure 2 above, to create a rail with one square edge and a ¾-in. maple tongue. Screws driven through this tongue into the MDF top secure the side rails. The bottom piece of mahogany should be ¾ in. thick, with the top piece slightly thicker to compensate for the thickness of the veneered MDF. I glue all the rails up at this time and then form the 30° beveled edges by running each piece through the planer with the jig shown in the top photo above. The beveled side rails can now be fitted to the veneered tabletop and benchtops glued and screwed in place. After fitting the support frame into the bridle joints on the legs, place the top in position. The frame and top can now be joined with countersunk screws run up through the frame into the under-

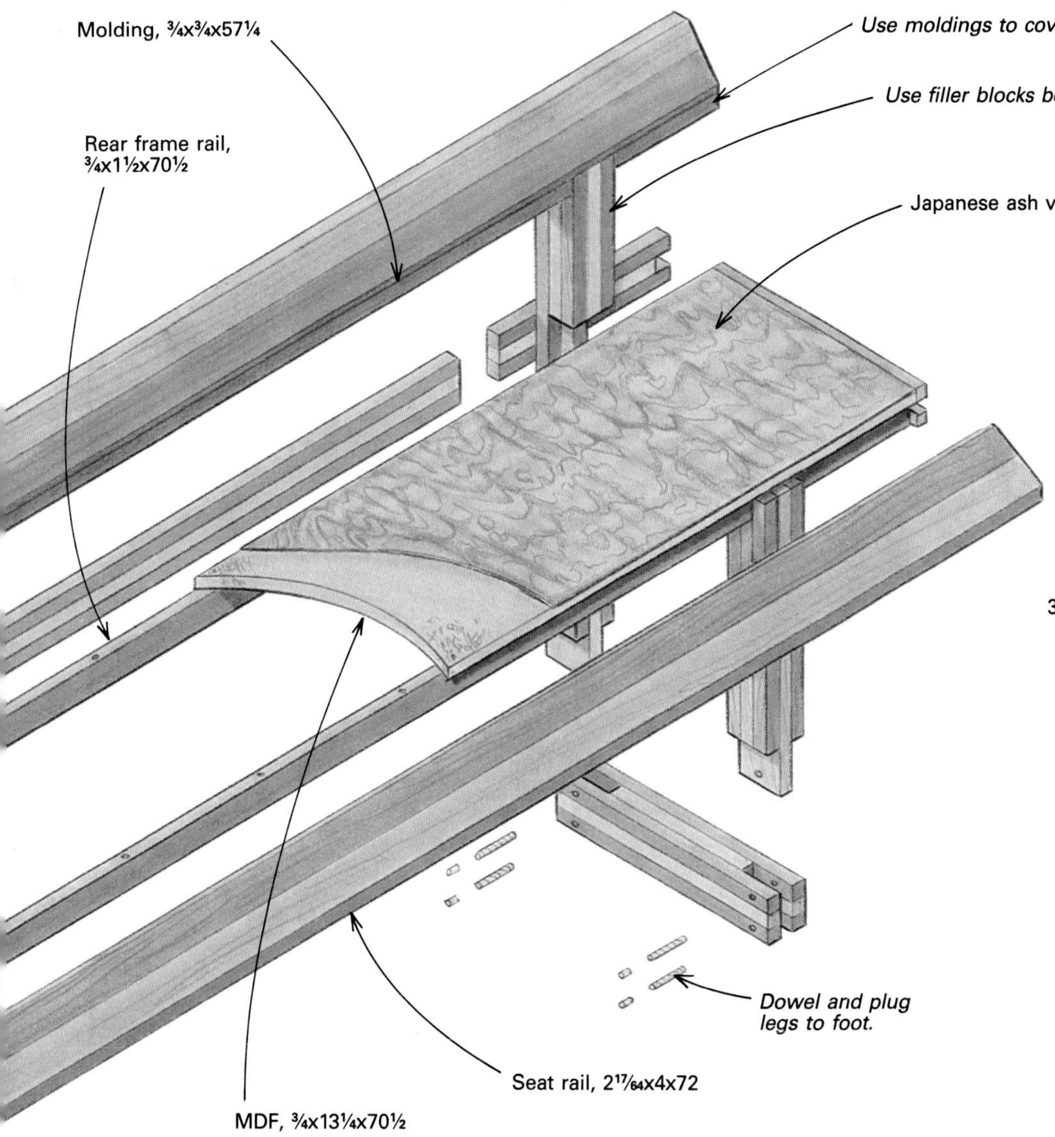
Molding, ¾x¾x57¼
Use moldings to cover tongue.
Use filler blocks between seat and backrest.
Rear frame rail, ¾x1½x70½
Japanese ash veneer, 1/64 in.
Dowel and plug legs to foot.
Seat rail, 2 17/64x4x72
MDF, ¾x13¼x70½

Detail B: Section of bench at crossmember

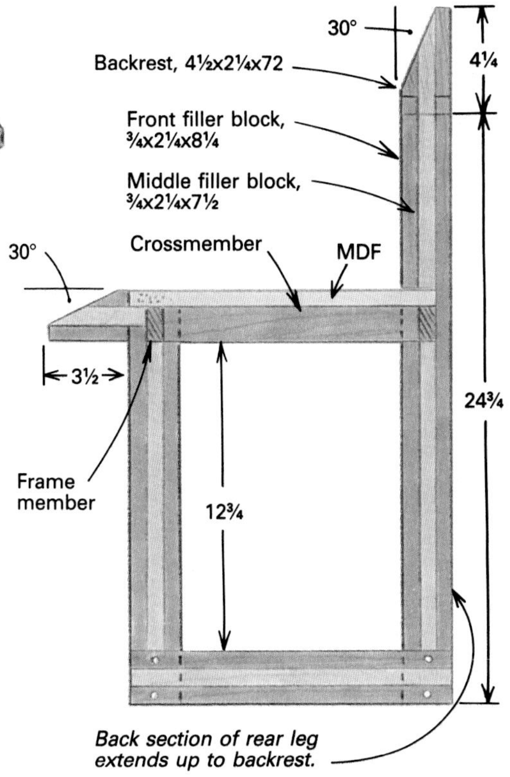
30°
Backrest, 4½x2¼x72
4¼
Front filler block, ¾x2¼x8¼
Middle filler block, ¾x2¼x7½
30°
Crossmember
MDF
3½
24¾
Frame member
12¾
Back section of rear leg extends up to backrest.

side of the top and through the ends of the crossmembers into the maple tongue of the side rails.

The ends of the table are finished with end molding that is glued up like the rails, with ¾-in.-thick stock on the bottom and middle and slightly thicker stock on the top. The dadoes in the ends that fit the tongues of the side rails are formed by making the middle piece of the lamination 1½ in. shorter than the top and bottom layers. The end crossmembers of the tabletop frame are now glued to the end moldings. This crossmember/molding unit is then fitted to the end of the table between the side rails and is glued and screwed through the crossmember into the bottom of the tabletop.

To complete the table, cut two end caps for the feet from the ends of the backrest rails. After fitting the tongue of the end caps to the mortises in the feet, glue and clamp the caps in place and screw through the mortise and tongue from the bottom of the foot.

Building the benches—The construction techniques for the benches are basically the same as for the table. Using my nine-piece joinery system, I constructed the U-shape leg units shown in figure 2 above. Again, attention to detail and fit at this point will yield tight-fitting joints that will require little handwork later. The leg-to-foot joints of the benches are doweled and plugged in the same manner as the table. Having constructed both leg units, I join them to the front and rear frame rails, which run the length of the bench minus the end moldings, as shown in the bottom photo on the facing page. The crossmembers are installed between the front and rear frame rails at the legs and at the ends of the rails with glue and screws. I attached the seat rail by screwing through the tongue of the rail into the bottom of the veneered MDF seat. The seat and rail butt against the back legs and are held in place with screws running through the frame members into the MDF. Glue mahogany moldings onto the tongue of the backrest before gluing the backrest in place on top of the legs. Applying the filler blocks to the rear legs and gluing the moldings to the back and ends completes the benches.

Before applying any finish to the table, I hand-sand the joints as needed to level tenons or clean up glue squeeze-out. Also, I check the rails surrounding the veneered surfaces to be sure they are even, and I sand the rails to eliminate any high spots. Avoid sanding the veneer or you'll risk cutting through it. I hand-sand the entire piece, except the veneer, working from 120-grit up to 250-grit sandpaper. Then, I lightly sand the veneer with 250-grit.

For a hard, durable finish, I spray on four coats of clear satin lacquer, sanding between coats with 250-grit paper to remove orange peel or overspray. Don't apply more than four coats; the additional coats will darken the color of the wood. After sanding the final coat with 400-grit paper, I rub out the finish with fine steel wool and polish it with Butcher's Wax. □

Dave Murphy is a serious amateur woodworker and a creative director with an advertising agency in Farmington, Conn.

Pedestal Tables
Sculptural bases and veneered tops

by Jim Wallace

When I design a table, I consider the pedestal as important as the top. Modern manufacturers often relegate the table base to the role of unobtrusive support, as if to say: "Paint it black and perhaps it will disappear." However, my tables are meant to be sculptural as well as functional, so the pedestal is an integral part of the design, not merely a support for the top, no matter how spectacular it may be.

My table designs are inspired by many sources: nature, art, architecture, fashion and graphics. The pedestal or "Post" in the bottom photo on the facing page was influenced by the decorative elements of Post-Modern architecture, hence the name "Post:Modern Table." My designs often are influenced by more practical considerations. For example, the top of the Post:Modern Table is veneered with 24 wedge-shape segments, partly because the satinwood veneer was available only in 5-in. widths and partly because I didn't have a press large enough to veneer the top as one piece.

Constructing these pedestal tables, with their sculptural bases and unique veneering problems, is a challenge in any shop, but especially so in my 300-sq.-ft. one-man shop. This small space also has forced me to limit my tool collecting. I have a 10-in. tablesaw, hand circular saw, 12-in. disc sander, belt sander, orbital sander, drill press, ⅜-in. drill, router, clamps and a compressor for spraying lacquer. In this article, I'll concentrate on describing some of my techniques rather than giving you plans for duplicating one of my tables. I want to show that even though you may not have a shop stocked with expensive tools, you needn't limit the creativity of your designs. Being from the school of "whatever works," I

have evolved some unorthodox methods for building tables and have come up with devices to compensate for many of my shop's shortcomings.

Whatever works – The multipurpose table shown in figure 1, below, simplifies many operations. It is constructed from 2x4s and plywood, with 32 casters mounted on 6-in. centers on the top. My mother says it looks like a geriatric skateboard, but she'll have to wait, because I'm still finding new uses for it around the shop. In figure 1, the table's being used casters-down, as a stand to hold the tops while the veneer is clamped. Turned this way, I also use it as a mobile workbench for moving large in-progress pieces from my small garage shop to my driveway, where I work whenever possible. Cutting up the large 4-ft. by 8-ft. sheets of birch plywood and particleboard needed to construct all my tables is a real chore for one person. Turned casters-up, the multipurpose table becomes an outfeed table the same height as my 10-in. Craftsman tablesaw, which is also on wheels for moving outside. The sheets slide neatly off the saw and over the casters, making the process an easy one-man job.

Because my pedestals are built with various sizes of polygons, I devised the adjustable jig shown in the photo below. It's basically a board with a pivot pin and a wide slot for an adjustable miter gauge. The piece to be cut is drilled in the center so it fits snugly on the pivot pin. The miter gauge, fitted with the appropriately angled fence (for example, 45° for an octagon, 30° for a hexagon), is set in conjunction with the saw's rip fence to cut the desired-size piece.

The circumference of each tabletop is embellished with a series

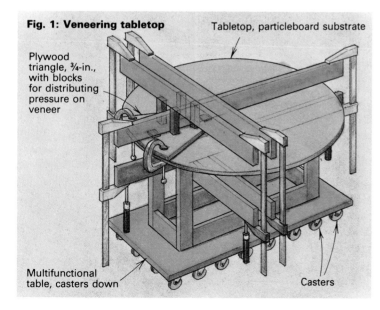

Fig. 1: Veneering tabletop

Tabletop, particleboard substrate

Plywood triangle, ¾-in., with blocks for distributing pressure on veneer

Multifunctional table, casters down

Casters

This jig for cutting polygons has the versatility to cut various shapes in a large range of sizes. Set up here to cut octagons, the jig can be adapted to cut hexagons by replacing the 45° miter gauge with one that has a 30° fence.

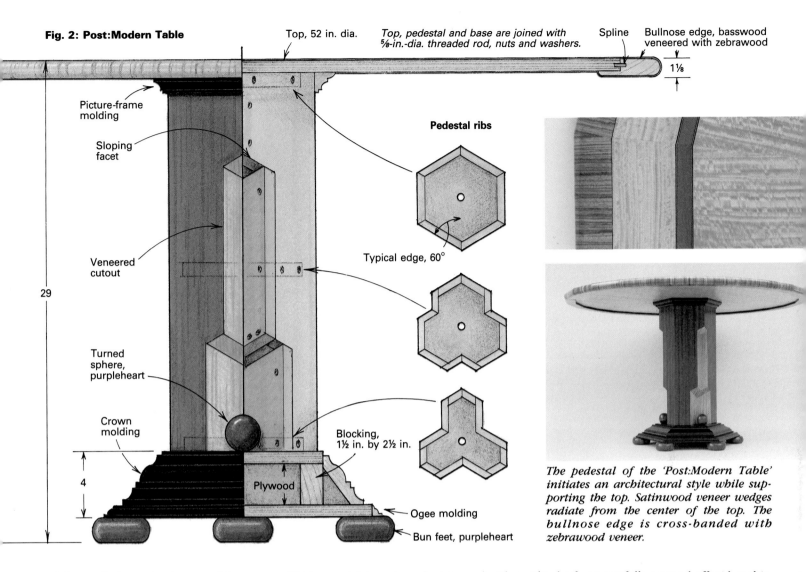

Fig. 2: Post:Modern Table

Top, 52 in. dia.

Top, pedestal and base are joined with ⅝-in.-dia. threaded rod, nuts and washers.

Spline

Bullnose edge, basswood veneered with zebrawood

1⅛

Picture-frame molding

Sloping facet

Veneered cutout

29

Turned sphere, purpleheart

Crown molding

4

Plywood

Blocking, 1½ in. by 2½ in.

Ogee molding

Bun feet, purpleheart

Pedestal ribs

Typical edge, 60°

The pedestal of the 'Post:Modern Table' initiates an architectural style while supporting the top. Satinwood veneer wedges radiate from the center of the top. The bullnose edge is cross-banded with zebrawood veneer.

of facets. Each top begins as a 4-ft. square of ¾-in. particleboard, on which I locate the center with diagonal lines and draw a 4-ft.-dia. circle. To cut the facets, I use a Masonite template guide based on the number of facets desired. As an example, I'll describe how to cut the 24 facets on the Post:Modern Table. I lay out three radii at 15° intervals and draw the chords between them at the edge of the circle. From this layout, I make a wedge of ¼-in. Masonite that covers the three radial segments. Then, I glue and nail three small strips to the wedge to serve as guides for the circular saw when cutting the facets. I lay one edge of the template on one of the radii, locate the point of the wedge at the center of the circle and screw the wedge to the top. I saw each facet with the circular saw base running against one of the little guide strips. Then, I unscrew the wedge and rotate it around the circle, overlapping one sawed facet and sawing two new ones each time I move it. Overlapping the cuts in this way will produce uniform facets. Any slight discrepancy can be eliminated when fitting the veneer and edging for the last facet.

Figure 1 on the facing page illustrates how I overcome the problem of veneering a 4-ft.-dia. tabletop without a veneer press. I divide the top veneer into wedge-shape sections and glue down two or three sections at a time, clamping them under a jig that covers ⅛th of the top. I span the triangular jig with 2x4s and clamp their ends to evenly distribute the pressure. Corresponding 2x4s running beneath the tabletop keep the substrate flat. Great pressure is not required, as long as the veneer is pressed flat while the aliphatic resin glue cures. I hold the veneer in place on the substrate with masking tape and put waxed paper between the veneer and the jig to keep the parts from sticking. I minimize glue squeeze-out by spreading a thin coat only on the substrate. Minor squeeze-out can

be trimmed with a utility knife or carefully popped off with a chisel. When I've glued down enough sections to cover 90° of the circle, I use a square and straightedge to trim the last wedge square. I repeat this at each 90° interval to eliminate any accumulated error as I go around the circle. I always veneer the underside of the table right after the top and apply finish to both sides to prevent warping.

Building the Post:Modern Table – The pedestal of the Post: Modern Table is a hollow, hexagonal column of particleboard, reinforced with three internal plywood ribs (see figure 2 above). The veneered cutouts in this pedestal are an example of the unique construction problems some of my designs present. I notched for the cutouts in the ribs and the sides before assembly and made the final cut at the top of each cutout with a hand circular saw after the hexagon was glued up. However, this required careful planning. In addition, there were some dangerous stop cuts on the tablesaw where I had to hold the side piece tightly on the saw table as I raised the angled blade up through the piece. In hindsight, it occurred to me that I could have assembled the pedestal as a complete hexagon and then made the cutouts with the circular saw. This is a more direct method, akin to carving, and eliminates a potentially dangerous tablesaw operation.

Figure 2 shows the finished pedestal and its parts. I cut out three identical ribs, using the adjustable polygon jig, and drill a 1-in.-dia. hole in the center of each rib for the all-thread rod that joins the top, pedestal and base. The pedestal's six sides are ripped to final width with the tablesaw blade tilted to leave a 60° bevel on the edges (so they'll form a hexagon when assembled). If I were to build this pedestal again, instead of prenotching the ribs and sides,

Drawings: Kathleen Creston; photos: Jim Wallace, except where noted

I would assemble the hexagon at this time, gluing and screwing the ribs in place inside the post and taking care not to put screws where the cutouts will be.

Mark the outline of the cutouts with a pencil and straightedge. Use a circular saw running against a guide board screwed to the side of the pedestal to make the 60° cuts along the long vertical lines. Relocate the guide as you work your way around the pedestal. The angled facets at the top of each cutout are cut with the circular saw riding on a jig that straddles the corner of the post and is screwed securely to the pedestal's sides. If your circular saw doesn't have the depth of cut for the top cutouts or where the cuts intersect the ribs, you can finish up with a handsaw. Sawkerfs that extend too far will be filled and veneered over. Particleboard pieces are custom-fit and glued and screwed into the cutouts and any remaining gaps. After filling all screw holes, sawkerfs and rough spots with auto-body filler, I sand all the surfaces smooth. Auto-body filler is perfect here because it cures quickly to a hard sandable surface, even when it's used to fill large areas. And, it's relatively inexpensive when purchased by the gallon. I *always* wear a dust mask when sanding it though, because the dust is an irritant.

Next, I make a paper pattern for the six facets of each cutout, cut the satinwood veneer close to the pattern's size and trim the veneer to fit into the inside corners. The veneer is glued down using cauls cut to fit over each piece and clamped across to the other side of the pedestal. After trimming the outside corners with a utility knife, I sand the veneer flush. The pedestal's main sides are veneered with padauk, two opposite sides at a time, using plywood

and 2x4s as cauls to distribute the pressure.

I borrowed a neighbor's lathe to turn the purpleheart bun feet and the spheres at the base of this pedestal. The lacquered bases for my tables are off-the-shelf white-pine architectural moldings, mitered and glued to a box made from two pieces of plywood with blocking in between (see figure 2 on the previous page).

The tabletop is veneered with satinwood wedges radiating from the center to a purpleheart border. The purpleheart is sandwiched between thin strips of satinwood and black imbuya, a Brazilian hardwood. The grain of the satinwood outer rim runs parallel with the table's edge, as shown in the top photo on the previous page. To cut the components for these veneer wedges, I clamp pieces of veneer between a pair of ¼-in. Masonite router templates, one pair for each of the shapes, and trim the veneer pieces to size with a flush-trim bit. Then the components of each wedge are assembled with veneer tape. Three of the wedges are then taped together and glued down using the triangular jig described earlier. The tabletop's underside is also veneered with satinwood, but with the grain running in one direction.

The bullnose edge is basswood wrapped with a cross-band veneer of zebrawood. I shaped four 4-ft.-long bullnose sections with a ¾-in.-dia. roundover router bit. To make the mold for veneering the bullnose, I resawed a 4x4 in half. I partially hollowed out the mating sides, cutting out most of the waste on the tablesaw and rounding the inside corners with a ¾-in.-dia. cove bit in the router. To test the fit, dry-clamp the halves of the mold together and try a veneer-wrapped section of bullnose. Continue making adjustments

Photo: Michele Russell Slavinsky

These are a few examples of the veneers available from Alpi of Modigliana, Italy. The fabric-like patterns, known as AlpiN-iN veneers, come in a wide color range and can even be made to order. The   *bird's-eye sample is made from veneers that are reconstructed into logs in such a way that when they are resawn into veneers, they mimic nature's grain patterns.*

Italian veneers lend an exotic touch

Veneers give me a greater variety in grain patterns, colors and construction techniques than I can get with solid wood. In addition, veneers allow more extensive use of rare and costly woods, helping to extend and preserve a dwindling resource. So it was with great excitement that I discovered Alpilignum veneers made by Alpi, a manufacturer in Modigliana, Italy.

These veneers are available in a wide range of patterns that simulate traditional wood grains, such as quartersawn oak, flat-sawn rosewood, bird's-eye maple and several varieties of burl. Alpi also offers a line of designer veneers, known as AlpiN-iN veneers,

in various colors and complex patterns that suggest woven textile designs. These veneers can even be custom ordered to your own designs.

To construct these patterns, sheets of veneer, sometimes precolored, are arranged into the desired patterns with the aid of computers and glued into a new "log." This log is then sliced into ⅟₃₉-in.-thick patterned veneers. Standard dimensions are 24½ in. by 133 in. and 24½ in. by 98 in. Because of strict quality control, the patterns and colors are true throughout an entire flitch; there is almost no noticeable variation from one sheet to the next. Be-

cause these veneers are made entirely of wood, they cut, lay up, glue, sand and finish exactly as standard woods and veneers.

Alpi also manufactures dimensioned lumber with inlaid vertical lines or geometric patterns.

Alpilignum veneers and other Alpi products are marketed in Canada and the United States by The Dean Co. Their main office, showroom and factory are located at Bee Street and Stafford Drive, Box 1239, Princeton, W.Va. 24740. They also have offices at Box 426, Gresham, Ore. 97030, and at Box 1818, 2006 English Road, High Point, N.C. 27261.   —*J.W.*

The gradually flaring pedestal of the 'LFI Table' (named with the customer's initials) blends into the subtly shaped underside of the top. The top's pattern is created in part by the herringbone design of the AlpiN-iN veneer (see sidebar, p. 26).

Fig. 3: LFI Table

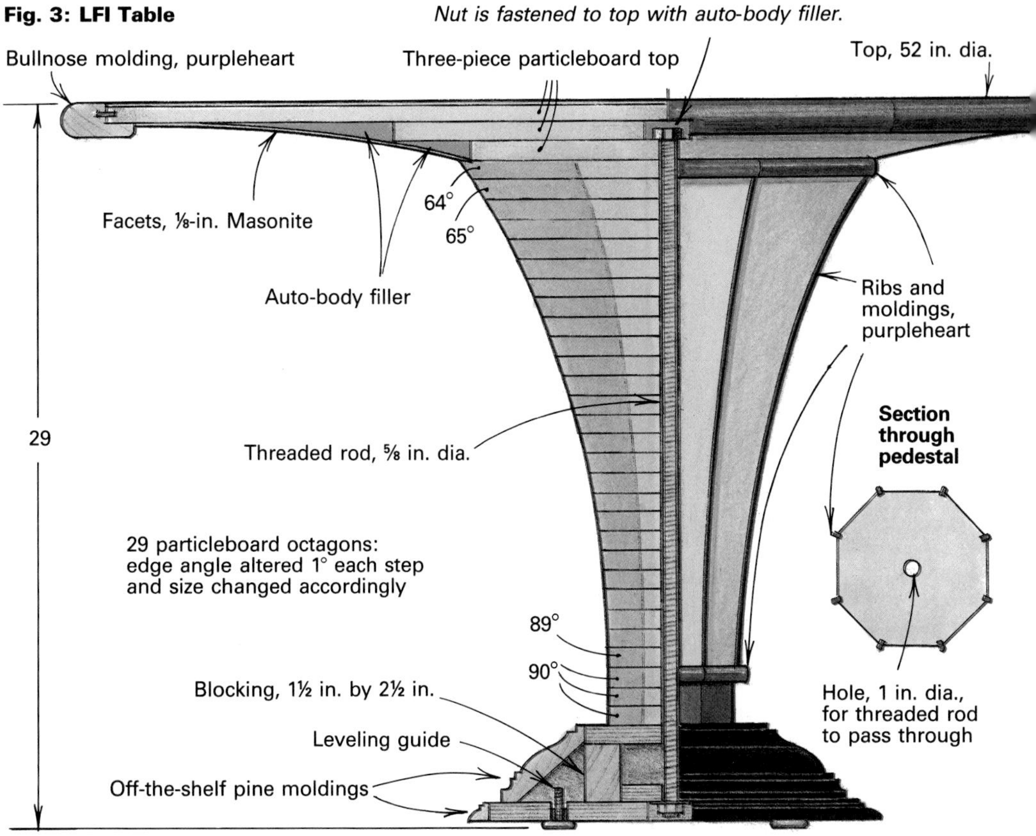

Nut is fastened to top with auto-body filler.

Bullnose molding, purpleheart

Three-piece particleboard top

Top, 52 in. dia.

Facets, ⅛-in. Masonite

64°
65°

Auto-body filler

Ribs and moldings, purpleheart

Section through pedestal

Threaded rod, ⅝ in. dia.

29 particleboard octagons: edge angle altered 1° each step and size changed accordingly

89°
90°

Blocking, 1½ in. by 2½ in.

Leveling guide

Off-the-shelf pine moldings

Hole, 1 in. dia., for threaded rod to pass through

29

on the mold with router and tablesaw until a tight fit is obtained. Then the mold's two halves are glued together and lined with aluminum foil to prevent the veneer from sticking to the mold. To apply the cross-banding, center the veneer over the mold's opening. Wet the veneer's surface with Titebond, and apply several clamps to press the veneer into the mold with the bullnose stock. After the glue cures 24 hours, the form can be tapped loose with a hammer. Excess veneer is trimmed with a block plane, and the 4-ft. lengths of bullnose are rabbeted to lap under the tabletop. I then miter each segment on the tablesaw and glue them to the edge of the top.

Before assembling the table, I finish its parts with several coats of lacquer. The underside of the top gets the same number of coats as the top. Then the top, pedestal and base are assembled, with ⅝-in.-dia. threaded rod running through the pedestal and the base. I inset a nut with auto-body filler in the underside of the top and recess a nut and washer in the underside of the base.

Building the LFI Table—The pedestal of the "LFI Table" (LFI are the customer's initials) is constructed by stack-laminating 29 ¾-in.-thick particleboard octagons (see the lower photo above). This is where the adjustable polygon jig really comes in handy. To form the flare in the pedestal, I decrease the edge angle of each octagon by 1° from the one before it and increase the width to compensate for the 1° flare (see figure 3 above). The octagons are tacked with small finish nails, to hold them in alignment during the glue-up. When all the octagons are assembled, I clamp the stack by tightening nuts on the ends of a ⅝-in.-dia. threaded rod passing through the 1-in. hole previously drilled in the center of each octagon. Then, I sand each curved side smooth. Cardboard templates are used as patterns for cutting the veneer for each side.

Veneering these curved sides presents a novel problem, requiring a novel solution. I cut an auto-tire inner tube into two C-shape pieces, filled them each with sand and closed the ends with bailing wire. I sandwiched the pedestal between layers of veneer, waxed

paper, ⅛-in. Masonite and rubber sandbags, then clamped them all together with bar clamps, using 2x4s laid across the sandbags as cauls. I was able to veneer all eight sides quite easily in four clamping operations. The veneer on the edges of each side was trimmed and then gently sanded before veneering the next two faces. A ¼-in. by ¼-in. groove was routed the length of each corner to receive the bandsawn purpleheart ribs. A purpleheart bullnose molding trims the transition from the flaring pedestal to the underside of the top, as shown in figure 3 above.

Using the same techniques described for the Post:Modern Table, I cut 16 facets on the edge of the top and veneer it with wedges of herringbone AlpiN-iN veneer (see the top photo above and the sidebar on the facing page). Next, I rout ¼-in. by ¼-in. grooves between each wedge section and around the faceted edge of the top and glue in a thin border of satinwood sandwiched between strips of black imbuya, which I had previously laminated and sawed into ¼-in. by ⁵⁄₁₆-in. strips. I leave these inlaid borders slightly proud of the surface to protect the top veneer while I work on the table's underside.

With the top upside down, I glue and screw two different size particleboard octagons to the underside to continue the flare from the pedestal (see figure 3 above). The steps between these two octagons are filled and evened out with auto-body filler, and as it is curing, I tack ⅛-in. Masonite wedges over each section to form the gentle flare. Any gaps between the Masonite wedges are filled with auto-body filler and sanded smooth. The facets created this way are then veneered one at a time, with the AlpiN-iN wedges weighed down with the rubber sandbags. The bags are heavy enough so clamping isn't neccessary, but a layer of waxed paper is needed to protect the veneer from the black of the inner tube. When the veneering is complete, I glue the solid purpleheart bullnose to the table's edge and sand the inlaid borders flush on the top. □

Jim Wallace, Institute of Business Designers, is project designer with The Bommarito Group, a commercial interior-design firm in Austin, Tex.

The oval coffee table, above, is one of 15 designs students choose from to build their first piece of furniture at the Leeds Design Workshops. The table has a solid-wood top and pedestal base, with edges that are profiled with rasps and spokeshaves.

Building Coffee Tables
Student projects from Leeds Design Workshops

by Suzanne Burns

A coffee table can be a challenging project for any wood-worker. It can be as intricate in design or as demanding in technical difficulty as any dining table or desk. Yet it is a small and manageable undertaking, well-suited for a relatively inexperienced woodworker. Because of this, a coffee table is the first major piece built by students at the Leeds Design Work-shops, a two-year school in furnituremaking and cabinetmaking in Easthampton, Mass.

Though students come to Leeds anxious to explore design, they don't design their own tables for this assignment. Instead, they choose, with the instructor, from 15 different tables, all designed and drawn by David Powell, who, with John Tierney, directs the school. The students use mostly hand tools and an occasional portable power tool to build their tables, because one project goal is to teach the proper and precise use of these tools. Design comes later, when the students have mastered basic woodworking techniques. Tierney says, "Customers will seek out these students in the future, when they are craftsmen, for the skills and versatility that can be fostered by hand tool use. Work-ing by hand changes one's perspective of what is possible—you

don't limit yourself to just what a machine is able to do. The control is more with the craftsman."

Powell designed each table to emphasize a different construction technique. While all the tables require basic joinery and shaping skills, some designs involve more advanced joinery or require coopering, carving or veneering. The instructors try to steer the student to the design that best suits the student's skill level. The objective is for a student to learn techniques while building a functional and attractive piece of furniture.

Each table created by Powell fulfills basic design criteria for a coffee table, yet the tables cover a wide range of styles—from Craftsman to Art Nouveau. The coffee table is simply a 20th-century piece of occasional furniture designed to hold drinks or books. It probably came into use with the advent of sofa seating or perhaps as a spin-off of the tea table. A coffee table is built long and low to match the height of a sofa. The top can be any size, but it usually isn't much more than 3 ft. or 4 ft. long and 2 ft. wide; otherwise, it takes up too much space in front of a sofa.

Despite the fact that students start from complete plans and are given all the dimensions, even the simplest table is not that easy

From *Fine Woodworking* magazine (July 1988) 71:72-75

to build: Students have just six weeks to make the table and are required to do everything but go out and harvest the tree themselves. Given rough planks of lumber, they must dimension the wood with a handplane, handsaw the joints, shape the edges, and sand and finish everything without the stationary machine tools they'll be taught to use after they've mastered hand tools. It's a tedious process and demands most students to push their abilities to the limit. Tierney says, "Nobody gets it right the first time, but by the time a student is done, he's developed a kind of confidence with handworking techniques that can't be had any other way."

When complete, the coffee table is reviewed by Powell and Tierney, who check every edge and surface against the measured drawing. They even use calipers and templates to make sure the student's work is within a hair of the correct thickness or shape. A table must be close to perfect before Powell and Tierney will pass it and allow the student to go on to the next assignment—a piece of casework such as a vanity or a display case.

Besides being good designs for student projects, Powell's coffee tables are also good-looking pieces of furniture. A close look at how students handle the construction of the tables can be very instructive. I'll describe three of my favorite tables and give you an idea about the technical difficulties you're likely to encounter if you decide to build one.

Oval table

This table consists of an oval-shape solid cherry top supported by a pedestal-type base. The base has two crossmember frames connected with four uprights to form the pedestal. One frame attaches to the underside of the top, and the other frame is shaped to form four feet that rest on the floor. Making this table involves basic handplaning and joinery skills, as well as spokeshave and rasp work to shape the edges of the top and base.

The 20-in.-wide top requires several boards to be jointed and then glued together. The Leeds students use jack planes and jointer planes to plane each board accurately to dimension and then to true the edges before gluing. They use smooth planes and block planes to level the top. The students cut the oval out with a bowsaw. If you don't want to use hand tools, you can joint and thickness the boards with a jointer and thickness planer and cut the oval with a jigsaw. The top's edge is shaped to a profile that's called an accelerating curve—one with a radius that changes around the edge. Although it takes longer to shape, the accelerating curve appears more dynamic to the eye than the fixed-radius curved edge you'd get with a roundover bit in a router. To hand-shape the edge, students make a cardboard template of the profile from a full-size blueprint, pictured at right, and then rough-shape the edge with a spokeshave and rasp, checking progress against the template. They refine and smooth the shape with sandpaper.

The eight pieces that make up the base must be cut to length, have their joinery done and be glued up before the edges get shaped. Waiting with the shaping makes it easier to clamp the base members, since the edges of the frame members opposite the joints will be square and flat. The two identical crossmember frames are made from the same wood as the top: 2 in. wide for the top frame and 4 in. wide

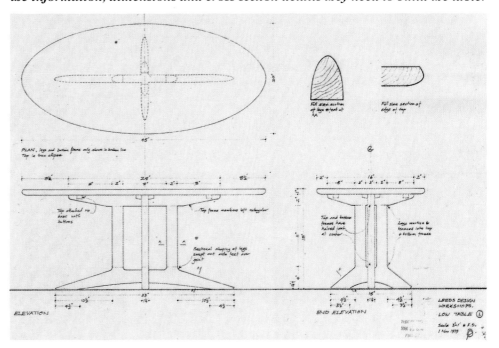

On the underside of the oval table, above, small buttons fit into grooves in the frame to hold the top rigid and flat, yet allow it to move across the grain in response to changes in humidity. A scaled-down blueprint, below, gives students all the information, dimensions and cross-section details they need to build the table.

for the bottom frame. The frames have a simple lap joint where they meet in the middle. Before gluing up the frames, chop the eight mortises and cut and fit the tenons in the ends of the uprights. The trick here is to keep everything perfectly square in every dimension by keeping the distances the same between the tenon's shoulders on the uprights' ends. If one length is off, either the top won't be level or the feet won't sit flat on the floor. Glue up the crossmember frames first, then glue

in the uprights to connect the two frames.

Before shaping the edges of the base members, taper the ends of the upper and lower frames toward the ends with a spokeshave or drawknife. You could also taper these ahead of time with a taper jig on the tablesaw. Like the top's edge, the profile on the base's edges is not a regular curve. Powell designed the base members to be elliptical in cross section for more visual interest. Shaping it requires a template, to check the shape, and a lot of patience with

a spokeshave, rasp and sandpaper. There are also recessed areas on the top and bottom sides of the legs that must be removed with a coarse file before shaping the elliptical edge profile. The bottom of the feet are chamfered slightly, after the edge shaping is done. The finished base is attached to the top with small buttons that screw to the top's underside and engage slots in the top frame, as shown in the photo on the previous page. This allows the solid-wood top to expand and contract freely.

Ribbon table

The second coffee table, known at Leeds as the ribbon table, is a graceful and very popular piece. Besides being a student project, the table is one of the Leeds shop's regular production models. With lines that make the wood seem like an undulating, continuous piece of fabric, the power and elegance of this table comes from the shaping that's done to the ends and edges of the top. Building the table is an exercise in coopering and carving, as well as planing and doweling.

Because this table has carving only on its ends and edges, you don't need to start with a 2-in.-thick plank. By using 6/4 lumber instead, the table will be lighter and you'll not waste as much carving time or material. Glue up an extra-large panel for the top that's about 10½ in. longer and 3 in. wider than the dimensions of the 4-ft.-long by 16-in.-wide finished top. This extra wood is sawn off and laminated to the ends and edges where needed to provide the necessary thickness for the carving. For the closest grain match, flip the pieces over before gluing them to the underside.

The end panels are glued up and shaped from the ends of the same boards used to make the top—so the grain will match. These panels are planed to an even-thickness curve, just like the end panels of the curved-dovetail table described on the next page. But the ribbon table's panels taper in thickness from ¾ in. down to ¼ in. at the sides so the thin edges meet the line of the carving at the top. After shaping, the panels are doweled into the thickness-ing pieces, located as shown in figure 1. This glue-up should be done before the top is carved so the carving will create a smooth transition from the top's ends and edges into the tops of the end panels and will maintain a continuous ribbon illusion.

The shape of the ribbon-like details at the top's four corners is shown by the three views in figure 1 at left. To begin the carving, rough-out the inside of the hollow in each corner by drilling away the waste in the deepest parts with a ½-in.

Building the sinuous-line ribbon table requires coopering of the end panels as well as extensive carving of the ribbon-like edges. To build up thickness for the carving, extra wood is glued to the underside of the top around its edges.

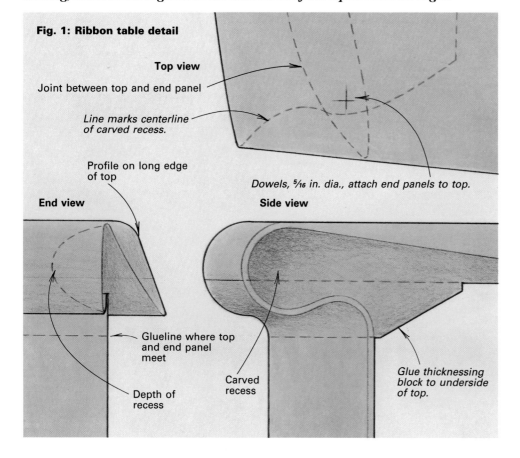

Fig. 1: Ribbon table detail

Top view

Joint between top and end panel

Line marks centerline of carved recess.

Profile on long edge of top

End view

Dowels, ⁵⁄₁₆ in. dia., attach end panels to top.

Side view

Glueline where top and end panel meet

Depth of recess

Carved recess

Glue thicknessing block to underside of top.

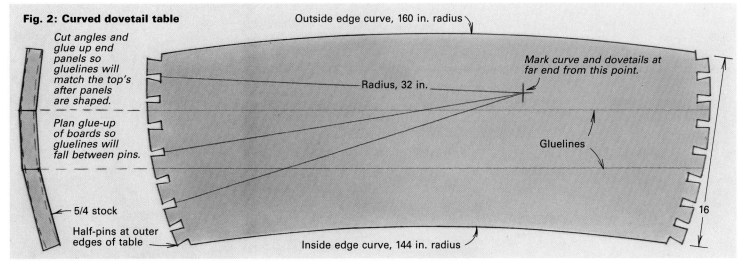

Fig. 2: Curved dovetail table

Cut angles and glue up end panels so gluelines will match the top's after panels are shaped.

Outside edge curve, 160 in. radius

Mark curve and dovetails at far end from this point.

Radius, 32 in.

Plan glue-up of boards so gluelines will fall between pins.

Gluelines

5/4 stock

Half-pins at outer edges of table

16

Inside edge curve, 144 in. radius

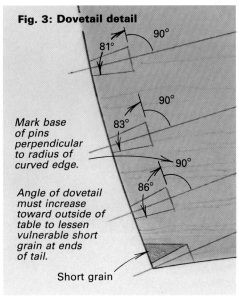

Fig. 3: Dovetail detail

90°
81°

90°
83°

Mark base of pins perpendicular to radius of curved edge.

90°

86°

Angle of dovetail must increase toward outside of table to lessen vulnerable short grain at ends of tail.

Short grain

This simple-looking table challenges the builder with laying out and cutting dovetails around a curved edge, as well as gluing up and coopering curved end panels. A subtle, large-radius curve along the table's length makes it more visually interesting than if it were straight.

twist drill chucked in a power drill or brace. The concave profile of the hollow can then be carved by scooping out the majority of the waste with gouges and then refining the shape with rifflers. The hollow tapers away as it wraps around under the top, as traced by the red profile line shown in figure 1. Next, carve the outside of each corner to define the recurving ribbon edge. Then, rough-out the curved overhanging lip on the table's ends with whatever seems to work best for you—a drawknife, a plane, gouges, or rasps and files. Take care not to undercut into the side grain of the end panel when carving the cove where the thicknessing piece meets the end panel: It'll spoil the smooth transition of the top flowing into the end. Refine and smooth the curves with scrapers and sandpaper. The profile of the long edges of the top are shaped last, using either a hollow-bottom plane, a regular plane or a spokeshave and sandpaper. Try not to overdo it with the sandpaper, and keep the ribbon edge crisp and well-defined.

Curved dovetail table

With its bench-like top and curved ends, this coffee table challenges its maker not only with tasks like coopering and handplaning a curved panel and cutting dovetails around a curved edge, but with a tricky layout as well. The table's 4-ft.-long top and ends must be made from the same boards so the grain will run continuously through the sides and top. But, the top and end panels can't be glued up into one big panel and then sawn apart into three separate pieces, because the top, viewed from above, is subtly curved. If you glue up a surface large enough to cut off the end panels adjacent to the top's ends, the grain in the panels will run diagonally instead of straight. Also, the end panels must be coopered so the same 5/4 lumber used for the top will allow the curve to be shaped (see figure 2). Carefully plan the layout of the top and end panels so the boards for these pieces can be cut out and glued up separately. When shaped and joined, the end panels' grain will match the top.

After the edge angles of the end panels

are coopered with a jointer plane, the panels are glued up and then shaped into smooth curved surfaces. After marking the radius on the endgrain with a cardboard template, use a convex-sole plane to shape each panel's concave inner surface. Take long, even strokes so the curvature will be even and not dip in the middle. The outside of the radius can be shaped with a regular jack plane: Start by planing a series of facets to follow the radius. When close to the final shape, switch to a scraper and then sandpaper to refine the curve and smooth the surface.

The curved dovetails that join the top to the ends are laid out radially around the top's ends. Once these are marked correctly, they're easier to cut than they appear. Take a straightedge aligned to a point that's at the center of the end's 32-in.-radius curve and mark the centerline of each pin on the table's top. Space the pins evenly around the curve. Next, draw the tails on the top. There's a bit of realignment you must do to the tails closest to the top's concave edge at both ends: Skew the angles of these dovetails, as shown in figure 3, so that the short grain at the outermost corners of the tails won't break off when you chop out the waste. Because it's easier to mark the dovetails on the table's top, it's best to cut the tails of curved dovetails first, then mark and cut the pins on the end panels. Tierney advises his students to saw for a perfect fit without trimming. He says it's easier to saw to the line than to try and clean out these dovetails with a chisel after sawing. After gluing, any unevenness is planed flush, and the top is planed flat with a smooth plane. □

Suzanne Burns is a reporter for The Valley Advocate *in Hatfield, Mass. David Powell and John Tierney assisted in the preparation of this article.*

Building a Pool Table

Starting from scratch with nuts-and-bolts joinery

by Paul M. Bowman

Fig. 1: Pool table

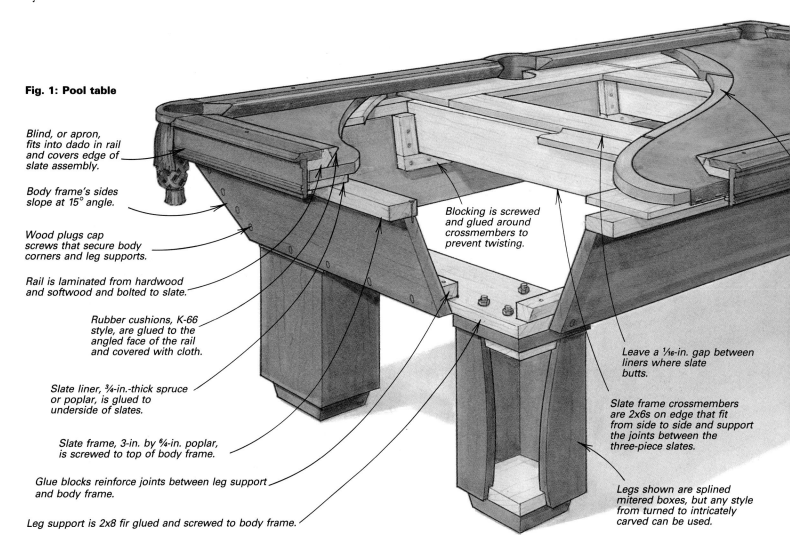

Blind, or apron, fits into dado in rail and covers edge of slate assembly.

Body frame's sides slope at 15° angle.

Wood plugs cap screws that secure body corners and leg supports.

Rail is laminated from hardwood and softwood and bolted to slate.

Rubber cushions, K-66 style, are glued to the angled face of the rail and covered with cloth.

Slate liner, ¾-in.-thick spruce or poplar, is glued to underside of slates.

Slate frame, 3-in. by ⁶⁄₄-in. poplar, is screwed to top of body frame.

Glue blocks reinforce joints between leg support and body frame.

Leg support is 2x8 fir glued and screwed to body frame.

Blocking is screwed and glued around crossmembers to prevent twisting.

Leave a ¹⁄₁₆-in. gap between liners where slate butts.

Slate frame crossmembers are 2x6s on edge that fit from side to side and support the joints between the three-piece slates.

Legs shown are splined mitered boxes, but any style from turned to intricately carved can be used.

The distinctive crack of the break, brightly colored balls rolling across the expanse of green and the "plop" of the ball dropping into the pocket—these are the sights and sounds of satisfaction to pool afficionados. But, few of them have the satisfaction of sinking balls into pockets on a table they've built themselves.

Building a pool table is somewhat intimidating, because of the size of the table and the weight it must support. In addition to the 400-lb. slate playing surface, a pool table must be able to support a person sitting on the edge while attempting a behind-the-back shot. On the other hand, aside from the compound angles, building a pool table doesn't involve anything that's beyond a competent weekend woodworker with the gumption to take on a large project.

The table described here is constructed much like many high-end commercial pool tables (see figure 1, above). Each section of the three-piece slate is glued to a wood liner and then screwed, but not glued, to the main table body, a box whose sides incline down and in at 15°. A 2x8 leg support is screwed and glued be-

tween the sides at each end of the box. The four legs are attached to these supports with lag screws or hanger bolts. Bolted on top of the slate are six rails, which support the cushions and pockets. An apron, or blind as it's called on pool tables, surrounds the rails and covers the edge of the slate assembly.

The choice of wood, the carving or other decoration on the table and the style of legs can be custom designed to suit an individual's tastes. But one thing is certain: The table must fit the slate, so buy the slate before you begin working. The slate comes from Italy or Spain, where it is cut to size and the pocket cutouts and holes are drilled for assembly hardware. The chart on the facing page lists common slate sizes, weights and playing areas. Unless you're buying 100 or more sets, you'll need to locate a local pool-table dealer in your area who is willing to sell you a single set. Don't buy slate that is not predrilled. You'll also need a set of #6 leather-covered pocket irons, type K-66 rubber cushions and facings, plastic sights for the "dots" in the rails and various hardware. After the table's built, you'll need cloth to cover the slate, balls, a triangle,

From *Fine Woodworking* magazine (March 1989) 75:38-44

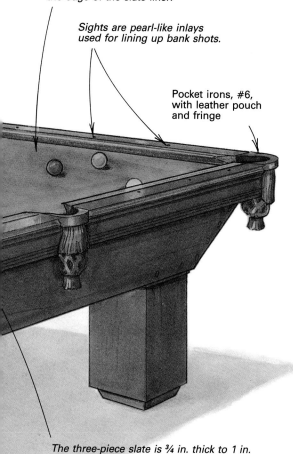

Cloth, 75% wool, 25% nylon blend, is stretched over the slate bed and stapled to the edge of the slate liner.

Sights are pearl-like inlays used for lining up bank shots.

Pocket irons, #6, with leather pouch and fringe

The three-piece slate is ¾ in. thick to 1 in. thick and comes with pockets cut out and assembly holes predrilled. Height from top of slate bed to bottom of leg should measure 29¼ in.

This walnut pool table, built by the author, has sloping sides and leather-and-fringe pockets, which are indicative of an antique-style table. The legs were purchased from a company that specializes in carving pool-table legs, and the relief-carved blinds are from a millwork-supply house. Once you've located the slates and accessories, there's nothing about building a pool table that's beyond the abilities of a competent weekend woodworker.

Figuring rail lengths

3-piece slate				Rail lengths (in.)	
Size	Weight (lbs.)	Slate description	Playing area between cushions	Side rails (4)	End rails (2)
1x45x85	398	Oversize 7 ft.	40x80	36½	37⅞
⅞x51x95	422	Oversize 8 ft.	44x88, std. 8 ft.*	40½	41⅞
1x51x95	484	Oversize 8 ft.	44x88, std. 8 ft.	40½	41⅞
1x53x99	528	Oversize 8½ ft.	46x92, oversize 8 ft.	52½	43⅞
1x57x107	612	Oversize 9 ft.	50x100, oversize 9 ft.	46½	47⅞

* The description of the slate size sometimes differs from the description of the playing area.

To determine if your room is large enough, take the desired playing area and add 57 in., the length of a standard cue, to all four sides. In tight spots, you can always use a shorter cue.

Formula for calculating rail length:

$$\text{Side} = \frac{\text{Playing length - side pockets (5 in.) -2⅛ in.}}{2}$$

$$\text{End} = \text{Playing width - 2⅛ in.}$$

cues and a bridge. The retail price of the slate and other supplies will come to about $800. Methods for covering the table and rails with the cloth are explained in the sidebar on p. 37.

Slate liner—The slate liner reinforces the brittle slate, anchors the staples holding the cloth and distributes the effects of the shims used to level the slate. You should use spruce or poplar 1x8 liners on the long sides of the table so there will be enough stock to accommodate the pocket cutouts. The rest of the liner can be from 1x4s. Be sure all the liner material is planed to the same thickness, or you'll be adjusting for the difference later. Butt the pieces together and glue the liner to the underside of the slate with Titebond glue or contact cement, as shown in the top, left photo on the next page. Hold the liner back about ¹⁄₁₆ in. from the edges where the slates butt so they can be pushed tightly together. Cut out the pockets in the liner by running a sabersaw blade along the slate cutouts. The ⅞-in.- or 1-in.-dia. holes along the slate's edge are for the bolts that will be used to attach the rails. These holes should be drilled

through the liner, along with the smaller countersunk holes for screws to hold the slate to the body.

Legs—There's no end to the design possibilities for pool-table legs: They can be square, tapered, turned or carved. The only limitation is that you leave a way to bolt or screw them to the table. The legs on the table in the photo above were purchased from a dealer who specializes in duplicating intricate carvings (see sources of supply, p. 37). The cross section in figure 1 shows the basic construction of simple, square legs. An official pool table should measure 29¼ in. from the bottom of the leg to the top of the slate. For the table described here, the legs should be about 15½ in. tall.

Body frame—The body sides are made from 11¼-in.-wide 6/4 flat and straight hardwood lumber. If you need to plane the pieces to flatten them, leave them as thick as possible. To determine the frame's dimensions, measure the slate's overall size and subtract 7 in. from each dimension, so the slate will overhang the body by 3½ in.

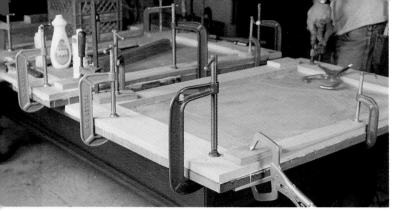

The ¾-in.-thick poplar slate liner is glued with Titebond glue and clamped to the underside of the slate. The slate's sides are lined with 1x8s to overlap the pocket cutouts, then 1x4 crosspieces are butted between them and held back ¹⁄₁₆ in. from the slate edges that will butt together.

To complete the body, the slate frame is screwed to the top edge of the body frame, and the crossmembers are installed to support the joints in the slates. Glue blocks, screwed below the crossmembers, add support. The slate frame stops short of the corners to allow pocket clearance, and a ¾-in. block ties the corner together.

all around. The incline of the sides is common, especially on antique tables. Joining these angled pieces, however, requires compound miters, so I initially crosscut the parts a couple inches longer than the final size to allow a little leeway for cutting these miters.

I prefer to cut the compound miters with a sliding tablesaw. However, a radial-arm saw will do. The arm of the saw should be swung 17° to the right of its normal, square position, and the blade should be tilted to 43¼°. Because the blade may wander in bevel cuts, I cut each end twice: I first cut about ¼ in. past my mark, then slowly trim to the line. You can cut the compound angle on both ends of each piece without changing the saw-arm setting. First, place the board to the left of the blade, with its bottom edge against the fence and its outside face down on the saw table. After cutting this end, roll the board over and slide it to the right of the blade. Measure and mark the long, top edge of the board and cut to length. After the angles are cut, rip the edges of all four box pieces at a 15° angle so the edges will be parallel to the floor when the slope-sided box is assembled. If you're using a scalloped bottom edge, shown in the photo on the previous page, saw the pattern now; be sure to leave the first 10 in. from each end square for the legs.

Assembling the body frame—Many commercial pool-table builders join the parts with nails, which are set and hidden with wood filler or molding. I prefer the additional strength provided by screws; the wood plugs covering the screws also add a nice detail. I drill plug holes for the screws that secure the corners and leg supports at the locations shown in figure 1. Then, I drill pilot holes through for the screws. I sand to 120 grit with a belt or stroke sander and use a vibrating sander after assembly for finer sanding.

I assemble the body frame on custom-made 20-in.-high sawhorses with 2x8x48-in. tops that can support the weight of the table and slate. The wide tops make it easy to assemble the sides, and the low height makes it easier to lift the heavy pieces of slate onto the completed body. Set the sawhorses where the body will be assembled, and level them in place, shimming beneath their legs, if necessary, to ensure that the body can be assembled square and true.

To assemble the four sides, I place the parts upside down on the sawhorses and brush a liberal amount of glue on the miters of two adjacent ends. Then, I carefully hold the corner in alignment and use a power screwdriver to run a 1½-in. #10 screw into one hole in the side and one in the end. I draw the corner tightly together with the rest of the screws, being careful not to strip out the end-grain holes. Repeat this process until the body is complete.

The next step is to cut and install a kiln-dried 2x8 leg support at each end of the body. Crosscut the ends with opposite 15° bevels so the supports fit snugly side to side. Then rip one edge of each at 15° to fit against the ends of the body. If you scalloped the bottom

edge of the body, bandsaw the leg support back away from the scalloped portion of the end so the support doesn't show. Screw and glue the supports in place, running 2¼-in.-long screws through the predrilled holes in the body frame and into the leg supports. Glue wooden plugs in all the screw holes, and sand them flush.

To drill for the lag screws or hanger bolts that attach the legs, make a plywood template the same size as the top of the legs and drill four evenly spaced ⁵⁄₁₆-in.-dia. holes. Place the template in the corners of the leg supports and drill through the template and the support. Use the same template when drilling the tops of the legs. Before I turn the table over, I round over the bottom, outside edge of the body and the four outside corners with a ⅜-in.-radius piloted router bit. With a helper, I turn the body over and reinforce the leg supports by gluing and screwing in hardwood glue blocks cut from scraps from the table sides (see figure 1).

A frame to support the slate completes the table's body. It's made from 3-in.-wide 6/4 stock and should overhang the body frame by 1¼ in. all around. Cut off the corners of the end pieces at 45° for pocket clearance, or let the parts come up short of the corner, as shown in the photo above, right. Screw and glue this frame to the top of the body. Install two crossmembers to support the joints in the slate. The crossmembers should be at least 1½ in. by 5½ in. (a standard 2x6) and cut to fit on edge from side to side. Glue them to the frame, and run a long screw into each of their ends from the outside of the frame. Screw and glue a block under the ends of each 2x6 crossmember for support. I usually also glue in side blocks to prevent twisting. With a sabersaw, cut out 6-in.-dia. arcs tangent with the body for the side pockets. Finally, round over the inside edges on the top of the frame so it's easier to insert wedges between this frame and the slate liner when leveling the slate. Now, set the slates on the body and slide them around until they're tightly together and centered on the frame.

The rails—The rails, more than anything else, make a slate-top table into a pool table. They can be made from a single piece of clear, straight hardwood, but hardwood and softwood laminated rails, shown in figure 2 on the facing page, reduce the possibility of warping and provide softwood for stapling on the cloth.

The most critical rail dimension is the cushion height. According to the Billiard Congress of America, the point of the cushion should be 1¹³⁄₃₂ in. from the bed of the slate on a standard table with 2¼-in.-dia. balls. The balls tend to climb a lower rail and be forced down under a higher rail. This height is determined by the 1¾-in. thickness of the rail in conjunction with the 15° angle of its face. If you vary the thickness of the rail, you must adjust the face angle to provide the proper cushion height, as shown in figure 2.

To make the laminated rails, you'll need six 1¾x3¼x48-in.

softwood boards (I prefer poplar because of its stability) and six ¾x3½x48-in. hardwood boards. Mill enough for one extra rail for tool setup and test cuts. Saw out a 2¼-in. by ¹¹⁄₁₆-in. rabbet in each piece of the softwood by making two cuts on the tablesaw. Glue the hardwood segments into this rabbet, and when dry, plane the hardwood flush with the softwood. Begin shaping the rail by ripping the 15° and 45° angles along the length of each rail's cushion face. On its top, cut a ¼-in. by ⁵⁄₁₆-in. groove about ⁷⁄₁₆ in. back from the 15° angled face. This groove is for the feather strip, which secures the cloth to the top of the rail. On the bottom of the rail, saw a shallow ½-in. by ¹⁄₃₂-in. rabbet where the rail cloth will be stapled. Finally, set the dado blade to just skim the back edge of the softwood as you cut a ¼-in.-deep dado for the blind into the hardwood. Mold the top edge of the hardwood with a router or shaper to add a detail and break the sharp corner.

Use the chart on p. 33 to determine rail lengths for your playing area, and crosscut the rails to length. These lengths are figured for #6 pocket irons, so be sure that's what you use. Bore ¾-in.-dia. holes in the rail ends; 2 in. should be deep enough for the pocket "ears" (see the left photo on p. 36). Center the hole 2½ in. back from the point created by the 15° and 45° angles of the angled face and ¾ in. down from the top of the rail. I drill the holes with a spade bit in an electric hand drill, using the bit's long shaft to align the hole.

Assemble the rails and pockets on the slate to check your playing area. Be sure the pockets are tight in the ear holes, and check the whole assembly for squareness. Tape pieces of cushion rubber onto rails across from each other, using double-faced tape, and measure the distance between their "noses." The measurements should be your desired playing area. If your measurements are long, you can trim the ends of the rails to leave the proper playing area.

Now you can cut the pocket angles on the rail ends with the radial-arm saw. The angles and sizes for the pocket openings are shown in figure 3 on the next page. The ends of the rails that border the corner pockets are cut with the blade tilted to 10° and the arm set at 52°. For the side pockets, the arm is reset to 15°. The angle in the rail's horizontal plane creates the correct-size opening for the pockets. The angle in the vertical plane serves to extend the cushion's nose around the ends of the cushions.

Cutting the pocket angles is much like cutting the opposite compound miters for the body: Cut one end, roll the board, move it to the other side of the blade and cut the other end. However, all the pocket-angle cuts should begin at the back of the feather-strip groove. So, cut the first rail to the right of the blade, with it's outside edge against the saw fence and its top side up so you can see where to begin the cut. The opposite cuts are made to the left of the saw blade with the top side of the rail face down. This makes it difficult to line the cut up with the feather-strip groove, so line up the first rail you cut with the other rails, bottom to bottom, to mark the location of the top-side-down cuts. The end rails get the 52° corner-pocket angle cut at both ends (in opposite directions), while the four side rails have one of their ends cut at 52° and the others cut with the saw arm reset to 15° for the side pockets. After the angles are cut, use a router to extend the shallow rabbet on the bottom of the rails, along the angled ends, for stapling the cloth.

The cast pocket irons are anchored in the ear holes with ⁵⁄₁₆-in. by 1-in. bolts run up through the rail. Drill 1-in.-dia. holes, deep enough to countersink the bolt heads and washers, directly below the threaded holes in the pocket ears. Then, drill a ½-in.-dia. hole through to the ear hole. The bolt should screw into the ears when the pocket is snug to the rail, and it should have enough play for minor adjustments during final assembly.

Attaching the rails–There are several different ways to attach the rails to the table: lag screws, mortised nuts, threaded inserts and threaded discs. Threaded discs, often referred to as metal rail plates in billiard-supply catalogs, are used most often, but they may be hard to find. I'll describe how to use them, but the same basic procedures apply for the other methods as well.

To locate the threaded discs, assemble the rails and pockets tightly together on the slate. Center the assembly by lining the

Fig. 2: Rails and blinds

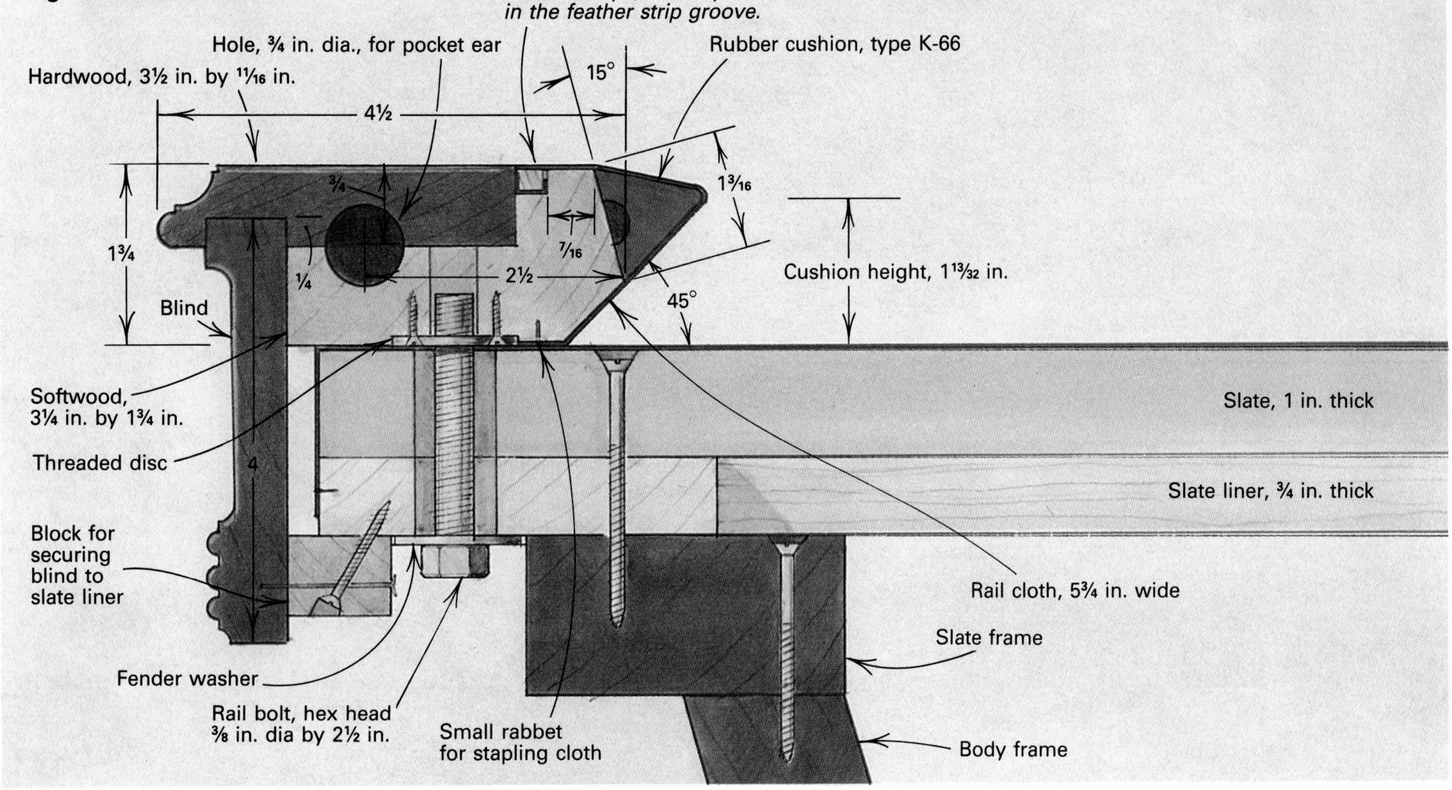
Feather strips, ¼-in. by ¼-in. softwood, are used to secure rail cloth in the feather strip groove.
Hole, ¾ in. dia., for pocket ear
Hardwood, 3½ in. by ¹¹⁄₁₆ in.
Rubber cushion, type K-66
15°
4½
¾
1³⁄₁₆
1¾
⁷⁄₁₆
¼
2½
Cushion height, 1¹³⁄₃₂ in.
45°
Blind
Softwood, 3¼ in. by 1¾ in.
Slate, 1 in. thick
Threaded disc
4
Slate liner, ¾ in. thick
Block for securing blind to slate liner
Rail cloth, 5¾ in. wide
Slate frame
Fender washer
Rail bolt, hex head ⅜ in. dia by 2½ in.
Small rabbet for stapling cloth
Body frame

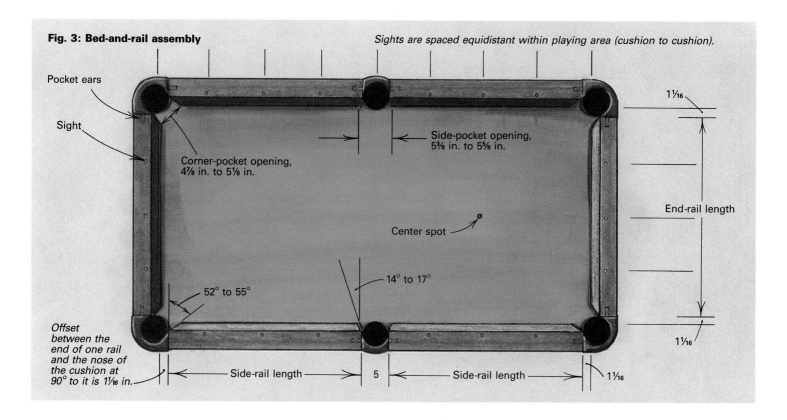

Fig. 3: Bed-and-rail assembly

Sights are spaced equidistant within playing area (cushion to cushion).

Pocket ears

Sight

Corner-pocket opening,
4⅞ in. to 5⅛ in.

Side-pocket opening,
5⅜ in. to 5⅝ in.

Center spot

1¹⁄₁₆

End-rail length

14° to 17°

52° to 55°

Offset
between the
end of one rail
and the nose of
the cushion at
90° to it is 1¹⁄₁₆ in.

Side-rail length

5

Side-rail length

1¹⁄₁₆

1¹⁄₁₆

Above, left: The pocket 'ear' is inserted into the hole in the rail's end, and a bolt is then run up from the bottom of the rail into the ear's threaded hole. The rails and pocket are upside down in the photo above, right. The ⁵⁄₁₆-in. by 1-in. bolt anchors the pocket ear in the rail, and the ³⁄₈-in. by 2½-in. rail-bolts screw into the threaded discs under the rails to secure the rails to the slate. The cloth is stapled and trimmed closely behind the pocket angle for a tight fit between the rail end and the pocket leather.

side pockets up with the slate cutouts and measuring the rail assembly's overhang all around the slate. Eye the side rails to see that they are straight, and double-check the whole assembly for square. Then, reach under the slate liner, and with a pencil, trace the holes in the slate onto the bottom of the six rails. Disassemble the rails, turn them over and mark the centers of the holes. The side rails, as well as the end rails, should be interchangeable with their counterparts.

Drilling for the threaded discs is done with a fence clamped to the drill-press table set for the holes' front-to-back alignment. First, countersink for the discs by drilling a shallow hole the disc's diameter. Then, change to a ⁷⁄₁₆-in.-dia. bit and drill 1 in. deep in the center of each countersink for the shaft of the rail bolt. Use one of the discs, its flat side facing and parallel with the cushion side of the rail, to locate the pilot holes for the discs' attachment screws. Then, screw the discs in place (see right photo this page).

Inserting the sights—The last step in preparing the rails is locating the sights used to line up bank shots. Figure 3, above, shows their placement. Divide the playing area's width by four, or its length by eight, to get the distance between the three sights on each rail. The end rail has one sight in the center and one, the calculated distance, on each side of the center. Place them halfway between the feather-strip groove and the back of the rail. The center of the side rails falls in the middle of the side pockets, so measure from that point.

Sights come in various sizes, shapes and materials. The round, plastic ones are the easiest to use. Just drill a hole the proper diameter and deep enough that the sight will stand just proud of the rail. Then, brush in a little glue and drive them in with a hammer and a wood block, to protect the sight. Once the glue is set, sand the sights flush using 120 grit on a belt sander.

The blinds—The blinds, or aprons, trim the rails and hide the edge of the slate assembly. They're about 4 in. wide and the same length as the rail they'll be attached to. If you bandsaw the ends with the curve shown in figure 2, they blend nicely into the pocket fringe, but you'll have to cut them long to allow for this curve. The blinds fit into the dado in the bottom of the rail and are held in place with blocking, which is glued to the backside of the blind and screwed to the underside of the slate liner. Glue two blocks to the back of each rail, making sure they won't be in the way when tightening the rail bolts. Drill an angled pilot hole in each one to screw the block to the liner. This makes for easy disassembly of the blinds when the rails are recovered.

Assembling the table—After the table parts have been stained and finished and the cushions have been glued to the rails and covered with cloth (see the sidebar on the facing page), you can set up the table. Place the table body upside down on the floor of the billiard room. Bolt the legs in place and then turn the table over. Level the table by using a carpenter's level and placing ⅛-in. plywood and plastic-laminate shims under the legs. Next, set the pieces of slate in place and screw them tightly to the body frame. A screwdriver bit in a hand brace simplifies this process. It's not a good idea to screw down the center of the slates along the joints unless you need to pull down a bowed slate, which is very uncommon.

Run your fingers across the four points where the slate joints meet the edge of the table to detect any difference in height. If there's a difference, loosen the screws in the lower slate and raise it by inserting a playing card or folded paper shim between the liner and body. Repeat this until the three slates are even at the table's edge. If your body frame is straight and true, the slates should be too. To double-check this, stretch a taut string from end to end, near the edge of the table, anchored to nails in the slate liner. Slip a coin or poker chip beneath the string at each end and use another chip as a gauge to test for equal clearance along the length of the slate. Next, the joints are felt their whole length. If one piece is lower, drive a 1½-in. by 6-in. softwood wedge, tapering up to ¼ in., between the slate liner and crossmember. One person can tap the wedge in place while a helper feels for the moment when the two pieces of slate are even. When the three pieces of slate are as even as possible, putty the joints with "Durham's Rock Hard" (available from local hardware stores) and a wide putty knife. Any gouges, scratches or screw holes in the playing area should also be puttied and sanded smooth. After the putty has hardened, use 120-grit sandpaper on a block to gently sand off any excess. Putty and sand again if necessary, then brush the table clean.

The bed of the table can now be covered with the cloth, as described in the sidebar below. Then, the rails and pockets are assembled on the covered bed, as shown in the photo (right) on the facing page. The rail bolts and washers are inserted through the slate liner and slate and finger-tightened in the threaded discs. Then the pocket-and-rail assembly is centered on the slate, and the end rail bolts are tightened with a socket wrench. Sight down the side rails and adjust them until they are straight, then tighten them down. To test their alignment, roll a pool ball down the side rails. The ball should pass the side pockets without catching a point of the cushion. Nail or screw the loose ends of the woven leather pockets to the underside of the slate liner, making sure that the balls will not escape through this opening. Lastly, slip the blinds up into the dado in the rails, and screw through the glue blocks into the slate liner.

Fine-tuning the table—To check the table for final leveling, hold a pool ball between your thumb and first finger about 12 in. above one of the rails. The line from your thumb to your finger should be perpendicular to the front of the cushion rubber. Drop the ball so it will strike the slate and the front of the cushion simultaneously. It should travel across the table at 90° to the cushion; if the table is the slightest bit out of level, it will roll toward the low point. As an alternate technique, grab a cue and shoot a ball slowly the length of the table, about 6 in. from the side rail. As the ball slows and stops, it will veer toward the low point, if the table's out of level.

The severity of the ball's drift, using either method, will help estimate the thickness of the shim needed under the leg toward the low point. Lift the table from the end so both legs are off the floor, and have your partner place the shims under the proper leg. If you pick up only the low corner, the torque is sure to break the puttied joints between the slates. Repeat this procedure around the table until the balls show no drift. □

Paul Bowman lives in Vancouver, British Columbia, Canada, where he works as a freelance writer. He builds pool tables on special order.

Sources of supply

Wholesale billiard-supply houses usually won't sell to individuals, so find a local dealer or pool-table manufacturer who will sell you the slates and accessories. If that fails, you can order everything you'll need, including slates, from the following supplier:

Tucker's Billiards, 3381 Ashley Phosphate Road, North Charleston, S.C. 29406

For machine-carved legs and decorative blinds:

Adams Wood Products Inc., 974 Forest Drive, Dept. I-3, Morristown, Tenn. 37814

Covering the rails and slate bed

by Eldridge Tucker

Experience has convinced me that the best cloth for pool tables is a blend of 75% wool to 25% nylon, with a weight of 22 oz. per linear yard. A purist might prefer all wool, but the nylon adds durability, and the heavy weight is well worth an extra couple dollars per yard. It comes 62 in. wide; you'll need around 3½ linear yards. Figure 4 at right shows how to cut the cloth for an 8-ft. table with a playing area of 44 in. by 88 in. Adapt this layout to the size of your slate.

Attaching the cushions: After the finish on the rails is dry, the cushions are glued to the angled face with either contact cement or yellow glue. The top edge of the rubber should be flush with the top of the rail. If you use yellow glue, use masking tape to hold the rubber in place until the glue dries.

After the glue has set, trim the rubber to length. Hold the rail so the cushion nose is down against a board or workbench, align a knife blade with the pocket angles and slice through the rubber from base to nose to extend the angle. Dip the knife blade in water for a smoother cut.

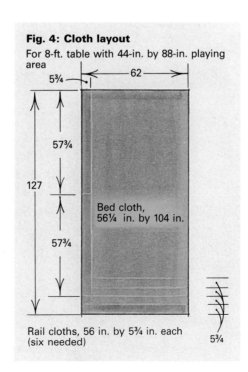

Fig. 4: Cloth layout
For 8-ft. table with 44-in. by 88-in. playing area

5¾
62
57¾
127
57¾
Bed cloth, 56¼ in. by 104 in.
5¾

Rail cloths, 56 in. by 5¾ in. each (six needed)

The cushion facings, made of laminated rubber and canvas, reinforce the cushion ends and cut down on the springiness of the cushion so the ball is not deflected too easily out of the pocket opening. Contact-cement them to the angled ends of the cushions and rails, flush with the beginning of the pocket angle and the top of the rail and cushion. Trim the facing's other edges to the contour of the rail with scissors or a knife. Break the top and front edges of the facing with sandpaper, as shown in the top, left photo on the next page, so a corner won't tear the cloth.

Covering the cushions: You'll need six ¼-in. by ¼-in. softwood feather strips to secure the cloth to the rails. Lay a feather strip in the groove on each of the rails so it's flush at one end, and mark the other end for length. Before removing the strip, make a line near its center, extending onto the rail and cushion, as a reference for lining up the strip when the cloth is being secured, as shown in the top, right photo on the next page. Remove the strip and cut it to length with a saw or chisel. Then, lay one of the precut rail cloths so its edge lines up on the joint between the wood and the rubber. Place the feather strip on the cloth above the groove, align the centerlines and tap the center of the strip partway into the groove. Work toward one end, tapping the strip partway in and pulling a little tension on the cloth in the direction you're working. Continue to the side-pocket ends, but stop about 6 in. back from the corner-pocket ends. While holding the feather strip down in the groove, pull about 2 in. of cloth through the groove below the strip, as shown in the right photo this page, to create a "pucker" so you can stretch the cloth around the angled cushion. Drive the last 6 in. most of the way into the groove to secure the cloth.

With a wood block, tap the length of the strip into the groove so it's just proud of the rail's surface. Trim the excess cloth by slicing with a knife against the cushion side of the protruding strip. Flip the cloth over the feather strip and cushion, and with a cloth-wrapped block, tap the strip flush with the rail's surface. Stretch the cloth tightly over the corner-pocket angle, and staple it to the rail right behind the facing and on the rail's bottom near the edge. The photo (right) on p. 36 shows where to staple. On the side-pocket ends, fold and tuck the cloth like you would wrap a gift, with the open part of the fold on the lower edge of the cushion. Pull the cloth tight and staple like you did on the other ends. Starting at the middle of the rail, stretch the cloth tightly over the cushion and staple it every 2 in. in the shallow rabbet on the rail's bottom. Trim the excess along this rabbet and close to the staples on the ends.

Covering the slate bed: After the slate's joints have been puttied, you can cover the slate bed. Start by lining the pocket cutouts with 1½-in. by 12-in. strips of cloth contact-cemented to the edges of the slate and liner. Brush the slate clean of any small particles left from sanding the putty, and lay the cloth down so it overhangs the slate evenly.

Figure 5, below, shows the steps for stretching the cloth over the slate bed. Always begin at the center of a side and staple

The cushion facing is contact-cemented to the angled rail end and cushion, then trimmed with scissors or a knife. The facing's sharp edge is eased with a sandpaper block so it won't tear the cloth when stretched tightly over the pocket angle.

the cloth every 3 in. into the edge of the slate liner. Work toward the corner pockets, pulling the cloth slightly in the direction you're working. Staple to within 2 in. of the pockets, to leave some play for stretching the cloth over the pocket cutouts.

Pocket cutouts: To stretch the cloth smoothly over the pocket cutouts, you'll need to make radial cuts in the cloth within the pocket areas, as shown below. Grasp the cloth at the pocket and pull it down gently to reveal the outline of the pocket cutout. With a razor knife, cut in the center first and then once or twice on either side to create triangular tabs. Always cut toward the cloth's edge. Again starting at the center, pull down firmly on the tabs and staple them in a neat line near the slate liner's bottom edge. Trim the cloth as close to the staples as possible, to avoid a loose flap that a hand may catch when retrieving the balls from the pocket.

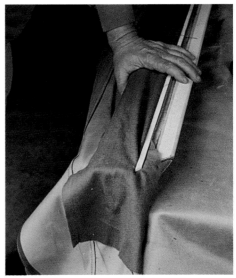

The feather strip is driven into the groove to within 6 in. of the corner-pocket ends. Here, about 2 in. of the cloth is pulled through the groove to create a wrinkle or 'pucker,' which helps stretch the cloth over the corner-pocket angle.

Trim the overhanging cloth around the table if it's long; if there's not too much excess, the blinds will hide it. Finally, cut circles out of the cloth with a knife for all the rail-bolt holes. If you just make an X-cut, the cloth will get caught in the bolt's threads. Now assemble the rails and pockets, and bolt them in place on the slate bed as described in the main article.

All that's left is to place the center spot for locating the rack of balls for the break. I run a string between the middle sights on two opposite side rails, at the end where the balls will be racked, and one between the middle sights on the end rails. Holding a level alongside the strings, I mark on the cloth the point where the two strings intersect and place the self-adhesive spot. Now you're ready. Rack 'em up. □

Eldridge Tucker has been in the pool-table business for 30 years. His shop, Tucker Billiards, is in North Charleston, S.C.

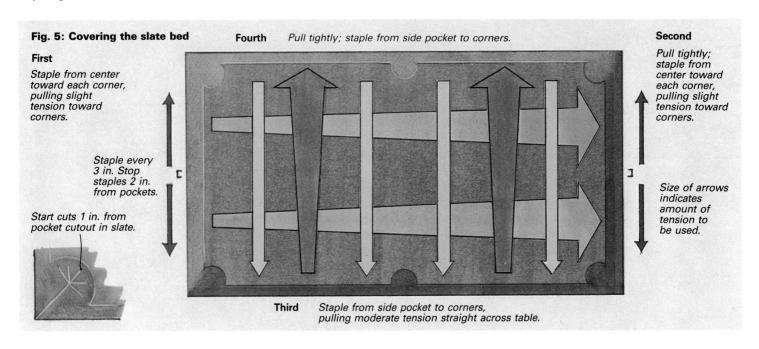

Fig. 5: Covering the slate bed

First
Staple from center toward each corner, pulling slight tension toward corners.

Staple every 3 in. Stop staples 2 in. from pockets.

Start cuts 1 in. from pocket cutout in slate.

Fourth   Pull tightly; staple from side pocket to corners.

Second
Pull tightly; staple from center toward each corner, pulling slight tension toward corners.

Size of arrows indicates amount of tension to be used.

Third   Staple from side pocket to corners, pulling moderate tension straight across table.

Fig. 1: Music stand

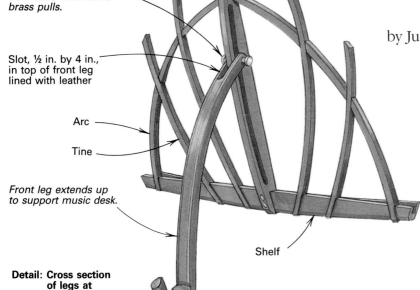

Vertical support

Stove bolt, #8, is 2 in. long.
Saw off head and cap
both ends with round
brass pulls.

Slot, ½ in. by 4 in.,
in top of front leg
lined with leather

Arc

Tine

Front leg extends up
to support music desk.

Shelf

**Detail: Cross section
of legs at
joint centerline**

Front leg has one
additional laminate.

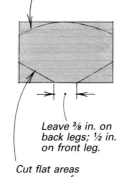

3/8

120°

Biscuit spline

Detail: Cross section of leg

Dome concave face.

Leave 3/8 in. on
back legs; ½ in.
on front leg.

Cut flat areas
on convex face.

Front leg

Back legs

Making a Music Stand

Working with laminated curves

by Judith Ames

The practical requirements of a music stand are simple: a stable base and a small desk to support sheet music. Beyond that, there's very little to restrict the creativity of the designer. My design for the music stand, shown in the drawing at left and the right photo on p. 43, is based on the repetition of simple curves to suggest the pleasant rhythms and patterns of music, or perhaps the peaceful motion of blades of grass blowing in the wind.

The three legs curve up from the floor and come together briefly, like intertwined melodies in a musical score, and then separate again to continue on their own paths; the back legs stop just above the joint, the front leg rises up to support the music desk. The desk consists of a shelf to hold the music, a vertical support that joins the shelf to the front leg, two arcs that connect the ends of the shelf with the top of the vertical support and the four tines that rise up from the shelf and intersect the arcs. A slot routed near the back edge of the desk's vertical support provides height and tilt adjustments in conjunction with the slot in the top of the front leg.

All the parts of the music stand are bent laminations except the desk's shelf and vertical support. Bent lamination is a process of gluing a stack of thin strips together while clamping them to a curved form. This bending method results in consistent curves with very little springback when the pieces are removed from the form, in contrast to steam bending, which can be somewhat unpredictable depending on the grain and quality of each piece of wood that's bent. Despite the consistency of the bent laminations, working with curves still presents challenges usually not encountered in the safe and secure world of straight lines and 90° angles. For example, building this music stand requires forms for laminating the curves, jigs to hold the curved parts while they're machined and individually fitting the curved parts together.

Laminating the curved parts—You need four different laminating forms for gluing up the curved parts: one for the back legs, one for the front leg, one for the arcs and one for the tines. Instead of sandwiching laminations between carefully fitted male and female forms, I just cut about 10 extra lamination strips from a secondary wood to use as caul strips when clamping the lamina-

From *Fine Woodworking* magazine (January 1990) 80:82-86

After eight hours the clamps are removed from one of the laminated legs. Note the unglued laminations that Ames uses as cauls to clamp the glued-up laminations to the form.

tions to the form (see the photo above).

To make the forms, glue and screw pieces of particleboard together face to face until the stack is about 1 in. thicker than the width of the pieces to be laminated. Each form should be about 1 ft. longer than the laminates that'll be glued up on it. Draw the desired curve on top of the particleboard stack and bandsaw to within ¹⁄₃₂ in. on the convex side of the line. The curves for the tines and arcs can simply be drawn with a compass; the tines have an 18-in. radius and the arcs an 11¼-in. radius. To duplicate the leg curves, use the grid pattern in figure 2 at right. The lower portion of the front and back legs are identical but they differ above the joint area. Mark the centerline of the leg joint on the form so you'll have a permanent reference for this all-important point. After bandsawing the curve, eliminate any wobbles from the form's curved face by working to the line with a horizontal edge sander or a rasp, taking care to keep the face square with the top and bottom of the form. Then, bandsaw a parallel curve 3 in. behind the working face so you can span the form with medium-size bar clamps, shown in the photo above. Finally, screw the form to a baseboard and coat the entire assembly, as well as the caul strips, with paste wax so glue will not adhere.

Because the music stand is so delicate, I recommend using a dense hardwood, like maple or cherry. Select straight-grain pieces for strength and to help hide the laminations. The bill of materials at right gives dimensions for the laminate stock, number of laminations for each part and the dimensions for each laminated part after it's been squared up for shaping. The arcs and tines are glued up twice as wide and long as their finished size. These curves are then bandsawn lengthwise and crosscut in half to give you four pieces from just the one glue-up.

Before ripping the lamination strips, mark a V on one side of the stock so you can keep the laminations in sequence while gluing. Rip the laminations on the tablesaw, using slow even pressure to keep the cut smooth, and, after every other pass, run the sawn face over the jointer to keep it flat and true.

In preparation for gluing up the laminations, assemble plenty of clamps and dilute some yellow glue with one part water to eight

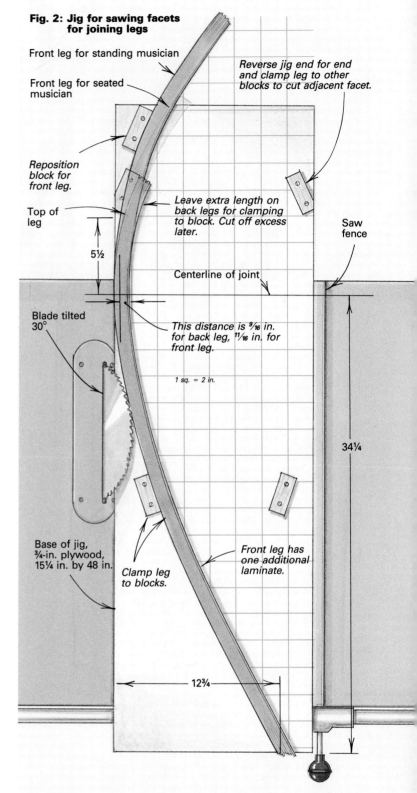

Fig. 2: Jig for sawing facets for joining legs

Front leg for standing musician

Front leg for seated musician

Reposition block for front leg.

Top of leg

5½

Blade tilted 30°

Base of jig, ¾-in. plywood, 15¼ in. by 48 in.

Clamp leg to blocks.

Reverse jig end for end and clamp leg to other blocks to cut adjacent facet.

Leave extra length on back legs for clamping to block. Cut off excess later.

Centerline of joint

Saw fence

This distance is ⁹⁄₁₆ in. for back leg, ¹¹⁄₁₆ in. for front leg.

1 sq. = 2 in.

34¼

Front leg has one additional laminate.

12¾

Bill of Materials

No.	Description	Stock size (in.)	Laminations, ⅛ in. thick†	Finished size (in.)
4	Tines, 18-in. radius*	1 × 1⅜ × 30	3	⅜ × ½ × 15
2	Arcs, 11¼-in. radius*	1 × 1⅜ × 4	3	⅜ × ¼ × 16
1	Front leg (sitting)	2½ × 1⅝ × 53½	9	1⅛ × 1½ × 53
1	Front leg (standing)	2½ × 1⅝ × 60	9	1⅛ × 1½ × 59½
2	Back legs	2¼ × 1⅝ × 46½	8	1 × 1½ × 46
1	Vertical support	½ × 1½ × 13½	None	Same
1	Shelf	1½ × 1⅝ × 18½	None	Same

* Arcs and tines are laminated twice as wide and long, and then resawn on the bandsaw and crosscut to length.
† Rip about 10 extra lams of each size to use as clamping cauls.

Drawings: Kathleen Rushton

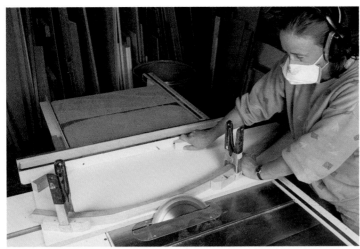

The facets for joining the legs are cut on the tablesaw by clamping the legs one by one to a jig. Position the leg on the jig by aligning the joint's centerline, which is transferred from the laminating form to each leg, with a corresponding line on the jig. The jig is reversed and the leg is clamped to the blocks on the opposite edge to cut the adjacent facet.

Taping a 15° wedge to the plate joiner's 45° angle attachment gives you the 60° angle needed to cut the slots in the facets where the legs come together.

parts glue, which allows a little more clamping time and makes the glue easier to spread. Lay out the laminates in sequence side by side on scrap plywood and spread the thinned glue evenly over their surfaces with a paint roller. Turn the pieces over and spread glue on the other side also. Of course, avoid spreading glue on the surfaces that will be the inside and outside of the glued-up curve. Quickly stack the laminates in sequence against the form and add the waxed scrap laminations. Then, clamp the strips to the form, starting in the center and working toward the ends. The laminations should be pressed down on the baseboard and clamped every couple of inches to ensure a smooth, continuous curve. Remember to transfer the centerline of the leg joint onto the glued-up leg and re-mark this point whenever necessary throughout all the subsequent machining; you'll need it to accurately saw the joint facets.

After eight hours remove the clamps and scrape off the excess glue. The laminations will shift slightly during glue-up so you should square up one edge of each piece by running it over the jointer while holding the convex face against the fence with a pushstick. Then with the trued edge down, thickness-plane the legs to 1½ in. and the arc and tine curves to 1¼ in. Bandsaw the arcs and tines in half lengthwise and plane the resulting halves to ½ in. thick.

Machining the legs—The cross-sectional detail in figure 1 on p. 39 shows the two adjacent facets that form a 120° angle on each leg where they join. The tablesaw jig, shown in figure 2 on the fac-

ing page and the top photo at left, registers the legs so all the facets are cut at exactly the same part of each leg's curve, ensuring that the facets are identical. The centerline, transferred from the laminating forms to the legs, is now used to locate the legs on the jig. When cutting the facets on the front leg, you'll have to unscrew the jig's upper clamping blocks and relocate them to accommodate the difference in the top part of the curve.

Refer to figure 2 for the dimensions of the jig's base, and use the grid pattern for marking the joint's centerline on the jig and gauging the placement of the legs. Align the leg's centerline with the corresponding line on the jig and screw the clamping blocks to the base. Then, reverse the leg and repeat the procedure to locate the blocks on the other edge of the jig. Now, clamp a leg to the blocks and with the sawblade tilted to 30° make test cuts, adjusting the fence until the angled cut just reaches the center of the vertical face of the leg. This cut is made on both back legs, and then the jig is turned end for end and the adjacent facet is cut on each leg while the leg is clamped to the blocks on the jig's opposite edge. Relocate the upper blocks and cut the facets on the front leg.

To index and strengthen the joint between the three legs, I use a plate joiner to cut a slot in each facet for a biscuit spline. A 15° wedge taped to the plate joiner's 45° angle attachment registers the slot at the proper angle (see the bottom photo at left). Clamp the leg securely to the workbench, and cut a slot that's centered vertically and horizontally in the facet; then, turn the leg over and cut a slot in the other facet.

Now, before shaping the legs, bandsaw the front leg's top to length, sand it to a dome shape and rout the ½-in. by 4-in. slot to hold the vertical support. Figure 2 gives dimensions from the center-line to the top of the front leg for either a standing or sitting musician. I cut the slot on the router table with a ½-in.-dia. straight bit. Run the leg's convex side down on the table and make three or four passes, raising the bit each pass until it cuts clear through. On the last pass go a bit farther so that the end of the slot is clean and straight. To increase the friction for holding the position of the desk later, line the slot with ¹⁄₁₆-in.-thick leather. Shape a block to fit snugly in the slot along with the leather and use it to hold the leather until the glue dries. With the block still in place, drill the ⅛-in. hole through the leg for the machine screw that clamps the desk in the slot.

Both the concave and convex faces of the legs can now be shaped to their final profiles (see the detail in figure 1 on p. 39). Use the tablesaw setup shown in the photo on the next page to cut the flat areas on the convex face that are parallel with the joint facets. With the blade still tilted 30°, raise it until it cuts into an auxiliary fence clamped to the rip fence. Then, make test cuts to set the fence so the angled cut comes about ³⁄₁₆ in. short of the vertical center of the face. Keeping the piece against the fence and in contact with the cutting edge of the blade, run each leg past the blade. Repeat the pass a couple of times on each surface to be sure you've trimmed as much as possible. Then, remove the sawmarks from the flat areas by hand-sanding with a block, carefully preserving the hard edges formed by the angled cuts.

To dome the concave face of each leg, I use a 1¼-in.-radius piloted roundover bit in a router table. However, because I don't want a complete roundover, I draw the desired arc on one of the leg's ends, which I then hold up to the bit and adjust the bit's height until it will cut very close to the line. Be sure to first run a test cut on the same width stock to see if you like the results. The flat area that's left at the center (where the bearing ran) is blended into the gentle arc by hand-scraping. Finally, sand the legs to 150-grit, smoothing the domed faces yet maintaining the hard lines where the curved faces meet the flat sides.

Now you're ready to glue the legs together; all three legs go together at the same time. Spread a very thin coat of yellow glue on all the mating surfaces, including the biscuits and slots. Go easy though: You don't want excessive squeeze-out. Glue one biscuit into each leg and then start them all at the same time into the mating slots in the adjacent legs. Squeeze the joint with your hands so the legs come together evenly. To provide firm, even pressure while the glue dries, tightly wrap a bicycle inner tube around the legs, beginning 3 in. above the joint and extending 3 in. below it. After about 30 minutes, remove the inner tube and carefully scrape away the worst of the squeeze-out. Let the joint dry for another hour before cleaning it with a chisel and 150-grit sandpaper.

To level the legs on the floor, bandsaw a hole in a 4-in. square of ½-in. plywood through which the leg will fit. Stand the tripod base on a flat surface, place each leg, one by one, through the cutout and scribe a line on each along the top of the plywood. With a handsaw, cut the legs on the line so they will sit flat. The base is now complete.

Building the music desk—The basic structure of the music desk is the inverted T formed by dadoing the vertical support into the back of the shelf. The dimensions for these two parts are given in the bill of materials on p. 40 and figure 3 below. To rout the adjusting slot in the vertical support parallel to the bandsawn curve of its back, I use a single-point guide fixture clamped to the router table, as shown in the left photo on the facing page.

The fixture is simply a piece of plywood with a ¾-in.-dia. dowel for the guide pin and a slot for the bit to protrude through. Clamp the fixture to the router table so the pin is 5⁄16 in. from the edge of a ¼-in.-dia. bit, which is set to cut ³⁄16 in. deep. Hold the vertical support's curved back against the guide pin and plunge it onto the rotating bit. Be sure to keep the curve pressed against the same point on the guide pin as you push the piece from right to left, and lift it off the bit when you're near the slot's end. Make three passes,

The convex face of each leg is shaped on the tablesaw using the setup shown above. The blade is tilted 30° and raised up into an auxiliary fence. Trim the corners of each leg's face by running the leg against the fence while maintaining maximum contact with the blade's cutting edge. Repeat the pass until the flat area you're cutting is uniform along the curve.

increasing the bit's depth by ³⁄16 in. each pass. On the final pass, when the bit cuts through the workpiece, start and stop the bit a little closer to each end to establish crisp ends on the slot. A note of caution: Any plunge cut can be dangerous. Hold the piece firmly and keep the work moving right to left: If you change direction, the router bit will try to grab the workpiece and pull it out of your hands.

Mill the shelf stock to the dimensions given in the bill of materials. Then, on the tablesaw, cut the 15⁄16-in.-wide dado, which will hold the sheet music, the full length of the shelf. Readjust the dado blade to cut the cross-grain dado in the center of the shelf's back for the vertical support. Before proceeding with shaping the shelf, you must first individually cut and fit the other parts of the desk to

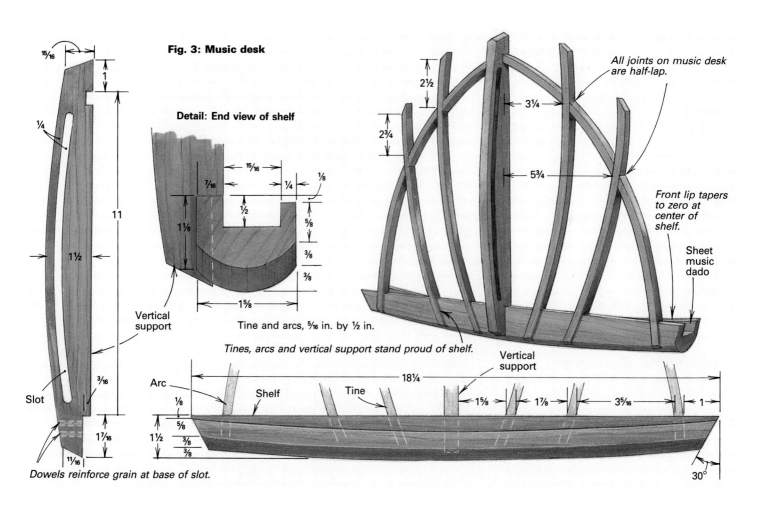

Fig. 3: Music desk

Detail: End view of shelf

Vertical support

Tine and arcs, 5⁄16 in. by ½ in.

Tines, arcs and vertical support stand proud of shelf.

Slot

Dowels reinforce grain at base of slot.

Arc

Shelf

Tine

All joints on music desk are half-lap.

Front lip tapers to zero at center of shelf.

Sheet music dado

Vertical support

Photo: Mark Van S

With a shopmade single-point guide fixture clamped to the router table, Ames routs the adjusting slot parallel with the back curve of the vertical support.

With the tines clamped in place, the author scribes along their edges. Next she hand-saws kerfs inside the scribed lines and then routs the dadoes.

The gentle curves of this cherry music stand, made almost entirely of bent laminated parts, combine to create a piece of furniture that harmonizes with the music it supports.

the shelf and to each other. Fitting these parts isn't difficult, but it must be done in the correct order as I will describe.

The first step is to fit the arcs to the shelf, but to do this you'll need to locate where you want the miters at the tops of the arcs to come together. Place the sheet music dado on the edge of a piece of plywood on which you've drawn a line perpendicular to that edge. The shelf should be back-side up and centered on the line. Now, measure 11 in. from the top back edge of the shelf and make a mark that intersects the perpendicular line; this is the high point where the arcs meet on the vertical support. Lay one of the arcs so its convex edge intersects the 11-in. mark on the plywood and crosses the shelf 1 in. from the end. Now, use a sharp knife to scribe along the sides of the arc for the dado in the shelf, and mark for the miter at the top by referring to the perpendicular line. Repeat the procedure for the arc on the other side, and then miter the top ends and cut the dadoes in the back of the shelf.

Next, cut the half-laps on the lower end of the arcs and fit them to the shelf dadoes. Then the bottom, front edge of the vertical support is notched and fit into the dado in the shelf. Assemble the shelf and the vertical support, and scribe and cut the dado at the top of the vertical support to receive the mitered top ends of the arcs. Now, assemble the shelf, the vertical support and the arcs (without glue) to form the desk's frame and place it face down. Measure at a right angle from the vertical support and mark the arcs and the shelf where the tines will intersect them (see figure 1 on p. 39 for dimensions). By holding the tines on the appropriate lines with spring clamps, you can scribe the location of the half-laps, as shown in the center photo above. Then scribe and cut the dadoes in the shelf's back and the rabbets on the arcs and tines to form the half-lap joints.

The method I use for cutting these small dadoes is to first make ¼-in.-deep kerfs, with a Japanese saw, just inside the scribed lines to mark the boundaries of the dadoes. Then, I can remove most of the waste quickly with a router without worrying about it pulling beyond the sawkerf. A small router with a 3-in. base designed for laminate trimming is ideal for this job. I carefully rout very close to the line and perfect the final fit with a hand chisel.

After fitting all the arcs and tines, you can finish shaping the shelf. Bandsaw the bottom curve and sand it smooth. Then, use the single-point guide fixture on the router table (see the left photo above) to trim the front rim of the shelf parallel with the bottom

curve. When trimmed, the rim's low point should be flush with the bottom of the sheet music dado at the center of the shelf; the low rim at the center makes for easy page turning, but because the rim rises at each end, it holds the corners of the sheet music open. It's a good idea to trim the rim in two passes to help you get the feel of it on the final cut; just move the fixture's pin closer to the bit for the final pass. When the rim is just right, cut the ends of the shelf so they slope in at a 30° angle. Sand the trimmed rim by hand and make a sanding block that fits inside the sheet music dado to clean it up.

Finally, dome the bottom of the shelf by sanding freehand on a horizontal edge sander or a belt sander clamped to the workbench. Use an 80-grit belt and draw the desired curve on the shelf's front and back. Holding the shelf at each end, rock it back and forth until you've sanded an even curve up to the line on the front. Then, draw the arc's profile on the ends and roll the shelf forward and back as you rock from end to end, to smooth the bottom to the profile. Be careful to maintain the hard edges. Repeat the process with a 150-grit belt, and then hand-sand to 220-grit.

Assemble the entire music desk one more time so you can mark and trim the top ends of the tines and vertical support and the bottom ends of the arcs and tines. The arcs and tines are slightly proud of the shelf's back and this detail is carried through by trimming their bottom ends about ¹/₁₆ in. below and parallel with the shelf's domed bottom. All the parts are disassembled and sanded to 150-grit. Glue the vertical support and the arcs to the shelf first, applying yellow glue sparingly to each joint and clamping with small spring clamps. After 45 minutes, unclamp the joints and clean off the excess glue. Then, glue the tines in place.

I finish-sand the entire piece with 220-grit paper and apply three coats of oil. I use a product called Profin, available from Daly's Inc., 3525 Stone Way N., Seattle, Wash. 98103, which is a mixture of polyurethane, tung oil, thinner and drying agents.

The vertical support of the music desk is clamped in place at the desired height and tilt by tightening round brass pulls (available from Ball and Ball, 463 W. Lincoln Highway, Exton, Pa. 19341) on both ends of a 2-in.-long stove bolt with its head cut off. I flatten opposite sides of the pulls with a few blows of a hammer; flattened pulls look more interesting and are easier to grasp between the thumb and forefinger to tighten or loosen the shelf. □

Judith Ames builds furniture in Seattle, Wash.

Staff

Laminated Spinning Wheel

Spokes without a lathe

by Albert Peetoom

Except for parts of the whorl and bobbin, this laminated spinning wheel was built without a lathe. A doubled-over loop of cord drives the spindle and whorl.

I built my first spinning wheel, the one in the photo above, while studying for my journeyman's papers as a boatbuilder. As the old hands patiently passed down their skills to us apprentices, it astonished me to think that after just four years I would be entitled to their rate of pay—how could I ever learn to be an accomplished woodworker in four years, or even forty?

So, in my spare hours, I sought other woodworking projects that would help round out my skills. One confidence-builder was a marquetry panel I made of a 150-year-old house in Aurora, Ontario, where I had lived when I was a child. The second project was inspired by the sight of a laminated ship's wheel at a boat show. I stared at the wheel for ten minutes, building it in my mind. But, of course, I couldn't justify building a whole ship as an excuse to make the wheel!

I don't remember who mentioned it first, but it turned out that my mother-in-law wanted a spinning wheel, and that's how this project began. Spinning wheels have been built for hundreds of years throughout the world. They were not only designed as machines, but also as attractive pieces of furniture. Today, antique wheels are sought for living-room decor rather than their spinning ability. Yet mine was to be a working wheel, and to ensure that it did its job, I started with the dimensions of the Norwegian raised-table wheel pictured in Bud Kronenberg's book *Spinning Wheel, Building and Restoration.* This book is, unfortunately, out of print, but at the end of this article I have listed another that should help in getting this wheel to run correctly. There are

several options for the spinning mechanism. The design shown here is meant for spinning fine-to-medium yarn at a skilled level.

Very briefly, a spinning wheel works by rotating a bobbin shaft (see figure 3) very rapidly. Wool fibers are fed in through the end of the shaft, which twists them up into yarn. The twisted wool feeds out through a hole in the side of the bobbin shaft and runs up a row of hooks on the flyer, which is glued to the bobbin shaft. On my wheel, the pulley attached to the bobbin is smaller than the one on the shaft, and so the bobbin turns faster than the flyer, winding up the wool as it's spun. The bobbin pulley has a flat-bottomed groove, so that it can slip a little as the bobbin fills.

I hope I can cover enough here that you will at least be able to make a spoked wheel without needing a lathe. For those interested in completing the full project, there should be enough hints in the drawings, photos and sources to finish the job, provided you are willing to add a measure of your own ingenuity.

I made my first wheel with one small jig that bent and glued each U-shaped spoke section separately. When I had them all done, I epoxied them together to form the wheel, then added the rim and the hub. One of my first reactions was to be grateful that epoxy was so good at filling gaps. Yet each lamination improved, and by the time I got to laminating the treadle, I could produce tight, seamless joints.

A spinning wheel does not have to be as strong as a wagon wheel, but it does have to be balanced and must run true. One of the things I learned along the way is that the best lamination is

From *Fine Woodworking* magazine (March 1987) 63:78-82

The key to a balanced wheel is an accurate form. Here the author bends steamed laminations into place for drying, after which they will be epoxied together into a rigid framework. The hub and rim are then added to complete the wheel.

achieved when the strips are pressed between a male-and-female jig. For my second wheel, I made the full-wheel jig shown in the photo above. To make a laminated wheel that turns true, it's most important that the clamping jig is made as accurately as possible. My jig is centered out around a ¼-in. hole through the plywood; this hole represents where the axle will be, and its importance will become clear as we go along. The dimensions of the jig can be taken from figure 3. Lay the lines out clearly and number all the jig pieces and their positions on the form. Use screws to fasten the teardrop-shaped sections, because they will be removed and re-fastened several times. Wedges, as shown, give adequate clamping pressure.

The wood to be bent and laminated should be clear stock with a relatively straight grain. I have used black walnut, red oak and Honduras mahogany. Walnut has excellent bending qualities. Oak must be cut slightly thinner than walnut to take the same stress without breaking. Mahogany is less pliable than oak and breaks more frequently, so extra pieces must be cut.

In making the first wheel, I began by soaking the strips in hot water before bending. I soon discovered that steaming makes things go much faster. My steam box is a simple long box made of plywood and heated by an electric tea kettle. I steam the strips for about four minutes, bend and wedge them into the form, then allow them to dry. Steamed strips will dry overnight, whereas soaked ones sometimes take days. When the strips are removed from the form there is some springback, but they retain

enough of the shape to be returned to the form for gluing.

For gluing, every part of the jig must be wrapped in light plastic sheeting to prevent the jig from becoming part of the finished wheel. In your glue-up procedure, make sure that the plastic doesn't puncture, because the wheel must pop off the jig with little effort and return there after clean-up so that the hub and rim parts can be added.

I used epoxy for the entire spinning wheel. If a laminate does not press quite tight, the glue will fill the void with no structural problems. The epoxy I used is made by Industrial Formulators of Canada, Ltd. (3824 William St., Burnaby, B.C.).

The epoxy's short working time—45 minutes—meant that I could not glue up the whole spoke assembly at one time. Instead, on the first day I glued three of the U-shaped spoke sections together, supporting the outer spokes with unglued laminations in the jig. After the epoxy had set up somewhat, but not fully cured, I removed the three-spoke assembly from the form and cleaned up the excess glue. In general, with epoxy, it's best to sand off the excess within 24 hours, when the glue is still pliable and cuts well without raising dust. If you allow the epoxy to fully cure (usually in two or three days, depending on the temperature) it chips off, taking wood with it. The hard glue dulls a cutting edge as well, so plan clean-up time carefully.

The second day, I glued three more spoke sections to the first; on the third day, I added the last two sections. Don't be surprised, as you add sections, if you have to unscrew parts of the

Photos, except where noted: Keith De Jong, drawings: Joel Katzowitz

Fig. 1: Adding the hub

1. Trim ends of spokes in form using sawtooth hole drill.

2. Cut hub with flycutter.

3. Insert hub, mark notches and bandsaw. Trace insert profiles, bandsaw, and epoxy hub assembly in place.

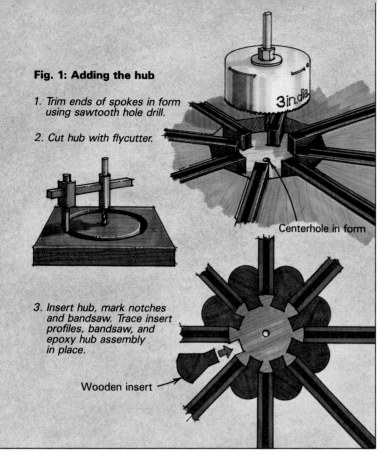

Centerhole in form

Wooden insert

Fig. 2: Grooving the rim

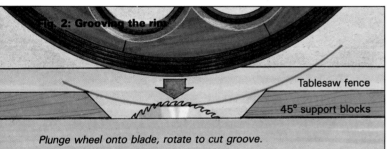

Tablesaw fence

45° support blocks

Plunge wheel onto blade, rotate to cut groove.

Fig. 3: Wheel dimensions

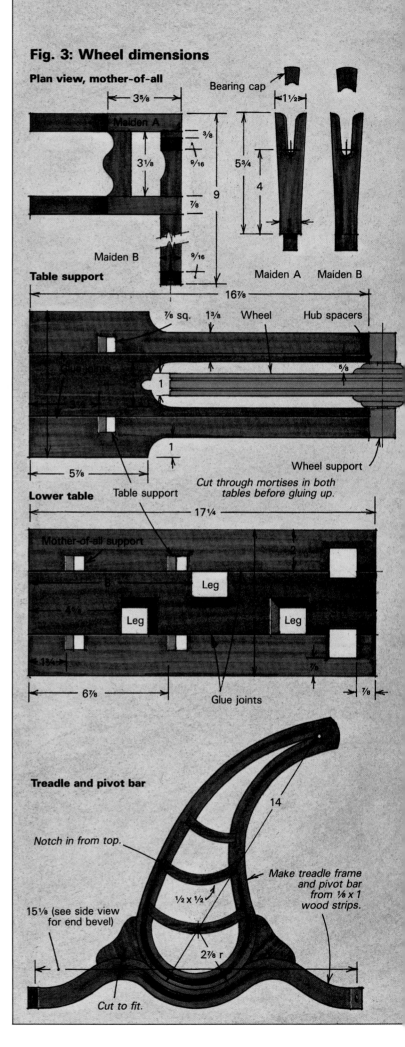

Plan view, mother-of-all

Bearing cap

Maiden A

Maiden B

Table support

Maiden A   Maiden B

⅞ sq.   1⅜   Wheel   Hub spacers

Wheel support

Cut through mortises in both tables before gluing up.

Lower table   Table support

Mother-of-all support

Leg

Leg   Leg

Glue joints

Treadle and pivot bar

Notch in from top.

Make treadle frame and pivot bar from ⅛ x 1 wood strips.

15⅛ (see side view for end bevel)

½ x ½

2⅞ r

Cut to fit.

form to remove and replace the wheel. It will be tight. The hub assembly, which will hold a ¼-in. axle, is added to the wheel as shown in figure 1. To make room for the hub to fit in the form, I bandsawed the points off the teardrop-shaped blocks. If this had been a production effort, I would have made entirely new blocks for the purpose, or even a whole second form. The importance of the centered axle hole now becomes clear—it's the pilot hole for trimming the spoke ends to length. When the hub insert is added, its centerhole lines up with the original hole in the jig, and becomes the pivot hole for truing the wheel on the bandsaw. I'll get to that in a moment, but first we have to add the rim.

The rim is composed of sections of solid wood surrounded by five strips of laminations to form what could be called the tire. The entire rim is ¼ in. thicker than the spokes for two reasons. First, aesthetics—I thought it would look better. Second, function—I needed the extra width on the tire for the two grooves for the spinning wheel's drive cord.

The solid-wood rim sections are bandsawn to shape and epoxied to the spoke sections on the form. I removed the original wedge blocks and added new ones for wedging the rim segments in place. To center the ¾-in.-thick spokes in the 1-in. rim, I shimmed the spoke assembly with ⅛-in.-thick strips, and added another layer of ⅛-in.-thick pieces on top, to allow a level surface for weighting the wheel flat as the glue cured.

After the epoxy had hardened somewhat, I removed the wheel and cleaned up the glue. Then I made a cove joint between the

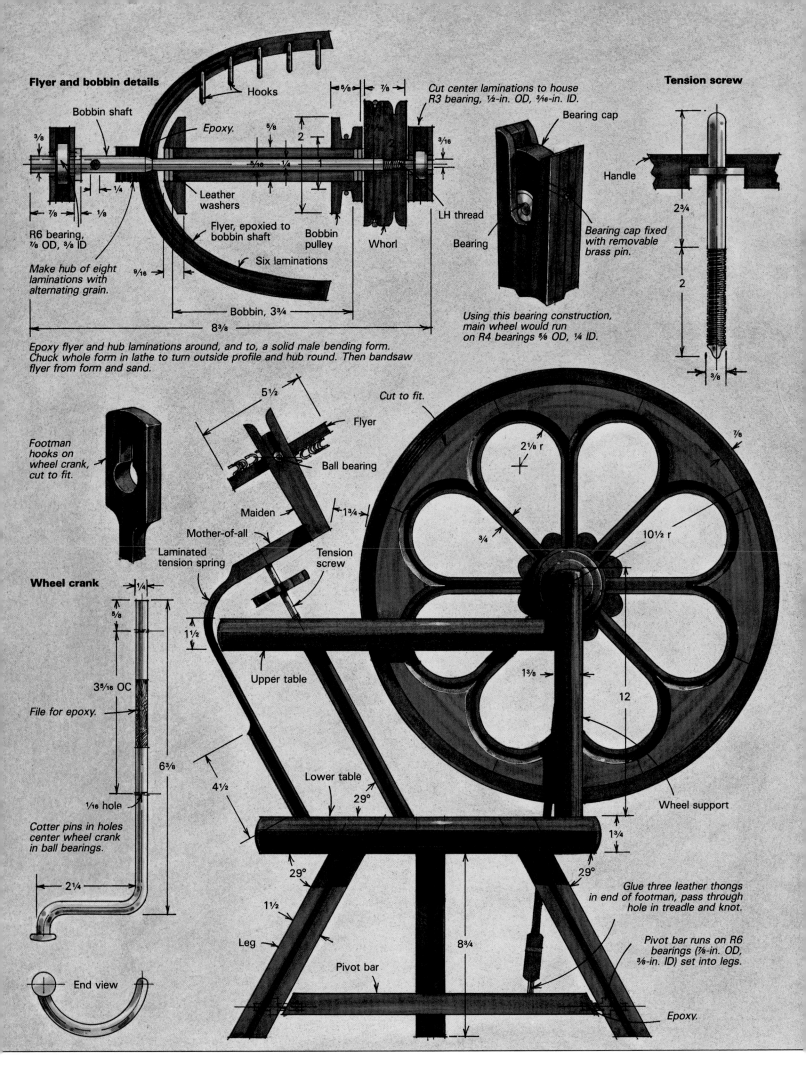

Flyer and bobbin details

Hooks

Bobbin shaft

Epoxy.

Cut center laminations to house R3 bearing, ½-in. OD, 3/16-in. ID.

Leather washers

Flyer, epoxied to bobbin shaft

Bobbin pulley

Whorl

Six laminations

LH thread

R6 bearing, ⅞ OD, ⅜ ID

Make hub of eight laminations with alternating grain.

Bobbin, 3¾

8⅜

Epoxy flyer and hub laminations around, and to, a solid male bending form. Chuck whole form in lathe to turn outside profile and hub round. Then bandsaw flyer from form and sand.

Tension screw

Bearing cap

Handle

Bearing

Bearing cap fixed with removable brass pin.

2¾

2

3/8

Using this bearing construction, main wheel would run on R4 bearings ⅝ OD, ¼ ID.

Footman hooks on wheel crank, cut to fit.

Flyer

Ball bearing

Maiden

Mother-of-all

Laminated tension spring

Tension screw

Cut to fit.

2⅛ r

¾

10½ r

7/8

1⅜

12

Wheel crank

¼

⅝

3 5/16 OC

File for epoxy.

6⅜

1/16 hole

Cotter pins in holes center wheel crank in ball bearings.

2¼

End view

5½

1¾

1½

Upper table

Lower table

29°

4½

29°

1½

Leg

Pivot bar

8¾

29°

Wheel support

1¾

Glue three leather thongs in end of footman, pass through hole in treadle and knot.

Pivot bar runs on R6 bearings (⅞-in. OD, ⅜-in. ID) set into legs.

Epoxy.

Cutting the tricky angled mortises for the legs (see figure 3) is a matter of sawing and chiseling before the table is glued up.

Forms to clamp parts with compound curves must be designed so that the clamping pressure occurs where needed, perpendicular to the centers of the bends. The crossbars in the finished treadle are bent and notched into place separately.

rim segments and the spokes using a ⅜-in. #7 gouge. My next step was to true the wheel round; for this I used a circle-cutting jig on the bandsaw.

I applied the outside laminations one at a time, cutting each layer to fit with butt joints. It doesn't matter whether each layer of the rim is a single strip or not—mine were two pieces each. I didn't bother to steam these strips, as the bend was not severe. The four inner layers are ⅛-in. strips of light and dark walnut; the outermost layer is purpleheart. For pressure, I used a web clamp. After the last outside lamination went on, I found that the wheel did not need truing; if it had, I would have used the axle hole as a pivot and trued the wheel with sandpaper and scrapers.

Those are the basics of making the wheel. To make the hub covers, I cut discs with a flycutter, then shaped them with an ogee bit in a router. The covers are epoxied to the hub and act as spacers so the wheel can stay centered in the uprights.

Here's a quick course in completing the spinning wheel. The uprights and the legs are notched right through the upper and lower tables. Instead of drilling and chiseling through a solid piece, I laid out the notches in such a way that they could all be cut from an edge before glue-up, as shown in the photo above. The two front legs come through the lower table at a compound 29° angle. Because of this, these legs are parallelograms in shape and must be cut by trial-and-error to fit.

Up to that time in my woodworking apprenticeship, these were some of the most complicated joints I had made. I have to confess that they would not meet my standards today. But I had viewed the project as a step in the learning process, and counted on the gap-filling properties of the epoxy to fill the gaps in my skills. When it came to fitting the legs, I had some difficulty keeping the epoxy from draining out of the joint. To remedy this problem, I simply covered the top of the notch with wide cellophane tape and turned the table upside down. The tape formed a dam to keep the glue in, and was sanded off after the glue cured. You can probably see some wide glue lines in the photo of the first wheel; the second wheel shows much improvement, and when I make a third wheel it will be better yet.

Here's another learning experience: On my first wheel, I supported the wheel-crank bearings by laminating them into the uprights. This method called for improvement because the bearings are inaccessible and the wooden support tends to wear with use. On the second wheel I used a bearing cap instead, as shown in figure 3, in much the same way as the bobbin shaft is kept in line on the maidens.

The drive cord is a single length looped double. A spinning wheel needs a sensitive, practical means of adjusting the drive tension. The standard practice is to use a wooden bolt and nut to draw or tilt the mother-of-all carrier. Instead, I mounted the mother-of-all on a springy lamination, to help even out the drive impulses. To tension and steady this assembly, a screw is threaded into the upper table; its top end fits into a metal sleeve in a 1-in. slot in the mother-of-all.

To make the threads for the tension screw, I drilled a ⁷⁄₁₆-in. hole through the upper table and covered the bottom with cellophane tape. I filled the hole with epoxy and, as it started to get thick, I put a waxed ⅜-in. bolt into the hole, cleaning away the excess epoxy as it was displaced. When the glue was good and hard, I heated the bolt with a soldering iron and turned it out. The epoxy threads were very tight at this point, but by rolling up some 120-grit sandpaper and running it up and down in the hole, I was able to get enough clearance.

For the hardware, your best bet would probably be to enlist the aid of a local metalworking shop or order from the firm listed in the sources. As a boatbuilder, I had an easy time getting the hardware custom made for a reasonable cost—about $100 and a case of beer. All the hardware that requires a bond to wood can be attached with epoxy. The section of metal that gets glued must be filed to create a jagged surface that will allow a mechanical bond with the glue.

My major problem, in terms of the time involved, was tracking down someone with an abrasive surfacer large enough to sand the wheel flat. That problem was finally overcome through dogged perseverance, and the first wheel eventually came out fine. This second wheel, built on a much more accurate form, may not need surfacing at all. We'll see. □

Albert Peetoom lives in Maple Ridge, British Columbia.

Sources of supply

A complete set of metal parts for this wheel can be ordered from Fairfield Manufacturing, 213 Streibeigh Lane, Montoursville, PA 17754. (717) 368-8624. Total cost for sealed bearings is $58.50; the crank, spindle, etc. total $83.45.

For fine tuning and running the wheel, try: *The Care and Feeding of Spinning Wheels* by Karen Pauli; 76 p., 1981, illustrated, paperback, $7.50. Published by Interweave Press, Inc., 306 North Washington Ave., Loveland, CO 80537.

The Custom-Fitted Chair

An exploration of ergonomics

by Tom Hurley

The routes by which some of us find our way into chair-making often become clear only in retrospect. In the early 1980s, I was spending a lot of time sitting in a badly frayed aluminum lawn chair, staring into space, mulling over project details and worrying about my Visa debt, its decimal point shifting one space to the right with each new cash flow crisis of my custom cabinetmaking shop. The seven years during which I'd tackled a variety of furnituremaking commissions hadn't included chairs, but had required turning rapidly from one unrelated piece to another, saying hasty goodbyes to unresolved design problems after barely saying hello. I was longing for depth in a specialty that would combine the economies of repetition with the chance to refine a single demanding product through several generations.

Shortly thereafter, the Toronto Transit Commission began replacing its fleet of ancient, rusting streetcars with new ones whose seats, compared with the generous cushy benches of the old, struck me as a backward step into ergonomic stinginess. This, for me, was the last straw in a world already crowded with chairs that were uncomfortable for normal-size people and punishing for anyone who strayed from the anthropometric norm. Chair design had always beckoned to me from afar as *the* major woodworking challenge, and I suddenly knew that the time had come, as it comes for many a restless maker, to take a whole-hearted run at the problem.

I settled into my lawn chair to ponder the three major options in producing a truly comfortable high-back chair: a single-model chair that would fit the average body, like that of my first customer, whose deposit check I'd just received; a user-adjustable chair that would meet a broader range of anatomical needs; and a one-off chair, custom-fitted to the body of the individual paying the bill. Distrusting ergonomic charts, which are based on that designer's phantom, everyman, I started planning a fitting jig that would reassure my first customer, in advance, of the comfort of his as yet undesigned new chair. As I bolted together a rough plywood framework with nineteen adjustable slats, I realized that a basic decision was already being made: I was suddenly in the business of building custom-fitted chairs.

While the first fitting session with the client was awkward, it provided the dimensions and contours needed to address the next phase of design: the visual and structural aspects of the chair. I didn't want a boxy-looking orthopedic device, but rather something light on its feet, with detachable cushions in a fully exposed hardwood frame, whose structure would allow for strength without sacrificing delicacy. I wanted a repeatable overall design that allowed individual chairs to incorporate different contours and dimensions to suit the body of the owner. With the help of full-scale drawings and bandsawn, hot-glued mock-ups, I arrived at a design to which I pinned the promotional name, "The Custom Chair."

Three completed chairs later, skinned knuckles told me I needed a more sophisticated jig for fitting customers, one that would be easier to fine-tune over a broader dimensional range. The result was a new sit-in device, shown on the next page. Its vertical plywood walls enclose a series of movable frames, each frame representing a seat or back slat in the final chair. A threaded rod at each end of a slat is fixed to a shop-made plastic gear. Nineteen bicycle chains, purchased from a suspicious clerk at a local cycle shop, connect the pairs of gears. Each slat can be rotated, raised and lowered under load, and moved back and forth in relation to its neighbors. Eight automobile scissor jacks enable simultaneous height and pitch adjustments to the independent seat and back assemblies. An extra set of drop-in back slats of varying curves make it possible to properly cradle the transverse contours of wide and narrow upper bodies.

This device turned out to be a valuable tool for subsequent chairs, allowing me to explore and confirm with test subjects the many comfort factors emphasized by other chair designers. Perhaps above all else, new customers welcomed the prospect of proper support for the S-curve of the spine, as well as for the transverse curvature of the rib-cage, which flattens out as it approaches the area of the shoulders. Above that, a neck roll cradles the head to complete support for the upper body. The fitting chair let me forget about orthodox ergonomic prescriptions and trust the individual body to seek its own proper seat length and height, plus an appropriate pitch that would neither jackknife the pelvic area nor send the sitter in a slow slide onto the floor. A pair of wooden arms, adjustable for pitch and height, provided clients with a sense of enclosure and security while they sipped tea and leafed through magazines during their fitting. The arms were set high enough to offer support without bunching the shoulders.

In retrospect, I should not have been surprised at the teasing I got over this contraption, which certainly symbolized my obsession with the project, and seemed to many to embody a kind of madness. In fact, given the requirements of flexibility and access to controls under load, it was the simplest version I could devise.

As my experience fitting customers grew, it became clearer just how subtle and complex is the full answer to the question, "What makes a chair comfortable?" There were many surprises, the first being the need to help the customer overcome the phys-

From *Fine Woodworking* magazine (March 1987) 63:42-46

Tom Hurley developed this chair-fitting device to tailor each of his chairs to its owner. The back and seat slats are adjusted by gears and bicycle chain, while jacks alter height and back angle. An adjustable template transfers contours to a full-size layout of the custom chair.

ical memory of the chair he or she was currently using. When it finally dawned on prospective buyers that here was a chance to utterly pamper their seated anatomy, the degree of sensitivity to minute changes always rose dramatically, sometimes to Princess-and-the-Pea acuteness. In the fitting device itself, establishment of the basic back contour gave way to fine tuning—perhaps an upper slat recessed ¼ in. for the points of the shoulder blades, then maybe a lumbar slat moved forward a similar amount to achieve a feeling of continuity in lower back support. Working against these subtle adjustments was my observation that at different times the same customer brought to the fitting chair varying degrees of muscular tension, with resulting differences in the perception of needed support. It became important to aim the final fitting at a set of contours and dimensions that encouraged the body to settle into its own most relaxed state.

Getting the right relative pitch for seat and back became crucial in order to combine the sensation of relaxed lounging with a posture sufficiently upright for reading and conversation. By starting with the back unit low and slowly approaching upright, I was able to find the precise point where the sitter's head was comfortably lined up on the spine, but short of the point where it would fall forward unless restrained. This was something no ergonomic chart could tell me. Pitching the back of the chair to take into account the head's center of gravity allowed the sitter to be upright, but still completely relaxed, without having to unconsciously tense muscles to maintain position.

When customers felt their arms were correctly and evenly supported, the fitting device arms were invariably at slightly different heights. This disparity, attributable to a combination of anatomical asymmetry plus the effects of being right- or left-handed, had to be compromised for the sake of visual balance. We all have slightly lopsided bodies, but nobody seems to want a lopsided chair.

As I had expected, customers tended to be people with non-average body types, engaged in largely sedentary work. It was gratifying to see a 6-ft. 3-in. psychotherapist feel for the first time a chair offering proper back support for long periods of sitting. Shorter-legged customers were relieved to be able to rest their lower legs at a comfortable 45° angle to the floor rather than have them dangle.

For one tall client weighing in at 280 lb., comfort consisted of extra width (24 in. as opposed to my usual 21 in.), a seat that took the strain off his ankles, plus long, sturdy arms for easier entry and egress. A lot of experimentation suggested the use in all chairs of terylene-wrapped, 1-in.-thick soft foam for the back cushion, and for the seat a dense, firm 4-in. foam designed to depress a maximum of 1½ in. under load. Cushion cover materials also have their implications for comfort, with leather promoting more forward slide than high-friction fabrics.

When fittings are concluded, the work of building each chair begins. The first task is the creation of a set of patterns from the contours and dimensions of the fitting device. Using a wooden jig with multiple adjustable fingers, I transfer precise slat-end positions from the fitting device onto paper. These markings are elaborated into a full-scale profile located on the paper above a baseline representing the floor. Taped to a vertical wall, this full-scale elevation profile allows me to confirm that the evolving chair matches the profile of the fitting device. I lay clear Mylar on this full-scale paper elevation and, with a pen, trace the final profile outlines plus leg and slat joint locations. With the help of carbon paper, I can now use these Mylar patterns to transfer the lines

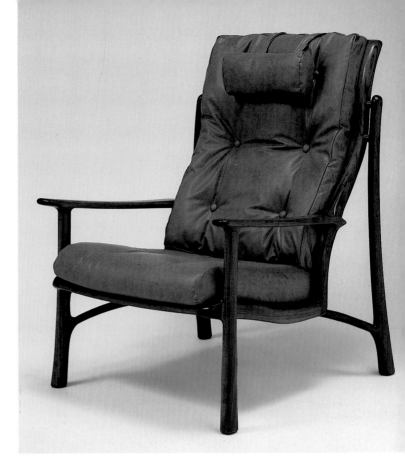

Hurley's basic chair is light on its feet and delicate; its design allows the alterations for each individual to be unobtrusive.

Rear struts connect the back legs and back seat slat to stiffen the structure. The pieces are butt-joined, doweled and epoxied.

directly onto the wood, flipping the transparent sheets over to get the mirror image for the opposite side. A separate set of Masonite patterns for the seat slat curves, and for the four graduated back slat curves, completes the layout before turning on the bandsaw.

When designing the basic chair, I had decided to work exclusively from 2-in.-thick roughsawn hardwood, achieving curves by bandsawing rather than by lamination or steambending. Wood species include the oaks, black walnut, white ash and imbuya. The basic structural unit providing both solid support for the cushions and the potential for custom contouring was the slat: 1¾-in. wide by about ¾ in. thick and usually 21 in. long, with edges radiused on the router table.

A personal penchant for slender structural members entailed

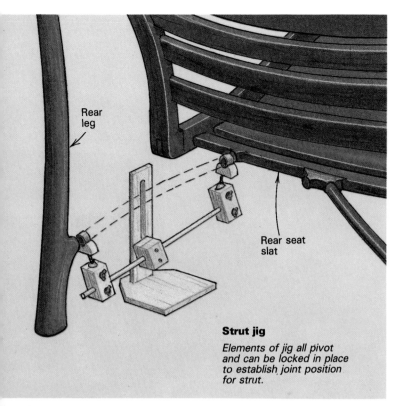

Rear
leg

Rear seat
slat

Strut jig

*Elements of jig all pivot
and can be locked in place
to establish joint position
for strut.*

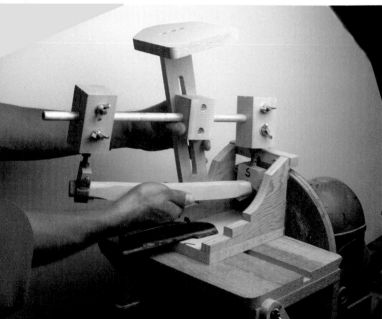

Hurley devised a jig to trim leg-to-seat struts at precisely the right length and angle. The copper rings are fixed in position against the joint faces on the chair, then the rough strut blank is inserted and its ends abraded.

the need to triangulate the framework in two critical places. The first was in connecting the bottom of each rear leg to the back of the rear seat slat with a strut, as shown on p. 51. The second was in reinforcing each front leg with a curved brace to the underside of the seat, which also serves to visually complete the side-view arc begun by the rear leg struts. Once the side members of the chair's seat and back are bridle-joined, I rout the slots for the slat splines to form what I call the chair basket—the chair minus its legs and arms. By suspending the basket against the full-scale drawn profile, I can mark for leg joints positioned to hold the basket at the desired height and pitch.

With each chair comprising about 40 separate parts, joinery be-

comes a preoccupation. The drawing on p. 53 shows the construction: Router-cut spline grooves join slats to side members; a pinned bridle joint joins seat and back side members; dowel-reinforced lap joints fix front legs to the seat; doweled butt joints serve elsewhere. The rear legs join the back with turned spacers fitted into counterbored holes. Wedged, through ½-in. dowels complete the joint. Since each chair is slightly different, I rely on a number of adjustable jigs to speed layout of the joint faces, to be trimmed on tablesaw or router table.

Joinery for the pair of dowel-reinforced, wishbone-shaped rear leg struts is difficult, since no two chairs offer the same distances or angles between the rear leg and the rear seat slat. I devised the jig shown at left to establish these dimensions. The jig's two copper rings are snugged flat against the joint faces and then locked tight in relation to one another. By wedging the rough-cut, overlong strut members into these two rings, I can abrade the ends against a disc sander. A bored-out acrylic plate keeps the ring from touching the sandpaper, while allowing the wooden member through for precise trimming. The ends of the wishbone-shaped struts are then bored to accommodate ⅜-in.-dia. dowels, which reinforce the butt joints to the rear legs and seat slat.

Plastic resin glue held the earlier chairs together, until tests convinced me of the advantages of woodworking epoxy, mainly for its strength in bonding small-section endgrain joints. (I use the West System Epoxy, made by Gougeon Brothers, Inc., 706 Martin St., Bay City, Mich. 48706.) Once the chair frame is glued up, final joint shaping and surface smoothing begins, with electric die grinder, rasps, files and sanding. Four coats of oil, followed by the installation of custom-sewn seat and back cushions, finish the chair.

After completing a number of chairs, I had solved the major production and design problems, and learned a great deal about chairs and their relation to the human body. I had also learned what it meant to forge ahead on the strength of obsession, and what it meant to incur runaway development costs in the face of dwindling hope of profit. I did not relish the idea of doubling the initial $2,500 price and thereby eliminate all but the most affluent clientele. The writing was on the wall—an inordinate degree of hand work combined with large amounts of time spent in customer fitting sessions made prospects dim. I decided to wind up the project, sold the fitting device to an industrial designer and carried home my own sample Custom Chair. Settled into its cozy contours I was finally able to reflect on the venture in relative tranquility.

Was it all worth it? Certainly not in terms of short-run return on investment. Yet with no models to follow, this was impossible to predict; it was a good idea whose promise could only be tested by going the distance. There is no other way to get a fix on design, production and marketing problems. When my probably overambitious solution threatened to bury me, I decided, with mixed relief and regret, to climb out of the hole. Yet the promise, I think, remains, perhaps for a custom chair somewhat less fastidious in its fitting, simpler in its design and production, and at a lower price. Certainly the clientele is there, with urgent needs currently being very poorly met. Meanwhile, the industrial designer in whose living room my fitting device now sits is not quite sure what to do with his impulsive purchase. At least for the moment, he can contemplate the possibilities in comfort.   □

Tom Hurley works wood and writes in Toronto, Canada.

A Framework for Comfort

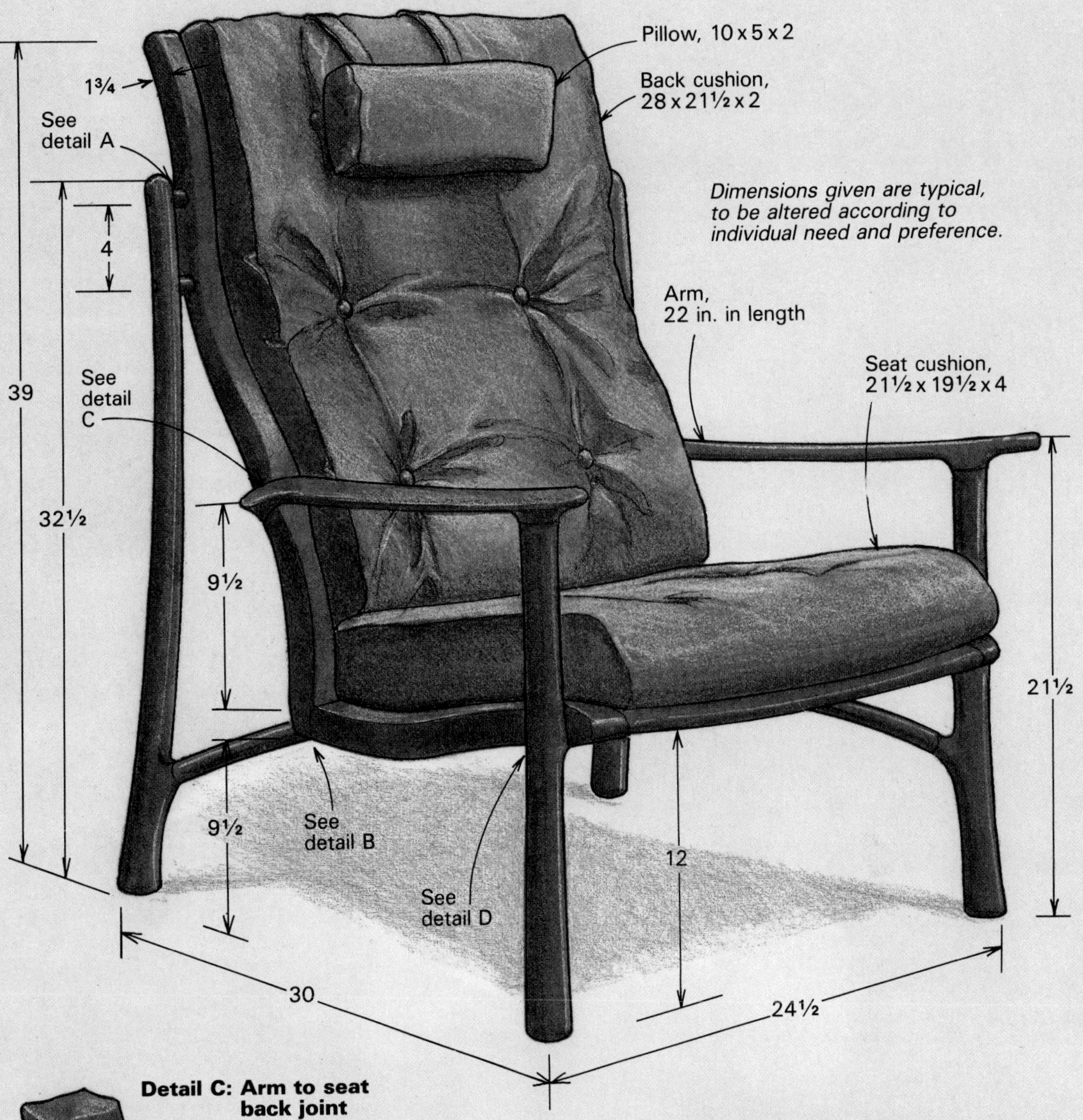

Pillow, 10 x 5 x 2
Back cushion, 28 x 21½ x 2
1¾
See detail A
Dimensions given are typical, to be altered according to individual need and preference.
4
Arm, 22 in. in length
39
See detail C
Seat cushion, 21½ x 19½ x 4
32½
9½
21½
9½
See detail B
12
See detail D
30
24½

Detail A: Seat back to leg joint

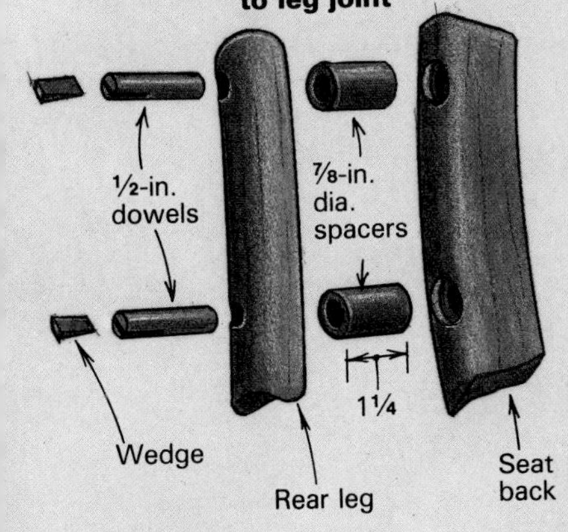

½-in. dowels
⅞-in. dia. spacers
1¼
Wedge
Rear leg
Seat back

Detail B: Seat back to seat bottom joint

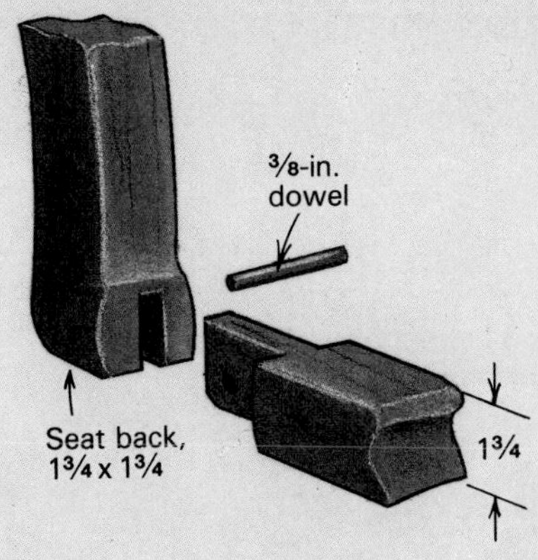

⅜-in. dowel
Seat back, 1¾ x 1¾
1¾

Detail C: Arm to seat back joint

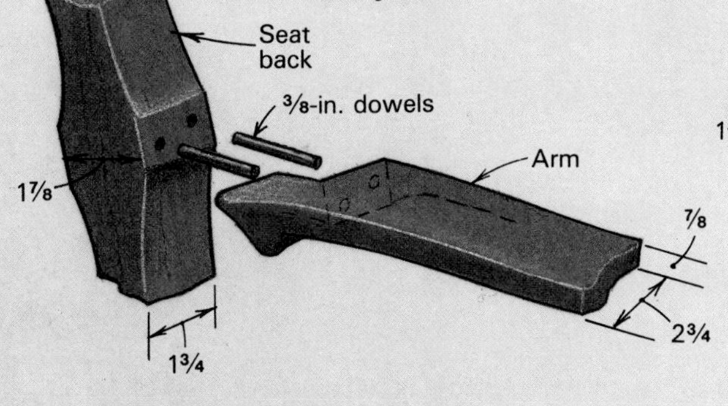

Seat back
⅜-in. dowels
Arm
1⅞
⅞
2¾
1¾

Detail D: Seat to front leg joint

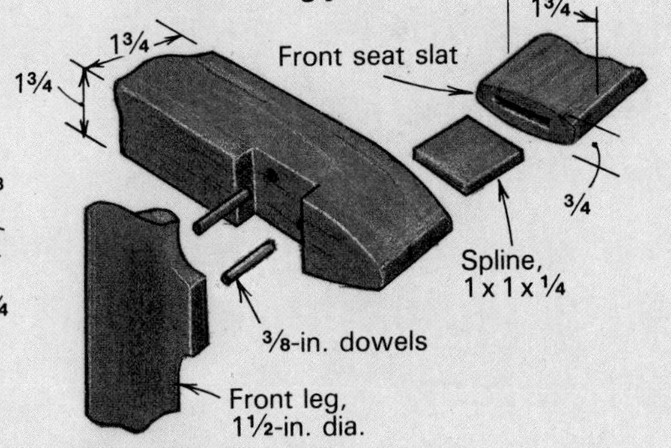

1¾
1¾
Front seat slat
1¾
¾
Spline, 1 x 1 x ¼
⅜-in. dowels
Front leg, 1½-in. dia.

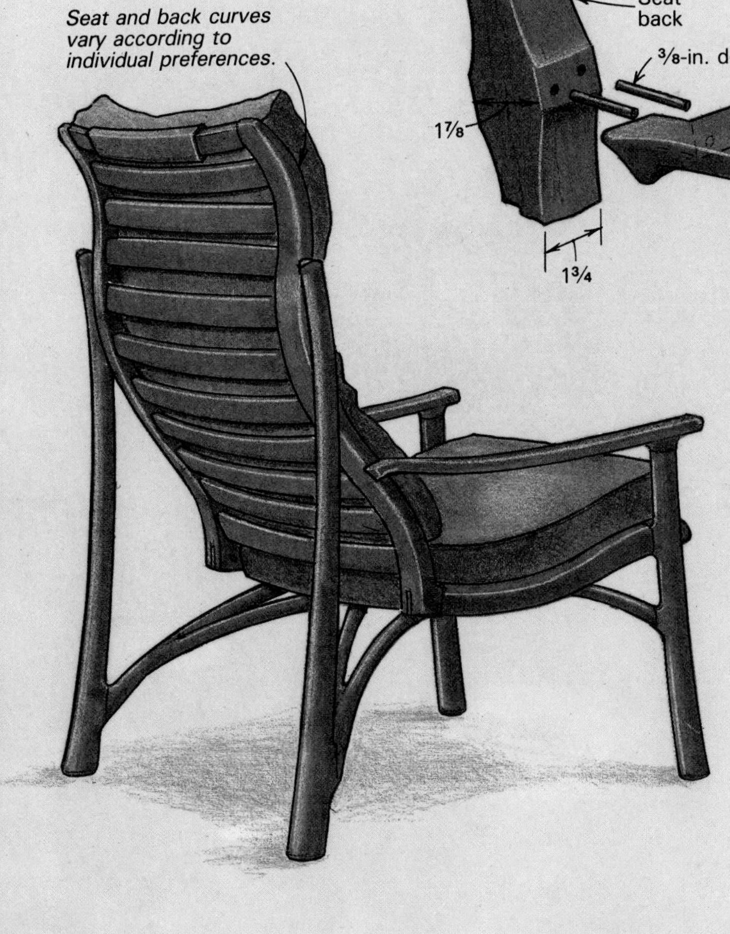

Seat and back curves vary according to individual preferences.

Detail: wishbone strut

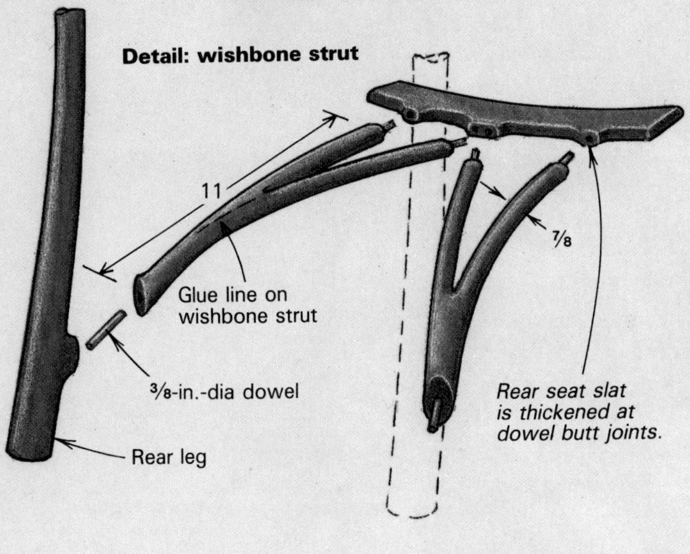

11
⅞
Glue line on wishbone strut
⅜-in.-dia dowel
Rear seat slat is thickened at dowel butt joints.
Rear leg

Making A Foursquare Chair

Comfortable seating with right-angle joinery

by Scott Dickerson

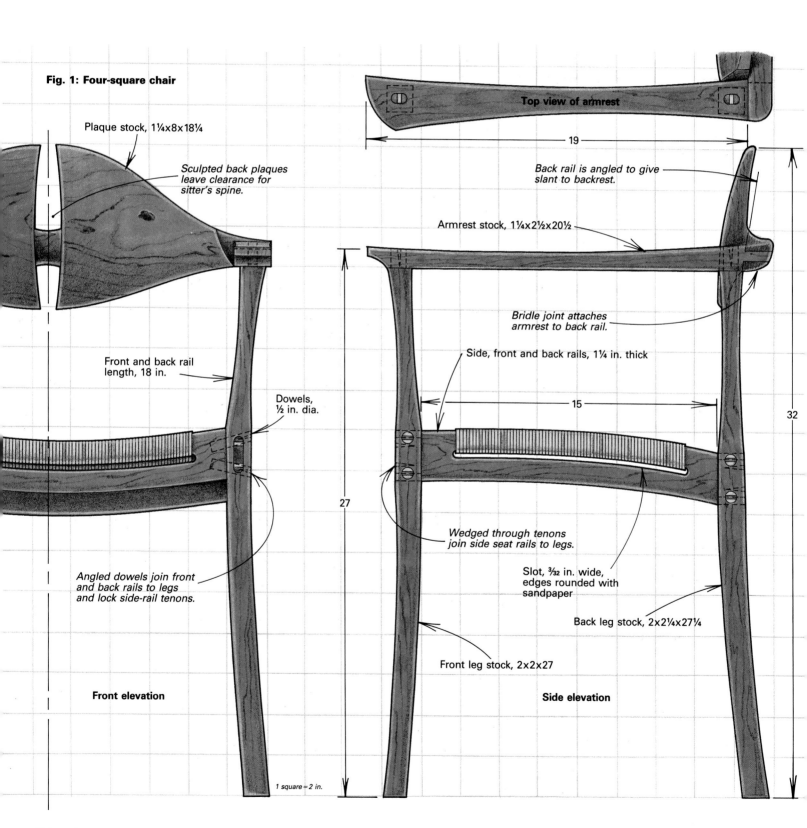

Fig. 1: Four-square chair

Plaque stock, 1¼ x 8 x 18¼

Sculpted back plaques leave clearance for sitter's spine.

Top view of armrest

19

Back rail is angled to give slant to backrest.

Armrest stock, 1¼ x 2½ x 20½

Front and back rail length, 18 in.

Dowels, ½ in. dia.

Bridle joint attaches armrest to back rail.

Side, front and back rails, 1¼ in. thick

15

32

27

Angled dowels join front and back rails to legs and lock side-rail tenons.

Wedged through tenons join side seat rails to legs.

Slot, ³⁄₃₂ in. wide, edges rounded with sandpaper

Back leg stock, 2 x 2¼ x 27¼

Front leg stock, 2 x 2 x 27

Front elevation

Side elevation

1 square = 2 in.

Drawings: David Dann

My client said he didn't know what he liked until he saw it, but added he had seen enough of my work to know he'd like me to design and build for him a dozen dining chairs with arms. I took this to mean I had freedom of expression, but being wiser from years of calluses and tendonitis, I knew better than to proceed with wild abandon. After years of making chairs with steam-bent or laminated parts, I've grown tired of the many rigors connected with these methods of chairmaking: breathing sawdust from sawing boards into thin strips for lamination, fooling around with the complex joinery of curved chair parts, and tightening and loosening an endless array of clamps during glue-ups. This commission appeared a good time for me to return to a style of chairmaking I'd worked in years ago and to create a simple, practical design I call a "foursquare chair."

I call my design a foursquare chair because all four legs join the seat rails, chair back and armrests at right angles. Building a chair with basic right-angle mortise-and-tenon joinery simplifies the construction immensely, and it reduces the number of hours it takes to make the chair, and hence, its cost. In this article, I'll discuss how I produced my foursquare chair, pictured at right, and the sidebar on p. 58 will tell you how to make a comfortable and attractive cane seat once the woodwork is done.

Design—I begin by making full-size drawings of the chair I have in mind. I rarely draw reduced-scale sketches, because they don't show much about the actual proportions and feel of the chair. A full-size drawing can be pinned to the wall at floor level. By standing back and giving it the squinty eye, I can tell a great deal about what the actual chair will look like before I begin construction. The most useful drawings for a chair design are side and front elevations, as shown in figure 1 on the facing page. I draw the side elevation first, because the shape and location of the surfaces that support the sitter—the slope of the seat, the profile of the backrest and the elevation of the armrest—are best seen in that view. I don't worry much about the chair's aesthetics until these crucial surfaces have been established. I also draw a top view of the armrest, to define its shape.

I draw on rag-vellum paper that has light blue ⅛-in. and 1-in. grid lines (available in rolls 20 yd. by 42 in. from Charrette, 31 Olympia Ave., Woburn, Mass. 01888). The square grid speeds up plotting the contact points, and you can count squares instead of using a ruler to determine the length of chair parts.

Starting with chair dimensions that I know to be comfortable from past chairs I've built, I draw the side rail of the seat 18 in. above the floor at the front and 17 in. at the back. This provides just enough incline to keep the sitter from sliding forward and out of the chair. For comfort, the backrest's surface should be large enough to firmly support the sitter's lower and middle back. In this chair, the backrest's surface should meet the sitter's back at about 10° reclined from the vertical. To support the forearms of most sitters at a comfortable height, I place the top of the armrests 9 in. above the front seat rail. I also make the armrests level and extend them all the way to the backrest.

With all the chair's sitter-support surfaces defined, I still need to plot the points where the legs meet the ground. I like the front leg directly beneath the front of the seat, so the chair cannot tip forward if a sitter perches on the edge of the seat. Likewise, if the back legs meet the floor 2 in. or 3 in. behind the front face of the backrest, the chair will resist any attempt by the sitter to cock the chair back on its hind legs, an abuse that will surely loosen the joinery of any chair.

To draw the front view of the chair, I follow a similar process. I make the seat on my chair 18 in. wide, so all but the largest person will have enough room between the armrests and full support in the seat. Armrests should be wide enough to offer support

The author's foursquare chair with its wrapped cane seat is comfortable and attractive. Though its parts are curved and shapely, the chair is constructed with mostly right-angle joinery, making it relatively easy to build.

for the forearms and hands. The armrests on my chair taper from 2½ in. wide to 1½ in. wide. If the legs meet the floor directly beneath the armrests, the chair won't tip sideways when the sitter leans over to pick up a dropped fork.

I draw the front outline of the backrest to provide the most support along the sitter's dorsal muscles that parallel the spinal column. These muscles cushion the load against the backrest's contoured surface. To prevent the backrest from pressing uncomfortably against the bony ridge of the backbone, I split the backrest vertically, allowing a slot for the spine's vertebrae. Thus, the form of the backrest becomes a pair of sculptured plaques, and I attach them to a rear rail that ties the two back legs together.

I complete both the side- and front-view drawings, much as a child completes the figure of a connect-the-dots puzzle. With the critical support points and surfaces defined, the remaining lines are much a matter of style, though I have to continually be aware of the comfort factor. For instance, the curved front and back seat rails make sitting in the chair more comfortable, and the rounded front ends on the armrests make them more pleasant to grip. I also have to factor in the limitations of my material: Because I wanted to use solid wood for this chair, the curvatures I chose had to be gradual, to avoid short-grain weakness that are inevitable in tighter-curved sections. I prefer the look of slender components, but make them thicker at the joints that need more strength. After refining the shapes and thicknesses of the various components, I am ready to engineer the chair's joinery.

Joinery design—The joinery in my foursquare chair is easy to execute, because so many parts join at 90° angles. Because dining

Once the backrest plaques are joined to the back rail and clamped to the bench, they are roughed to shape with a small motorized block plane. The author then uses spokeshaves and scrapers to refine and smooth the forms.

With a ½-in. spiral-fluted straight bit in a plunge router, the author cuts through mortises in the chair's armrests and legs. The chair parts are clamped inside a plywood jig, which guides the router base as it cuts the mortises. Two adjustable stops clamped to the top of the jig's sides act as stops to determine mortise length.

chairs are among the most brutalized furniture in the home, I use interlocking dowel and tenon joinery to help the chairs survive the stress of being sat on, of being dragged and of being balanced on their rear legs. Further, interlocking joints help prevent parts that are joined cross-grain from separating due to differential wood movement caused by humidity changes.

The side seat rails join the four legs with through mortises and tenons. I make the legs thick enough at the joints to prevent racking forces from breaking through the mortises. Also, I wedge the ends of the side-rail through tenons to prevent them from pulling out. Because there isn't enough room to also mortise and tenon the front and back rails to the leg, these rails are joined by angled dowels. The dowels are driven through holes drilled in the side of the legs, penetrating deeply into the ends of the front and back rails. The angle creates a dovetail-like effect that makes the joint inseparable once assembled, and because the dowels pass through the edges of the side-rail tenons, they also lock those joints.

The armrests join the tops of both front and back legs with through tenons rising from the legs. Although the chair doesn't have stretchers bracing the legs below the seat, the armrests reinforce the front-leg to side-rail joint and keep the chair from rack-

ing. The chair's connecting back rail is joined to the armrests with a bridle joint. The tenon is cut on the armrest, leaving more wood on the back rail, which needs the extra stock for strength. The armrests also have shoulders on their inside faces, which buttress against the back rail and keep it from racking. The backrest joins the back rail in a glued long-grain to long-grain joint—the strongest joint possible.

Construction—I start construction by making up a cutting list for the chair parts, specifying the dimensions of the final parts, as drawn on the plans. Next, I make patterns for the parts that will be shaped so I can quickly make identical parts for all 12 chairs. I use ⅛-in.-thick white Marlite (a Masonite-like product used in bath enclosures, which is available from local hardware stores) for the patterns, but its white surface is very slick, so I scrub it lightly with sandpaper to provide some tooth for the pencil lines. I transfer the lines for a part from the full-size plans using carbon paper between the plans and Marlite. The patterns are then bandsawn out, and the edges are smoothed with a rasp and spokeshave.

I decided to use cherry for my chairs to harmonize with the interior of the client's home. First, I joint, thickness-plane and cut all the parts to rough dimensions. At this stage, I make the parts at least ¼ in. oversize in width and thickness and allow 1 in. extra in length. For maximum efficiency in making a whole set of chairs, I perform each of the operations described in the following paragraphs on all chair parts before moving on to the next step.

I start with the backrests, and following the Marlite pattern, I mark and bandsaw out the shape. Because some of the edges of the backrests are difficult to sand after being glued to the back rail, I spokeshave and sand all edges of the plaques. Next, I dress the back rail to final dimensions and cut the bridle-joint slot on each end with a tablesaw. I then cut a 10° bevel on the rail's front face and glue the backrest plaques in position on the rail. A ¹⁄₁₆-in.-deep rabbet jointed on the back sides of the plaques keeps them from slipping when clamped.

After the glue dries, I'm ready to shape the faces of the backrest plaques. I rough out the shapes with a Porter-Cable motorized block plane (see top photo this page), then use a spokeshave and cabinet scraper to refine the form—a rigorous job, but I've always enjoyed the satisfaction of shaping wood to final form by the judgment of eye and hand. After the plaques are done, I spokeshave, rasp and sand the back rail to final shape.

As with all the other shaped parts, the joints of the armrests should be cut while the armrests are still square pieces, because it's easier to reference a square part to the saw fence. The tenon that joins the back-rail bridle joint is cut on the tablesaw, holding each armrest vertically in a sliding-tenon jig to cut the cheeks, then crosscutting the shoulders using the miter gauge. I also cut the angled shoulder on the inside edge of each armrest on the tablesaw. The direction this 10° shoulder slants to meet the angled face of the back rail determines whether an armrest will be a right or left arm. One of the chairmaker neuroses I've developed over the years is the "right-left top-bottom paranoia." To avoid confusion and mistakes, I separate my armrests and other right-left parts into different piles and mark them accordingly.

Next, I cut the mortises that join the armrests with the front and back legs. For this, I use a plunge router fitted with a ½-in. spiral-fluted straight bit and a shop-built mortising fixture (see bottom photo this page). The armrest clamps in the plywood fixture, while the top rails of the box-like fixture guide the router base. Two adjustable stops limit router travel to determine the length of each mortise. I cut two mortises in each armrest, one for each leg. This same jig does the mortises in the legs for the

Above: The leg-side rail assembly is secured in a bench vise while the author roughs the leg to shape with a drawknife. The joints for the rails and armrests are cut while the legs are still square and easy to align. Right: Once the chair is assembled and held together with light clamps, the author bores dowel holes to join the legs to the front and back rails. The angles of the slanting holes aren't crucial, so they're eyeballed to speed the job along.

side-rail tenons. The tenons atop the legs are cut on the same tablesaw tenoning setup described earlier. Because router-cut mortises have rounded corners, all tenons must be rounded to match. I do this with a rasp and file, and I think the rounded tenons look better than square-cornered tenons would with the curves of my chair.

Next, I cut out the side profile of each armrest on the bandsaw, following the side elevation, then I refine it with spokeshaves and sandpaper. I cut the top outline to pattern, leaving the front end square to provide a flat clamping surface when I glue the armrest to the back rail. I also leave some extra width on the armrest at the back tenon so I can clamp across the back to pull the bridle joint tight. After smoothing the edges of both armrests, I glue them to the back rail.

Before sawing the side seat rails to shape, the tenons should be cut on the ends. I employ the same tablesaw setup I used for the leg tenons, cutting the rail's tenon shoulders square with the ends of the still-square rail blanks. Although the side seat rails are curved and the tenons join the back legs lower than the front legs, the tenons will still fit squarely into the leg mortises (see figure 1, p. 54). Once all the joints are cut and fitted, you can shape the tenonless front and back seat rails and round their edges. I don't shape the legs yet, because it's easier to hold them in a vise after they've been glued to the side rails.

Assembly—Before gluing up the legs and side seat rails, I cut two wedging slots in each tenon and bandsaw a whole coffee can full of wedges. After gluing and clamping, the wedges are driven in the tenon ends, to tighten the tenon in the mortise. With the leg-and-rail assembly held in my bench vise, I begin shaping the legs using a spokeshave, rasp and cabinet scraper, as shown in the smaller photo above. While shaping, I follow the plans, using both my eye

and touch to bring the shapes to final form. Leave the joint surface area unshaped where the front and back rails will join the legs. This area is shaped later, after assembly is completed.

To drill the ½-in. dowel holes in the front and back rails, I dry-clamp the rails in place with the right and left sides of the leg assemblies, taking care not to put clamps where I'll need to drill. To bore the holes, I use a brace fitted with a double-twist auger bit that's marked at a 2½-in. depth by a file groove on the flutes. I eyeball the angle of the holes to approximately 10°, the upper one slanting down and the lower one slanting up into each rail end, as shown in the larger photo above. The dowels are cut about 3 in. long (the excess is trimmed off later), chamfered on one end and kerfed on the other to accept a wedge. If the dowels fit too snugly in their holes, reduce their diameter by driving them through a dowel-sizing plate (available from Woodcraft Supply, 41 Atlantic Ave., Box 4000, Woburn, Mass. 01888).

Because the dowel holes are angled, the chair, less the arms and backrest, must be assembled in one step. I use four small bar clamps for the initial squeeze before wedging the dowels and two heavy bar clamps to snug the joints up tight. Moving quickly before the glue dries, I spread yellow glue on the ends of each rail and into the dowel holes with a stick, then butter each leg at the joint. A single glue-dipped dowel is then driven into each rail end. Holding the rails in a vise while installing these starter dowels with a mallet helps keep everything in order. Then, I push the legs onto the angled dowels in the rails, first one side, then the other. The second dowel for each joint is then driven home. When all the dowels are in place, I clamp the chair with the bar clamps and drive the wedges into the kerfed dowel ends. The excess dowel is cut off flush with the leg's surface with a small handsaw. I then attach the bar clamps directly across the rails, using a softwood pad under each clamp face to distribute the pressure and avoid iron-staining the wood. I finish by removing the bar clamps and wiping up the glue squeeze-out with a damp sponge.

After the glue dries, I finish shaping the legs around the rail joints with rasps and sandpaper, then glue the armrest/backrest assembly on top of the legs. After this assembly dries, I clean and shape around the armrest joints and finish shaping the armrests. This is easier if the chair is clamped securely by its side rail in a bench vise. Next, the long slots for the seat caning are cut in all four seat rails with a sabersaw. I start by drilling three closely spaced pilot holes at one end of the curved rails with a ³⁄₃₂-in. drill bit, then follow along the holes using a coarsely set blade in the sabersaw

to create the ³⁄₃₂-in.-wide slot. The edges of the slot are rounded, first by roughing out a chamfer in the slot with a countersunk bit in an electric drill, then by running a strap of 80-grit sandpaper reinforced with masking tape back and forth through the slot, like a shoe-shine cloth. I sand the chairs and rub in several saturation coats of Watco Danish oil before caning the seats, so all surfaces can absorb the oil evenly. When the last of the oil fumes has dispersed from the shop, you're ready for the last step—caning the seats. □

Scott Dickerson divides his time between chair design and land-use planning. He lives in Harborside, Maine.

Wrapping a cane seat

by Janet Redfield

The wrapped-cane seat I use to upholster my husband's foursquare chairs has a tightly woven center section with a subtle diamond pattern on the top. The underside is a simple over-under pattern, which hides the splices and tied-off cane ends. Wrapping and weaving the seat pattern (see drawings below and at right) seems complicated, but it's far simpler once you have the cane in hand.

To begin, you need a bundle of common-size cane (available from H.H. Perkins Co., 10 S. Bradley Road, Woodbridge, Conn. 06525); a small spool of #34 beading wire (available in craft shops); small, sharp scissors; an 18-in.-long, ⅛-in.-dia. dowel or rod with a dull point on one end; and a bucket of water.

It can take from seven hours to seven days to cane a chair, so set the chair on a table at a comfortable work height. Open the bundle of cane and hang it up so you can remove one strand at a time. Pull out five or six of the longest strands, cut out cracks, brittle black spots and other imperfections, and discard

any strands less than 5 ft. long. Soak the strands in a bucket of water for 10 minutes. Meanwhile, cut several 2¼-in.-long pieces of the beading wire to splice the canes later. With the chair facing you, mark the center of the front seat rail with masking tape, to help locate the pattern.

The first step in the actual caning is to wrap and stretch a straight pattern of cane all running side to side. This provides a warp for the pattern to be woven into from front to back later on. Take one cane from the bucket and dry it off. Note the cane has a shiny, rounded top side that must face up on top of the seat. Insert 10 in. of it, flat and dull side up, through the slot on the outside of the left side rail. Wrap the 10-in. end around the left, front chair leg and temporarily tape it down. Remove any twists in the cane, and begin wrapping and stretching the warp through the slots in the right and left rails, following the sequence shown in figure 2 below. Repeat the process, alternating

wrapping the cane around the rail with stretching it between the rails, moving from front to back. As you run out of cane, refill the bucket so all strands soak at least 10 minutes. You'll form two layers of cane, one at the top of the seat and one at the slots. Do not pull the cane tightly, because it will tighten up as it dries; it should flex 1 in. up or down at the center of the seat. Also, slide the wraps so they're tight against each other on the side rails.

Several strands of cane are needed for the warp, so you need to splice pieces together. When you reach the end of one cane, cut the strand closest to the back approximately 4½ in. in from the inside of the left rail on the bottom of the seat, so your splices will be covered when you weave the seat later. Notch the cane and wrap the splice with wire, as shown in figure 2 below, and continue wrapping. When you have wrapped five or six rows, untape the cane from the front leg and tie it off, as shown in figure 3

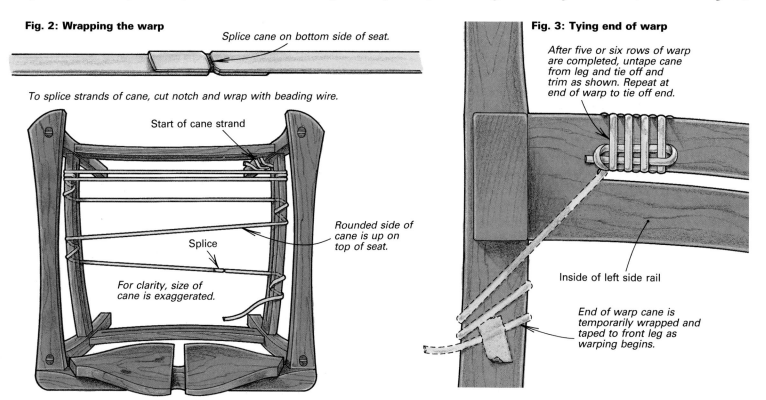

Fig. 2: Wrapping the warp

Splice cane on bottom side of seat.

To splice strands of cane, cut notch and wrap with beading wire.

Start of cane strand

Splice

For clarity, size of cane is exaggerated.

Rounded side of cane is up on top of seat.

Fig. 3: Tying end of warp

After five or six rows of warp are completed, untape cane from leg and tie off and trim as shown. Repeat at end of warp to tie off end.

Inside of left side rail

End of warp cane is temporarily wrapped and taped to front leg as warping begins.

Fig. 4: Cane-seat weave pattern

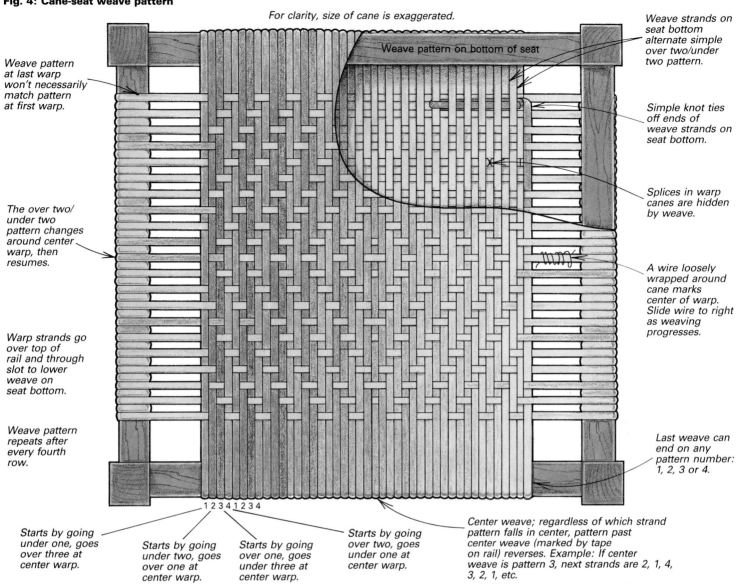

For clarity, size of cane is exaggerated.

Weave pattern on bottom of seat

Weave strands on seat bottom alternate simple over two/under two pattern.

Weave pattern at last warp won't necessarily match pattern at first warp.

Simple knot ties off ends of weave strands on seat bottom.

The over two/under two pattern changes around center warp, then resumes.

Splices in warp canes are hidden by weave.

Warp strands go over top of rail and through slot to lower weave on seat bottom.

A wire loosely wrapped around cane marks center of warp. Slide wire to right as weaving progresses.

Weave pattern repeats after every fourth row.

Last weave can end on any pattern number: 1, 2, 3 or 4.

1 2 3 4 1 2 3 4

Starts by going under one, goes over three at center warp.

Starts by going under two, goes over one at center warp.

Starts by going over one, goes under three at center warp.

Starts by going over two, goes under one at center warp.

Center weave; regardless of which strand pattern falls in center, pattern past center weave (marked by tape on rail) reverses. Example: If center weave is pattern 3, next strands are 2, 1, 4, 3, 2, 1, etc.

---

on the facing page. Continue wrapping and splicing until you have filled the side slots. Check to see that the warp strands are all straight and not too tight. Finally, tie off the end of the last cane as you did the first.

Now rest the chair on a soft surface upside down on its arms, with the back toward you. Due to their growth nodes, you must feel each cane to find the direction it slides easiest in, and weave it in that direction. Insert a cane, rounded side up, through the outside of the slot in the back rail. Weave it through the bottom warp strands, going over two canes, under two, over two, under two, as shown above. Continue weaving toward the front. Pull the cane through the front slot until only 3 in. dangle out at the back rail. Align this first woven cane so it is perfectly straight and in line with the end of the front and back slots on the chair's left side (viewed from the top). Now turn the chair over, with the front facing you. Bring the cane hanging from the front slot over the top of the front rail and begin weaving the top of the seat, following the pattern of row

#1 in figure 4. Depending on the number of warp strands, you may end the weaving going over or under one or two strands at the back of the seat, but that's okay. Wrap the center warp strand loosely with wire, so you can locate it easily and slide it to the right as you work.

Flip the chair over and insert the weaving cane through the outside of the back slot. Now weave the seat's underside in an alternating over-two under-two pattern. Insert the strand through and over the front rail as you did above, pull the woven cane tight and begin weaving row #2. Next, weave the seat bottom, then row #3, seat bottom and row #4. When you reach row #5, repeat pattern #1, and then rows #6, #7 and #8 copy rows #2, #3 and #4 respectively. This pattern continues to the middle of the chair, marked with masking tape. Then you must flip the pattern and reverse the four-row repeat you did on the first half of the seat. Whether the center strand is the same as rows #1, #2, #3 or #4, the strand just right of it follows the weave pat-

tern of the next lower-numbered row.

When a cane runs out, thread a new one in on the seat bottom. Cut off the previous strand two-thirds of the way from the back. Insert a new strand through the front slot, weaving it toward the back so it's woven over and under in the same pattern as the previous strand at least 6 in. past the old strand. Push the new strand up over the old one, overlapping the two. Push the pair tightly together.

As you near the end of the rail slots, the woven canes will be tight and weaving will be difficult. On top of the seat, the 18-in. dowel will ease the weaving process: Slide the tool into the warp, following the correct row pattern, then thread the strand alongside it and pull the tool out. When you're done weaving, tie off the first and last canes under the seat, as shown in figure 4. Remove the center wire and masking tape, and pop the seat with your finger. It should twang—a sign that you can sit down and relax. □

Janet Redfield is a stained-glass artist. She lives in Harborside, Maine.

Three Benches

Park seating with a Japanese flair

by John Goertzel

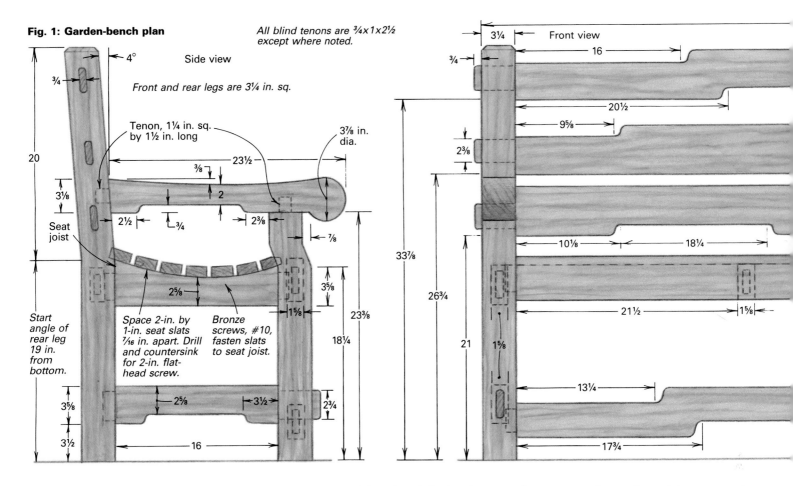

Fig. 1: Garden-bench plan

All blind tenons are ¾ x 1 x 2½ except where noted.

Side view

Front and rear legs are 3¼ in. sq.

4°

¾

Tenon, 1¼ in. sq. by 1½ in. long

3⅞ in. dia.

20

3⅛

Seat joist

23½

⅜

2

¾

2½

2⅜

⅞

33⅞

23⅜

18¼

26¾

Start angle of rear leg 19 in. from bottom.

Space 2-in. by 1-in. seat slats ⅞6 in. apart. Drill and countersink for 2-in. flathead screw.

Bronze screws, #10, fasten slats to seat joist.

2⅝

3⅝

1⅝

3⅝

3½

2⅝

3½

2¾

16

Front view

3¼

¾

16

20½

9⅝

2⅜

10⅛

18¼

21

1⅝

21½

1⅝

13¼

17¾

Benches are a delightful addition to any yard or garden. They add a decorative touch and provide a pleasant spot for quiet conversation, contemplation or for simply enjoying the outdoors. But the bench I built has a special purpose: It serves as a memorial to H.G. "Jerry" Sanders, a conservationist who was the leader of a successful grass-roots effort to preserve one of the last-remaining stands of old-growth forest on south Whidbey Island, about 30 miles north of Seattle, Wash., in Puget Sound.

The 6-ft.-long bench shown in the photo on the facing page is large enough to seat three or four people. It has the look of a traditional English-garden or park bench, but with an Oriental twist suggested by the back stretchers, which are stepped much like the roof line of a Japanese temple. And, as is common with Japanese furniture, the joinery itself is also a strong visual element. Mortise-and-tenon construction is used with waterproof epoxy resin to connect the bench members. The only hardware are the bronze, square-drive screws fastening the slats to the seat joists. The bench is permanently installed with bolts that extend from the bottom of the bench's legs and are set in concrete.

Wood selection and bench design—Intended for public use, the

bench had to be ruggedly constructed to withstand the wear and tear of the anticipated traffic and the rigors of the Pacific Northwest climate. I didn't want the bench to be dwarfed by the background of giant Western red cedars, so I went with a hefty construction, which seems appropriate for the size of the bench and in scale with the neighboring trees.

Selecting the right wood for your climate can eliminate much of the maintenance and periodic refinishing that might otherwise be necessary. I wanted my bench to weather naturally and blend with its environment. Little light filters through the old-growth forest, so the area remains damp for long periods of time; thus, I was limited to durable, moisture-resistant varieties, such as teak, cedar or redwood. I chose Alaskan yellow cedar, because it is durable, more dense and structurally stronger than Western red cedar or redwood. It is also very aromatic and cheaper than teak. I selected the most-attractive pieces, those with straight, tight grain and those containing a minimum of knots and sapwood, which would eventually rot. And, much of the air-dried and check-free wood I purchased was full-dimensional, rough-surfaced 4x4s and 5x5s, enabling me to build the bench without laminating any of its parts.

If you can't get West Coast species, woods such as white oak, which

From *Fine Woodworking* magazine (May 1989) 76:54-59

Fig. 1A: Stretcher transition detail

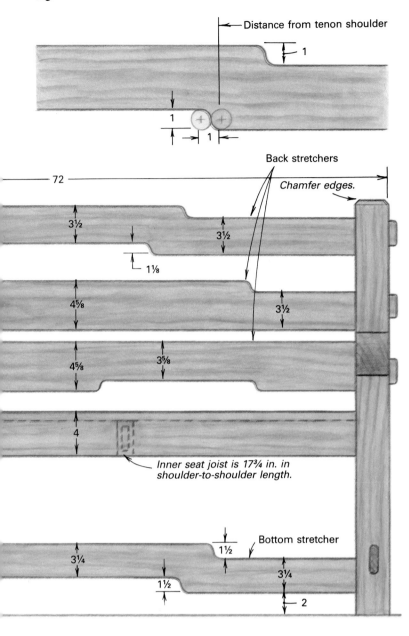

Distance from tenon shoulder

1

1

1

72

Back stretchers

Chamfer edges.

3½

3½

1⅛

4⅝

3½

4⅝

3⅝

4

Inner seat joist is 17¾ in. in shoulder-to-shoulder length.

Bottom stretcher

1½

3¼

1½

3¼

2

had been influenced by ideas from Asia. Some of their designs were based on strong horizontal line patterns, such as the cloud-lift patterns found in the tiered, roof-beam construction of traditional Chinese and Japanese buildings. In developing my final design, I modified the traditional English park bench, like the ones you find in quality mail-order gardening catalogs, to incorporate this same kind of strong but delicate-looking tiered construction.

The dimensions of the finished bench are 72 in. long, 38 in. high and 24 in. deep (see figure 1 at left). The back of the bench is composed of three horizontal supports, each of different width with offset curving transitions. The shape of the back, created by all its pieces joined together, is important, because the back is visually dominant and therefore strongly suggests the bench's theme. I've continued the Japanese flavor into the elegant, flowing shape of the arms, front legs and leg spreaders. The through mortises with protruding tenons connecting the back members to the leg posts focus ones attention on the joinery, further emphasizing that Asian touch.

I was determined to make the bench pleasant to sit on, so I decided on a gently sloped back and a slatted, concave seat, both of which are comfortable and attractive. This design also makes it possible for rain water to run off the bench easily. The back of the bench is straight, but the whole assembly angles back at about 4°. The three horizontal members of the backrest are hefty and positioned to provide plenty of support.

Building the bench—I start by rough-cutting all pieces to length and by truing up the stock. Most of the pieces must be shaped, but I cut all mortises and tenons first, while the pieces are still rectangular (or square). I rough-cut the mortises with a ¾-in. Forstner bit in a drill press. For the through mortises, a lumber scrap placed under the workpiece prevents the bit from tearing out the wood. I pare the walls carefully with a chisel, but leave the corners rounded. I find it easier and faster to round the tenons to fit rather than square the mortises.

The tenons are cut with a dado blade on the tablesaw, as shown in the photo at the top of the next page. Because many of the bench parts are large and awkward to handle, I built a crosscutting jig to guide the stock across the dado blade. This jig is much easier to use than the miter gauge when working with large pieces. My crosscutting jig has two parallel hardwood strips

is used in boat construction, will work. Black locust, cypress or other woods used for roof shingles and outdoor decks are also options. Softwoods are generally more dimensionally stable over a wider range of humidity than hardwoods and may be easier to work, but if you expect your bench to receive hard use, stick with the hardwoods.

Because Sanders had lived for years in Japan, I wanted this bench to reflect his great appreciation of the Japanese aesthetic. I first intended to base the design on traditional Japanese park benches, but was surprised to discover that such benches are not part of the country's culture. Public parks as we know them did not exist in Japan until about 150 years ago. The compounds of shrines and temples, which are not parks per say, are laid out with narrow, meandering walkways, and visitors can admire the landscaping as they stroll through the grounds. Occasionally, backless stone stools, designed to be a part of the landscape, are found in private gardens. The benches found in newer Japanese parks are mostly due to modern Western influences, and as such are reminiscent of benches sporting bright commercial advertising at bus stops in this country.

In looking for new inspiration, I remembered that several architects from the American Arts-and-Crafts tradition of the early 1900s

The author's bench is in a forest on Whidbey Island, Wash., amid a stand of Western hemlock, Douglas fir, sitka spruce and grand fir. Nearby is a 400-year-old Western red cedar, 31 ft. in circumference.

Above, Goertzel cuts the angled dado on one of the bench arms while the stock is still square. Afterwards, he'll use a bandsaw to rough out the shape of the arm to the marked outline.

glued to the bottom of a large sheet of ½-in. plywood. The strips fit the saw's miter grooves. The workpiece rests against a fence on the jig, which slides easily and provides good control when making crosscuts. The jig is simple and effective. After cutting the tenons, I round the corners with a rasp to fit them to the mortises.

At this point, I'm ready to shape the parts. I use the tablesaw and bandsaw to cut all the pieces within ¹⁄₁₆ in. of their final size. Handplanes, power- and hand-sanding with 80 grit and 120 grit quickly shape and smooth the pieces to their final form. Yellow cedar has a pungent odor and is an irritant to some people when it is being sanded or cut, so it's important to wear a respirator when working with this wood.

After dry-clamping the bench to check for fit and squareness, and to work out the assembly sequence, I'm ready to glue it up. I use epoxy resin, because it is strong, waterproof and a good gap filler. The epoxy "Cold Cure," available from The Wooden Boat Shop, 1007 N.E. Boat St., Seattle, Wash. 98105; (206) 634-3600, is especially formulated for cold temperatures and is often used by boatbuilders in the cool maritime climate of Puget Sound. Alternative glues, such as resorcinol or those with a urea-formaldehyde base, would also be suitable. I glue up the two end sections first and then lay them aside while I glue the seat joists to the front and rear seat stringers. Lastly, I glue these three sections together, along with the three back spreaders and the lower spreader that connects the front legs. Having an assistant available can help the assembly and glue-up go smoothly and quickly in a single stage. I use a rag soaked with acetone to clean away any excess glue before it has a chance to set up. Finally, I fasten the seat slats to the joists with countersunk, 2-in., square-drive #10 bronze screws.

I sand the bench once more, this time with 150 grit, to remove any remaining defects and to clean the surface in preparation for applying the finish. Two coats of 1:1 mix of Daly's Sea Fin Teak Oil (Daly's Inc., 3525 Stone Way N., Seattle, Wash. 98103; 206-633-4200) and Flecto Exterior Varathane (The Flecto Co., Flecto International Ltd., Box 12955, Oakland, Calif. 94604; 415-655-2470) varnish are applied. The mixture seals more quickly and more thoroughly than oil by itself. The finish doesn't prevent the bench from weathering to a natural gray color, but it does help prevent checking and warpage as the bench adjusts to its outdoor environment.

To install the bench in its permanent location, drill ½-in. holes 5 in. deep in the center of the bottom of the legs. Drive in ½-in.-dia. by 10-in.-long galvanized hex-head bolts and set them into wet concrete pads. The bench is elevated approximately 1 in. above the concrete, to keep the legs as dry as possible and to prevent moisture absorption by the endgrain of the legs. □

John Goertzel is a woodworker and builder. He lives on Whidbey Island, Wash. His company, Threshold Construction, specializes in passive solar structures. Sue Ellen White-Hansen is a freelance journalist and coauthor of this article. She also lives on Whidbey Island.

Walnut settee by the sea

by Thomas Hughes

I designed this walnut bench to provide a comfortable seat large enough for three people to enjoy a magnificent vista of the Pacific Ocean from the living room of an Arch Cape, Oreg., beach house. Almost 7 ft. long, the bench, shown at the top of the facing page, provides ample space to place drinking glasses or snack dishes. It also complements a framed, glass-top coffee table I built for the owners of the house.

The bench's apparent simplicity is deceptive. Contoured front and back rails reinforced with concealed metal brackets support a suspended seat made from contoured, laminated slats. The legs cant inward at the bottom, giving a visual lift to the bench, but this requires joining the legs to the aprons at an angle. These joints are not difficult to cut, though, if you lay them out carefully.

Bench design—I always make sketches to help sort out my ideas. Once I have a good sense of the piece, I usually make dimensioned scale drawings, along with full-size renderings of complex joints and other details. These drawings are needed to make this bench, but more importantly, they give me a better feel at this stage of whether or not my idea will "work." Finally, I build full-scale models from wood, cardboard and other scrap materials so I can study the design from a variety of angles and refine my ideas.

Three-dimensional models also give me a way to test the bench for comfort and to resolve construction details. I knew from my sketches that a framed, slatted seat would work well visually, but I needed to determine the most comfortable shape. To do this, I bandsawed different profiles from ¾-in. particleboard and set them on improvised pedestals so I could sit on them. Then, I kept modifying the shapes until one felt good. Next, I made a full-size end-view drawing of the bench seat to help determine how the front and rear rails should be shaped so they blend smoothly with the contoured slats (see figure 2 on the facing page).

I wanted the slats to be as thin as possible so the bench would appear light and the seat would give a little when a person sat down. I decided ⅜-in.-thick slats would be best, but this creates a structural problem in attaching the slats to the rails. Dovetails work, but appear too busy for my taste. I decided to use metal brackets: one end fitting into a mortised slot in the rails; the other end screwed to the bottom side of the slat. This solution enhances the feeling of lightness, because there's a ⅛-in. gap between the slats and the rails. The seat appears to be free-floating. This arrangement also increases the "springy" feel and adds to the bench's comfort.

I use 4-in.-wide stiles at both ends of the seat frame and an off-center middle stile, as shown in figure 3 on p. 64. The middle stile, the focal point of the bench, is made from a highly figured piece of walnut bordered with sapwood. By cutting the walnut into two pieces separated by a curved, tapering gap with the sapwood oriented toward the outer edges of the stile, interest was added. I left each outside edge irregularly shaped, as I had found it after removing the bark. Aside from design considerations, this two-piece

The author's 7-ft.-long walnut viewing bench will accommodate three people. Hughes designed the bench for a beachfront home overlooking the Pacific Ocean in Arch Cape, Oreg. The bench's slatted, contoured surface makes for comfortable seating.

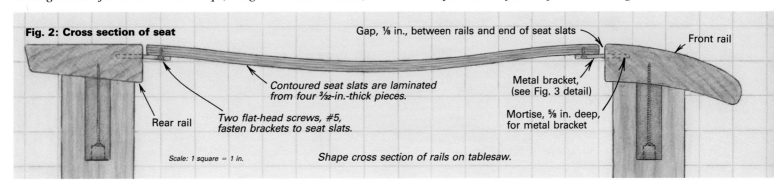

stile is useful as a convenient, built-in table surface.

The front and back aprons are tenoned into the leg tops. Screws counterbored up through the aprons fasten to the underside of the bench seat. The I-shape leg-stretcher assembly is also tenoned into the legs. While experimenting with my full-scale model, I discovered that I liked the appearance of the legs canted slightly inward from each side at the bottom, as shown in figure 3 on the next page and in the photo above. These odd angles complicate layout and cutting, so I make full-size patterns for the canted parts.

Construction—I start by building the lower frame, then do the seat. I pay particular attention to setting up my power tools and building special fixtures for odd-angle cuts. The old adage "measure twice, cut once" is good advice here.

I rough-cut stock for the legs to length and then square it up. The top and bottom of the legs are cut at a 6° angle, to allow for the leg cant. In addition, the tops need to be trimmed to match the contoured shape of the underside of the seat frame's front and back rails. I transfer the angles for these onto the ends of the legs directly from my full-scale drawing before cutting them on my tablesaw. I also mark the orientation of each leg, to avoid confusion.

I use the full-scale drawing again to mark the location of the mortises on the legs where the aprons and leg stretchers will be joined. To account for the leg cant, I tilt the drill-press table 6° before roughing out the mortises with a ⅜-in. brad-point drill bit. The leg stretchers are joined to the legs at 90°, but are skewed 6° from the leg vertical, so I return the drill-press table to its horizontal position before roughing out these mortises. I pare the mortise walls and square the ends with a chisel.

Next, I cut stock for the aprons and stretchers to length and square it up. The tenons are easily laid out directly from the full-scale drawing. I cut the shoulders on the tablesaw and then switch to a dado blade to remove the waste from the tenon cheeks, cutting shy of the intended depth. I use my router with a ½-in. dado clean-out bit (Carbide Saw & Tool Co. Inc., 2337 E. Burnside, Portland, Oreg. 97214; 800-777-7798) to bring the tenon cheeks to

their final size. I also rough out the apron tenons on the tablesaw, but because the shoulders here are angled, I cut them by hand using a Japanese Kaisoku Noko saw (Grizzley Tools, Box 2069, Bellingham, Wash. 98227; 206-647-0801 or 2406 Reach Road, Williamsport, Penn. 17701; 717-326-3806). I then clean up the apron tenons and shoulders with a chisel. I prefer the Japanese saw over a backsaw, because the Japanese saw cuts on the pull stroke, which I find more accurate and easier to control.

After drilling and counterboring holes in the aprons for screws that I'll use later to fasten the frame to the bench seat, I dry-clamp everything together to check the fit of the frame members. I make any necessary final adjustments and then reassemble and glue with Titebond. Now I'm ready to work on the bench seat.

I make the frame for the seat first. The mortises and tenons are cut in the rails and stiles as described above. To cut the tenons in the irregularly shaped middle stile pieces, however, I screw both stile sections to a squared-up piece of ¾-in. particleboard. The screws run up through the particleboard and into the underside of the stiles. (Even though these screw holes don't show, I still fill and sand them later.) After aligning stiles on the particleboard to replicate the way they will fit in the frame, I use the square particleboard edges as reference surfaces for cutting the tenons.

I'll later make and install metal brackets to support the floating seat slats. These brackets will fit into mortised slots in the front and rear rails. I rout these slots next, while the stock for the rails is still square. The mortise locations are taken directly from the full-size drawing; the top, inside edge of each rail is used as a reference, because this edge will not be affected later, when the rails are shaped. The mortises are cut with a plunge router with a ⅛-in. straight bit (available from Wisconsin Knife Works, 2710 Prairie Ave., Beloit, Wisc. 53511; 800-225-5959 or 608-365-9581 in Wisconsin; catalog #60006), using the shopmade mortising jig as shown in figure 4 on the next page.

To contour the length of the front and rear rails, I transfer the profile of the rails from the drawing to the ends of the rail stock. The back rail requires only two angled rip cuts on the tablesaw:

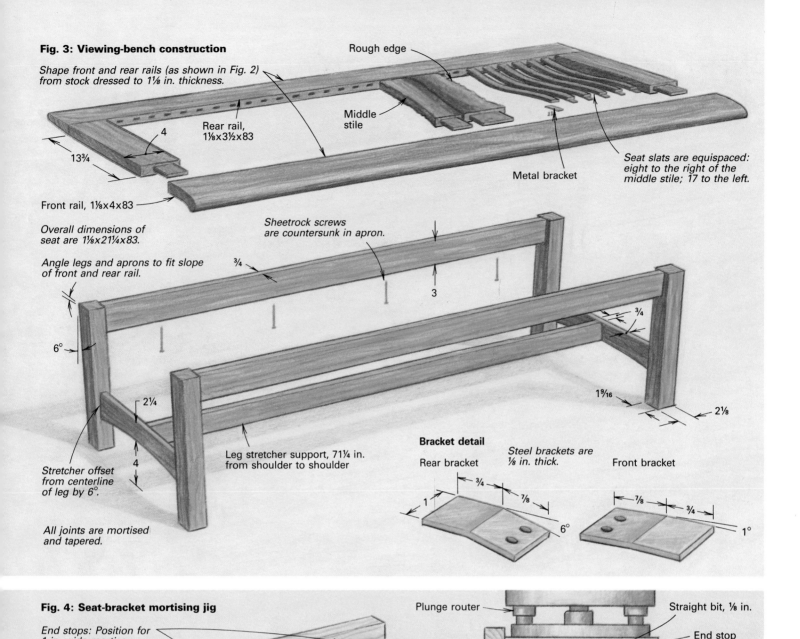

Fig. 3: Viewing-bench construction

Shape front and rear rails (as shown in Fig. 2) from stock dressed to 1⅛ in. thickness.

Rough edge

Middle stile

Rear rail, 1⅛x3½x83

Metal bracket

Seat slats are equispaced: eight to the right of the middle stile; 17 to the left.

4

13¾

Front rail, 1⅛x4x83

Overall dimensions of seat are 1⅛x21¼x83.

Angle legs and aprons to fit slope of front and rear rail.

Sheetrock screws are countersunk in apron.

¾

3

¾

6°

2¼

1⁹⁄₁₆

2⅛

Leg stretcher support, 71¼ in. from shoulder to shoulder

Stretcher offset from centerline of leg by 6°.

4

All joints are mortised and tapered.

Bracket detail

Steel brackets are ⅛ in. thick.

Rear bracket

Front bracket

1

¾

⅞

6°

⅞

¾

1°

Fig. 4: Seat-bracket mortising jig

End stops: Position for 1-in.-wide mortise.

Fence

Top surface of rails sits flush against bottom fence.

Bottom fence

Mark center of mortise to align rail to jig.

Plunge router

Straight bit, ⅛ in.

End stop

⅜

Clamping block

Bottom fence

Front or rear rail to be mortised

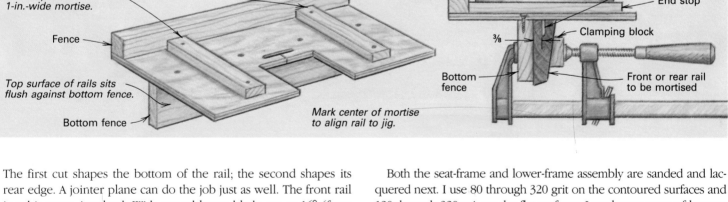

The first cut shapes the bottom of the rail; the second shapes its rear edge. A jointer plane can do the job just as well. The front rail is a bit more involved. With my tablesaw blade set at 16° (from vertical), I make a rip cut to remove most of the waste from the top surface of the rail. Then, using a ⅜-in.-wide dado blade, I rip along the underside of the rail to rough out its shape. The first pass is the deepest cut, extending just shy of what will be the rail's inside, bottom edge. The next pass, adjacent to the first, is made a bit shallower, but again, shy of the profile line drawn on the end of the rail stock. I continue in this way until I've completely carved out, in rough form, the concave shape on the stile's bottom surface. I use an old wooden jack plane (the sole and blade made convex to a 5-in. radius), a belt sander and hand-sanding to refine the shape and smooth the surface to its final form. I use Titebond glue when assembling the stiles and rails to form the seat frame.

Both the seat-frame and lower-frame assembly are sanded and lacquered next. I use 80 through 320 grit on the contoured surfaces and 120 through 320 grit on the flat surfaces. I apply two coats of lacquer sanding sealer (available from Imperial Paint Co., 2526 N.W. Yeon St., Portland, Oreg. .97210-1895; 503-228-0207), rubbing with 00 steel wool after each application. Finally, I apply two coats of semigloss lacquer. Each of these coats is rubbed down with 0000 steel wool.

The brackets connecting the slats to the rails are made from 1x1x1⅛-in. mild bar steel. I buy mine cut, drilled, bent and filed smooth at a machine shop for about $150. Each bracket has two ⁵⁄₃₂-in. holes drilled and countersunk for #5 ⅜-in. flat-head screws. After masking the ends of the brackets, which will later be inserted in the mortises, I prime them with Rustoleum spray primer and finish them with a coat of flat-black Rustoleum spray paint (available at local hardware stores). When the brackets are dry, I cement the brackets in the mortised rails with epoxy resin. Be sure to use only a moderate amount of epoxy, because squeeze-out can ruin the lacquer finish. If I do get some squeeze-out, I clean it up immediately with flat toothpicks.

At this point, I'm ready to make the contoured slats for the seat. These can be steam-bent from solid stock, but I decided to make mine by laminating four 3/32-in.-thick strips. I start by rip-cutting 3/16-in.-thick slats on the tablesaw from 1 5/8-in.-wide stock. I plane the slats to their final 3/32-in. thickness. I use a shopmade form to glue four slats together, again using Titebond glue. After jointing one edge, I rip the slats to width on the tablesaw. The slats

are then placed back into the form, which I use as a kind of sled to cut the slats to length on the tablesaw. To complete the slats, I hand-sand them with 80 through 320 grit, gently rounding their edges, and finally apply three coats of Watco Natural Oil. I rub the slats down with 0000 steel wool after each coat. The last step entails fastening the slats to the metal brackets with screws and assembling the seat to the frame with screws that go up through the front and rear aprons and into the underside of the seat rails. □

Tom Hughes lives in Arch Cape, Oreg., and specializes in designing and building custom furniture.

Art-nouveau garden bench

by Bim Burton

Art nouveau, with its flamboyant, free-flowing curves, was the rage at the turn of the century. The briefly popular style leaned heavily on nature for much of its inspiration, so it was natural that the Chelsea Flower Show, England's most prestigious horticultural event, would celebrate its 75th anniversary by trying to re-create a spirit of the era. I was invited to design and build a garden bench for the show that would echo this theme. My oak bench, shown below, is large enough to seat two people. Its slatted construction makes for an open, airy appearance, and the effect is accentuated by the interplay of light with the line and structure of the bench.

Although the bench is ruggedly constructed, I avoided complex joinery in building it. I used butt joints and countersunk screws throughout to secure all the bench's parts. Screws make the bench

quick to assemble and add a decorative touch. The shape of the slatted back is the result of a freehand sketch. Each slat is wedged between the two rear seat planks and screwed to the bottom rail. I drilled a hole near the top of each slat and threaded yacht rope through. The rope is knotted between each slat to fix the spacing and provide stability, but it also allows for a little "give" to the backrest, adding to the bench's comfort. The bench has armrests, but they are not structurally necessary, so can be added on or not according to one's personal taste. After sanding, I finish the bench with several coats of exterior varnish. □

Bim Burton designs and makes furniture at Workshop 119 in London, England.

Photo: Courtesy Kim Ivrey and 'Practical Woodworking'

This distinctive bench was especially built for display at the 1988 Chelsea Flower Show in London, England. The bench's lines, reminiscent of styles popular at the turn of the century, would make the bench a bright spot in any garden or yard.

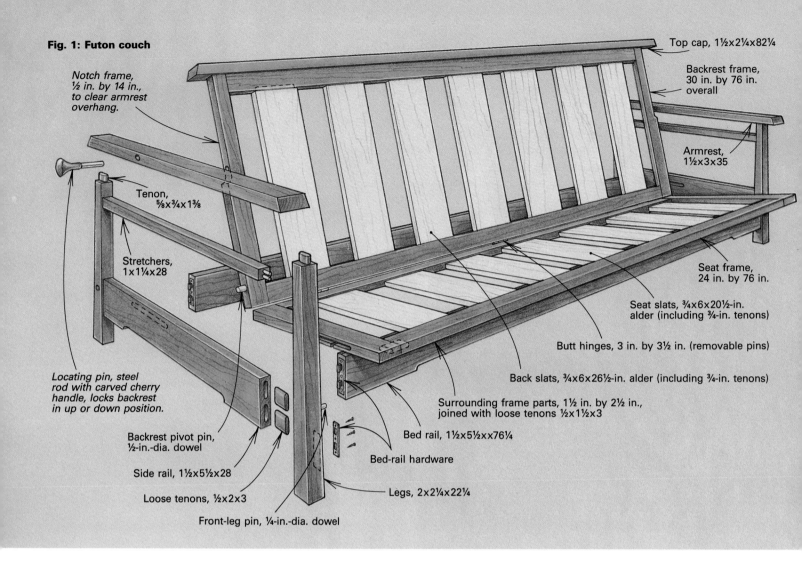

Fig. 1: Futon couch

Notch frame, ½ in. by 14 in., to clear armrest overhang.

Tenon, ⅝x¾x1⅜

Stretchers, 1x1¼x28

Locating pin, steel rod with carved cherry handle, locks backrest in up or down position.

Backrest pivot pin, ½-in.-dia. dowel

Side rail, 1½x5½x28

Loose tenons, ½x2x3

Front-leg pin, ¼-in.-dia. dowel

Top cap, 1½x2¼x82¼

Backrest frame, 30 in. by 76 in. overall

Armrest, 1½x3x35

Seat frame, 24 in. by 76 in.

Seat slats, ¾x6x20½-in. alder (including ¾-in. tenons)

Butt hinges, 3 in. by 3½ in. (removable pins)

Back slats, ¾x6x26½-in. alder (including ¾-in. tenons)

Surrounding frame parts, 1½ in. by 2½ in., joined with loose tenons ½x1½x3

Bed rail, 1½x5½xx76¼

Bed-rail hardware

Legs, 2x2¼x22¼

Making a Futon Couch
Pivoting backrest converts from seating to sleeping

by Gary Rogowski

A futon is simply a mattress-size cotton shell filled with cotton batting to a thickness of 4 in. to 6 in., then tied through, like an overstuffed comforter. Ideally suited for the small quarters and austere interiors of Japanese homes, futons have been traditional bedding in Japan for more than 2,000 years. They are laid down over tatami mats on the floor for sleeping, then rolled up in the morning for daytime storage or removal to the outdoors for airing. However, because sitting and sleeping on the floor is not customary in the West, we've adapted the use of the futon to suit both our habits and our interiors. That adaptation is in the form of a contemporary-style, wood-frame couch that lifts the futon off the floor and converts it from a couch to a bed and back again (see the top photos on the facing page).

At first, the idea of sleeping on a 4-in.-thick cotton mattress may strike you as lumbar torture, but the futons now available in the United States are made 6 in. thick and are filled with 100% cotton batting or a cotton and polyester blend. When used on a frame, they often have a 2-in.-thick, high-density foam core sandwiched between 2-in.-thick layers of cotton batting. Futons are available in standard mattress sizes from twin to king and can be purchased with a fitted, zippered case in a wide variety of colors and patterns.

The futon couch described here consists of two side frames for the armrests and legs, connected by two long bed rails that lock into the side frames with standard, knockdown bed hardware. Two larger frames are hinged together and convert from seat and back-

Drawings: David Dann

The hinged seat and backrest frames, along with a simple system of pivot pins and slots, allow the author's cherry couch frame (above) to be converted to a bed (below). A futon is the perfect mattress for this application, because of its flexibility.

Photos above: Jim Piper

rest for the couch to a sleeping platform for the bed. The backrest frame pivots on two ½-in.-dia. dowels that fit into slots routed in the side rails. After the backrest has been laid down flat, the platform is slid forward about 3 in. to center it over the bed rails. As the platform is slid forward, the seat frame is guided by ¼-in.-dia. dowels that are glued into the front legs and run in slots routed in the edge of the seat frame. Two steel locating pins with carved cherry handles are inserted through holes in the armrests to lock the backrest in the upright position, or through holes in the back legs to lock the platform in the sleeping position.

Design—Although smaller than an overstuffed hide-a-bed, a futon couch is still a fairly large piece of furniture and must be tailored to fit comfortably in the room for which it's planned. Make sure of the futon size before you begin your frame, and check if there's room to convert the couch to a sleeping platform. My couch was built so that a double-bed, 54-in. by 76-in. futon would fit on it lengthwise between the armrests. You'll note in figure 1 on the facing page that the seat and backrest frames are different widths. I determined the front-to-back depth of the seat frame by measuring the seat of a couch that I found comfortable. When sizing the seat frame, take into account the thickness of the backrest portion of the futon, and make sure that the seat isn't so deep that it interferes with your knees, forcing you to dangle your feet up in the air. When the futon is folded in the couch position, it will extend beyond the wood frame, providing a softer front edge. In the bed position, the total width of the two frames should equal the full width of your futon; both of these frames should be the same length as your futon.

Two other important details are the size of the armrests and the method for securing the futon on the frames. I made my armrests wide enough and thick enough to sit on, because contrary to the wishes of your Aunt Shirley (the same Aunt Shirley that would cover your futon couch in clear plastic if she had the chance), people will invariably sit on the arm of your couch. To ensure that the futon stays on the couch, sew straps onto the back of the futon cover where it folds for the backrest. When these straps are tied to the backrest slats, they prevent the futon from shifting forward.

I recommend you make full-scale joinery drawings to work out the construction details. This will help you see how each joint looks and how it will be cut. A full-scale drawing of the side of the couch will help you visualize the motion of the couch as it is transformed into a bed so you can plan for the placement of the pivot pins and slots.

Joinery—I used about 30 bd. ft. of 6/4 cherry for the side, seat and backrest frames. The legs require about 5 bd. ft. of 8/4 stock. Because I knew the back of my couch would be up against the wall and would not show, I used alder instead of cherry for the slats, about 20 bd. ft. of ¾-in.-thick stock. I've learned through experience to rough-mill all my parts and then remill them to final dimensions. I crosscut 1 in. over in length and rip ⅛ in. over in thickness and width. This way, if the wood wants to move, warp or cup, as it invariably does, my final milling will straighten, flatten and smooth it exactly to the dimensions I need.

The side frames are constructed with loose tenons fitted into mortises plunge-routed in the ends of the side rails and the sides of the legs. Loose tenons simplify my cutting list and eliminate the hassles of sawing tenons on the ends of long pieces. In addition, cutting twice as many mortises, once you're set up for them, is often faster than setting up, cutting and fitting integral tenons. The photo below, left, shows one of the jigs I use to mortise with the plunge router. The slots in the jig are cut out on a router table to the same width as the template guide that's screwed to the router base. The jig is positioned on the joint area and clamped in place. The router is placed over the jig, with the collar in one of the slots; a ½-in.-dia., carbide-tipped, spiral mortising bit is used to rout the mortises, as shown in the photo below, right. The same jig is used to rout the mating mortise. Because the inside face of the rail and the inside of the leg are flush, I simply clamp the jig's fence to the inside of each of the pieces. If they weren't flush, I would clamp a spacer, the width of the desired "set back," between the jig's fence

A single jig is used to rout the mating ½-in.-dia. mortises for the loose tenons that join the side rails to the legs. In the photo below, left, the jig is clamped to the end of the side rail. In the photo below, right, the author routs the mating mortise in the leg. The jig's slots are cut on the router table to fit the template guide screwed to the base of the Hitachi plunge router.

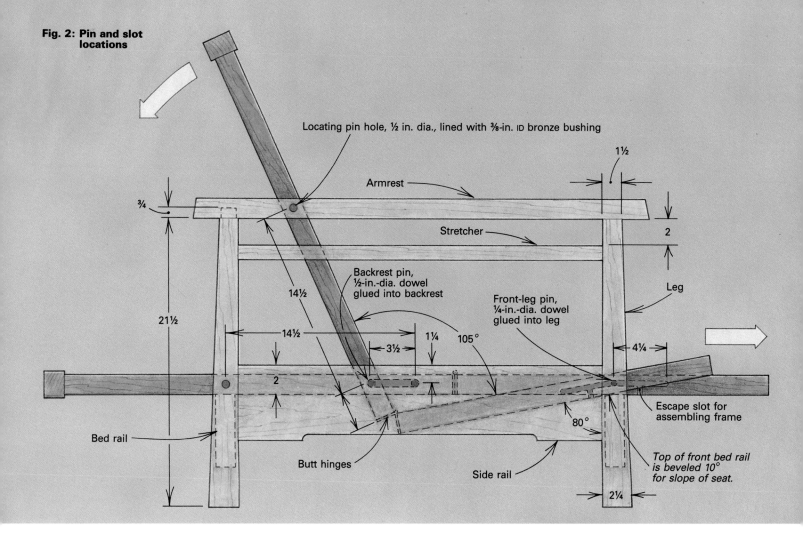

Fig. 2: Pin and slot locations

Locating pin hole, ½ in. dia., lined with ⅜-in. ID bronze bushing

Armrest

1½

Stretcher

2

¾

Backrest pin,
½-in.-dia. dowel
glued into backrest

Front-leg pin,
¼-in.-dia. dowel
glued into leg

Leg

14½

21½

14½

1¼

105°

3½

4¼

2

80°

Escape slot for
assembling frame

Bed rail

Butt hinges

Side rail

Top of front bed rail
is beveled 10°
for slope of seat.

2¼

and the piece that is to be inset. For extra insurance, I always pin these loose tenons with dowels. Sometimes I hide the pins on the inside of the joint, but they can be made decorative by using a contrasting wood for the pin.

I make the loose tenons by ripping lengths of solid stock on the tablesaw thick enough and wide enough to fit the mortises. I round over the long edges with a ¼-in. roundover bit on the router table to match the curved ends of the mortises left by the ½-in.-dia. router bit. Then, I crosscut the tenon stock to length, cutting it slightly short to allow space for excess glue and to ensure the joints come tightly together.

I mill all the side-frame parts to final dimensions and rout the mortises in the side-rail ends and in the legs using the mortising jig I made for the 1½-in.-thick stock. I chose not to use loose tenons on the armrests and leg tops; instead, I cut integral tenons on the 1½-in.-sq. tops of the legs so I could have as large a tenon as possible. I saw the tenons on the tablesaw before tapering the outside edge of the legs so I have all straight sides to work from. I fit the tenons to the ¾-in.-deep, ⅝-in. by 1⅜-in. mortises that I rout and chisel in the underside of the armrests. Then, I draw the taper on the legs, bandsaw them and clean the tapered side up on the jointer. I don't bother with a taper-cutting jig for tapering only four legs. I have all my legs cut and cleaned in the time it would take to set up a jig for the proper taper.

The only other joints I use on the side frames is another form of loose tenon–dowels. The stretcher below the armrest is doweled with two ¼-in.-dia. dowels per end. The dowels are more than strong enough to hold the stretcher in place, as no stress will be put on the joint.

The two long rails that connect the side frames and support the

sleeping platform are essentially the same as the bed rails that join the headboard and footboard of a conventional bed. On the couch in the top photo on the previous page, I glued the bed rails into the side frames with loose tenons, but this makes it difficult to move the couch and impossible to remove the platform frames. Instead, I recommend using bed hardware so the couch can be completely disassembled. Crosscut the bed rails ¼ in. longer than your platform frames (which are the same length as your futon), and saw a ¾-in. bevel on the back edge of the front rail (see figure 2 above) so that whether seat or bed, the seat frame is always bearing on a flat surface. Rout the mortises into the legs for the hardware before gluing up the sides frames, so you can run your router fence along the untapered inside edge of the leg. Mortise the mating hardware into the end of the bed rails. Because this hardware relies on screws to hold it in place, I use 3-in.-long screws in the endgrain of the rails.

Sand all the side-frame parts to 180 grit before gluing them up. I glue the loose tenons into the side rails first, spreading glue on all the surfaces with a brush or stick. Then, I glue the dowels into the stretcher and spread glue into the mortises on the legs. Use clamps to pull the joints home, making sure the frame remains square by comparing the diagonal measurements. If there's room for more clamps, glue on the armrests now; if not, wait until the glue dries and then glue them on.

While the side frames are drying, I assemble the seat and backrest frames. The finished frames will be ¼ in. shorter than the length of your bed rails so they can pivot and slide freely between the side frames. The widths of the frames will be based on your futon's width and the depth of your couch seat, as described in the section on design. There are seven alder slats in each of these frames to support the futon. I use slats instead of plywood panels, to provide air circulation around the cotton futon. This helps the cotton batting hold its fluff and reduces the chance that any dampness will lead to mildew. If you use plywood for the platform, be sure to drill a series of holes to ventilate the futon.

Although the frames themselves are joined with loose tenons and pinned, I tablesaw ¾-in.-long integral tenons on the ends of the slats. The cherry for the frames is milled to size and crosscut to length, then the mortises for the loose tenons in the corner joints and the mortises for the slats are made with a plunge router and jig. The slat mortises are ¾ in. deep, ½ in. by 5½ in., evenly spaced along the inside edges of the long frame pieces. On the 6-in.-wide alder slats, I tablesaw 5-in.-wide tenons to fit the mortises. The 5-in. tenons fit within the 5½-in. routed mortises without having to round over the cheeks of the tenons to match the rounded ends of the mortises.

Before sanding and gluing up the backrest frame, you'll need to bandsaw a ½-in. notch 14 in. down from the top of the end pieces, to clear the overhang of the armrest when the backrest is up (see figure 1 on p. 66).

Sand your frames and slats to 180 grit. Glue the slats into the long frame pieces first. Then, glue the loose tenons into the ends of the frames, brush glue on both the tenons and the mortises, and clamp on the frame's end pieces. After the clamps are removed from the frames, I pin all the loose tenons with ¼-in. dowels and sand them flush. I round over the outside edges that will be exposed with a ⅜-in. roundover bit. Don't round over the top rail of the backrest if it's to receive a cap piece, or the long edges of the frames that get hinged together.

Pins and slots—Converting the couch to a bed depends on two pivot points, as shown in figure 2: one where the backrest pivots in the side rails; the other where the seat frame slides past the front legs. The first of these is the most crucial: The ½-in.-dia. dowels glued into the sides of the backrest frame pivot and slide in slots routed in the inside of the side rail; these dowels help support the load on the seat and act as the pivot for the backrest. The other pins are ¼-in.-dia. dowels glued into the front legs; they slide in slots in the side of the seat frame and anchor this frame in both the couch and bed positions. The slots are long enough so the sleeping platform can be slid forward until it's centered over the bed rails.

You should note that the slots for these two sets of pins are, somewhat mysteriously, not the same length. This is because as the backrest frame is laid down, pivoting on its pin, the arc of the pivoting frame pushes the seat frame forward approximately 1 in. Therefore, the slot in the seat frame must include this 1 in. of travel, plus the 3 in. of travel as both frames are slid forward to center the sleeping platform. Adding the ¼-in. diameter of the front-leg pin, the slot in the seat frame must be 4¼ in. long; the slot in the side rail for the backrest pin, adding the ½-in. diameter of the pin, must be 3½ in. long. In addition, notice that the distance between the backrest pivot pin and the locating holes for both the couch and bed positions must be the same.

My seat slopes back at an angle of 10° with the backrest angled 105° from the plane of the seat. You might want to measure the angles on a chair or couch that you find particularly comfortable and then adjust the placement of your pins and slots accordingly. To calculate for any such changes, cut two sticks: one as long as the width of the backrest, the other as long as the width of the seat frame. Hinge these two sticks together and use them in conjunction with a full-scale drawing of your side frame to see how the frames will pivot and slide, and to determine the placement of the

locating pins. Refer to figure 2 on the facing page or your full-scale drawing when laying out the pivot-pin holes and slots; carefully measure and mark their locations on the appropriate pieces.

I recommend using a doweling jig or some other guide to ensure that the holes for the pins will be straight and true. Drill a ½-in.-dia. hole 1 in. deep into each side of the backrest frame, and glue a 2-in. length of ½-in. dowel into each of these holes. Next, drill ¼-in.-dia. holes ½ in. deep in the front legs, and glue in 1-in.-long, ¼-in. dowels. Then, clamp the seat frame in a vise and use the plunge router with a fence attached to cut the ½-in.-deep slots, one in each end, for the ¼-in.-dia. front-leg pin. Make an entrance and escape slot to allow for assembly of the seat frame near the center of each of these slots. The side panels are then clamped to the top of the workbench, and again using the plunge router with a fence, I rout the 1-in.-deep slot for the ½-in.-dia. backrest pin. After the slots are completed, I find and mark the centers for the ½-in.-dia. holes in the armrest and rear leg for the locating pins and drill them through, again using a doweling jig. To make sure these holes won't become sloppy with use, I line them with bronze bushings and use 4-in. lengths of ⅜-in.-dia. steel rod epoxied into carved cherry handles for the locating pins. Bronze bushings are readily available at well-equipped hardware stores. I use 1-in.-long bushings with an outside diameter of ½ in. and an inside diameter of ⅜ in., driving them into the holes from both sides and sawing off the excess. The handles, although almost an afterthought, will probably be the first thing noticed, so take your time and have some fun with them.

Now you can mortise for the three butt hinges that join the large frames and glue the cap piece onto the back frame. Sand the rounded-over edges of the frames and clean up any glue squeeze-out with an orbital sander and 180-grit or finer sandpaper. Finally, oil or lacquer the four separate frames and two bed rails. When the finish is dry, wax the pivot pins and slots well with paraffin so they'll slide easily.

Assembling the couch will be easier with two people. Begin by locking the back rail to one side frame. With the hinge pins removed so the large frames are separate, lay the backrest frame on the back bed rail and insert the ½-in.-dia. backrest pivot pin into the slot on the side frame. While your helper holds the first side frame and the backrest together, align the opposite backrest pivot pin with the slot in the other side frame and simultaneously connect the mating hardware of the back bed rail with the second side frame. Now you can connect the front bed rail to both side frames. Put the seat frame in place by lining up the escape slots routed in the sides of the seat frame with the front-leg pins and by inserting the three hinge pins to join the two platform frames. Mark the edge of the backrest frame for the locating pins, double-checking their placement in both the upright and sleep positions. Drill the ½-in.-dia. holes 1 in. deep with the doweling jig, line them with bronze bushings and insert the carved locating pins. To dismantle the couch frame, reverse the procedure described above. ☐

Gary Rogowski designs and builds furniture in his Portland, Ore., shop.

Sources of Supply _____

Steel rod and bronze bushings for the locating pins can be found at well-equipped hardware stores. Knockdown bed hardware is available from W.C. Winks Hardware, 903 N.W. Davis, Portland, Ore. 97209; or by mail from The Woodworkers' Store, 21801 Industrial Blvd., Rogers, Minn. 55374-9514. Futons can be purchased from Northwest Futon Co., 400 S.W. Second, Portland, Ore. 97204; or check your local Yellow Pages under futons or bedding.

Designing a Bed
From paper to prototype

by Ian Kirby

We are all capable of handling woodworking design decisions up to a point, but beyond a certain level most people become frustrated and switch off. An analogy would be the way we treat ourselves when we are sick. For a minor illness, we may prescribe the same treatment a doctor would have prescribed, but beyond a certain point of illness or injury we know we need a doctor—a professional who will use a combination of training, experience and analysis to arrive at a course of treatment.

Like a doctor, a trained designer has methods, techniques and pathways—a well ordered, well organized route that establishes the problem then solves it. Creativity plays a part, but it's a common saying among designers that the work is 99% perspiration and 1% inspiration. Everyone is creative to a considerable degree; design methods are the tools that bring creativity out.

In purely graphic terms, the design process might look something like the drawing below. We start at a point that represents the need for a design, whatever that need might be. From this point, we research and gather data in an increasing amount—try-

ing not to exclude possibilities—until we reach the center circle in the drawing. This center circle is where the data are considered and developed. The path leads off to the right in a narrowing triangle wherein the broad design is worked out, then its details, then the implementation of the design and finally, its evaluation. What's called for to the left of the center circle is divergent thinking, to the right of the circle, convergent thinking.

The diagram represents the signposts to the discipline of design. In this article about designing a particular bed, I will attempt to point to the places where we see some link between this ideal pathway and the job in hand—in other places the link is too obscure to unravel in this amount of space.

False leads—The most common misunderstanding is that to design you should have some knowledge of how to make the item. In reality it should be argued that, for a student, this knowledge is the greatest design barrier you could wish for since your design thinking is tethered within the knowledge. It causes convergent thinking early in the design process, at a time when diver-

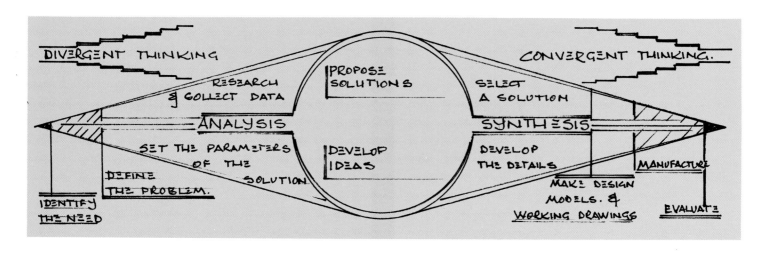

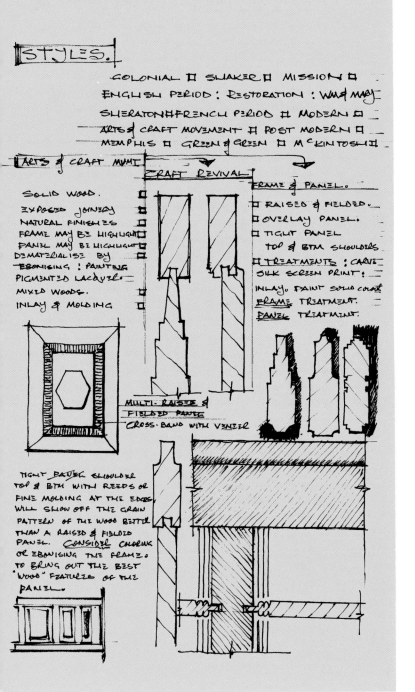

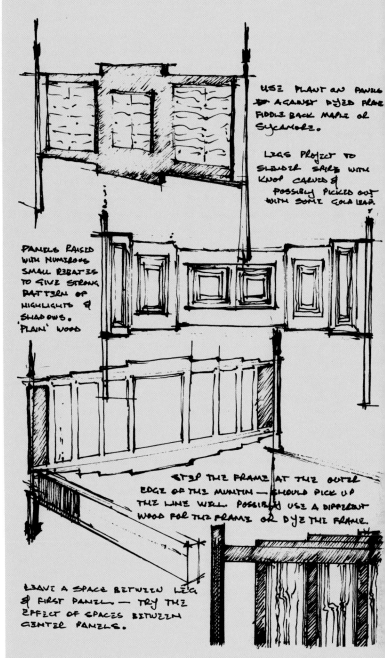

gent thinking is called for. In practice, you will find that the mind resists the disciplined method. All sorts of shortcuts pop in at all sorts of times—we have creative leaps that seem to bypass groundwork. Yet if the groundwork is not completed, a designer is unable to be objective about the solutions. To assist in continuing on track, sudden inspirations can be recorded with drawings and notes in order to empty them from your mind.

To know when not to re-invent the wheel yet keep to the pathway is part of the process of growing up as a designer. As one becomes more accomplished at problem solving, the design pathway seems to be somewhat lost—it isn't of course, but the double-edged sword of experience comes into play and makes observing the designer at work a complex operation.

The problem—Having explained the design method in general terms, I'm going to pick up the specifics that went into the bed design. The bed was to be designed for a client who was neither relative nor friend, but a business client. This is worth noting because the initial sorting out process is too easily passed over when you are dealing with someone you know—too much is as-

sumed by both parties—not enough questions get asked.

In our first meeting some general parameters had to be set. The bed was to be the main piece in a small group of bedroom furniture to be sold in a store specializing in blankets and bed linens. The bedclothes are of wool, mohair, linens and silks. The weaves and colors are unusual, the finishing details superb, the whole accent on quiet, understated quality.

I explain this to illustrate the unspoken messages in the surroundings, which will be underscored by the conversation about the work in hand. In most cases the client has no idea that this is going on, it is something you have to work on alone. The client will be quick to tell you what he or she thinks you need to hear, including solutions to the problem, but a client's express wishes are often misleading and can be costly. You wind up building a million-dollar mansion on a quarter-acre sub-division. It's often expressed as the client having a champagne taste and a beer budget.

The store's ambiance suggested furniture of a similar image. After listing all the materials one might use for a bed, natural polished wood seemed to be the most in keeping with the tone

From *Fine Woodworking* magazine (July 1986) 59:76-79

Dimensions

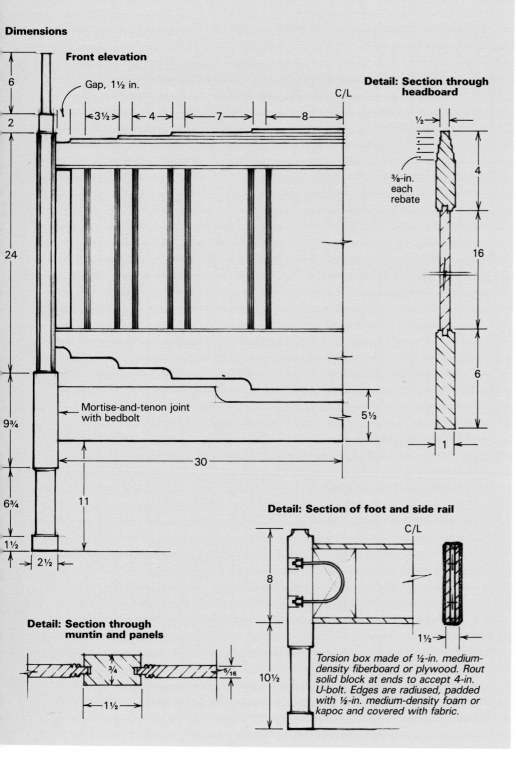

Front elevation

Gap, 1½ in.

←3½→ ←4→ ←7→ ←8→

6

2

24

Mortise-and-tenon joint
with bedbolt

9¾

6¾

11

1½

2½

30

**Detail: Section through
muntin and panels**

¾

⁵⁄₁₆

←1½→

**Detail: Section through
headboard**

C/L

½→ ←

⅜-in.
each
rebate

4

16

6

1

5½

Detail: Section of foot and side rail

C/L

8

10½

1½→ ←

Torsion box made of ½-in. medium-
density fiberboard or plywood. Rout
solid block at ends to accept 4-in.
U-bolt. Edges are radiused, padded
with ½-in. medium-density foam or
kapoc and covered with fabric.

Stick to standards

The spaces allowed inside a bed's frame must leave enough room so that standard springs and mattresses will fit. Spring units are sized to fit within the bed's rails, whereas matching mattresses are sometimes wider so bedclothes can overhang the side rails. The following dimensions are in current use, but it's best to check the actual springs and mattresses you plan to use.

Twin	39 in. by 75 in.
Double	54 in. by 75 in.
Queen	60 in. by 80 in.
King	76 in. by 80 in.
California King	72 in. by 84 in.

California King is a sensible proportion for a large bed, but springs and mattresses are generally not available except on the West Coast. Twin and Double are usually available in the 80-in., extra-length size. Adjust the length of the bed's rails to suit.

If you design a bed with a high footboard, allow about 2 in. of clearance in the length so that heavy winter bedclothes can be tucked in at the foot. This clearance can be smaller if the bed will be used in warm climes—it should not be larger than necessary, because too much space is an invitation for the mattress to slide down, which then allows pillows to drop between the mattress and the headboard. Similar clearance is necessary for a bed with side rails that extend above the box spring. This is seldom the case these days, as the box springs are usually higher than the side rails.

The bed in this article can be built in any of the four larger standard sizes by changing the width of the center panel in the headboard (and of course the length of the headboard's top and bottom rails). The dimensions of the other panels remain the same. —*I.K.*

---

the owner wished to project. Making such an important decision early in the process may not be possible on every occasion—it may not be wise either, because it does close some doors. The next step is to research and record all the options within the one form of bed—natural wood, that is a beginning point once again.

I earlier described the client as the store owner. In reality there are two clients and the second one now becomes paramount—the buyer. Most design work sets the selling price parameters very early in the process, yet if too much consideration is given to the cost at an early stage then ideas get bypassed. The aim is to go for the best ideas, then cut costs later.

The style—Another important decision that is frequently sifted out early is the style of the furniture: Shaker, Mission, Colonial, the European styles, Art Deco, Post Modern, Memphis—they

each define the form of the piece within a wide set of boundaries. Don't typecast things too tightly into styles, but use the words as shorthand so that you and the client have a path to follow without going in every conceivable direction at once.

A style that was suited to the situation was arrived at by considering all sorts of factors. Does the style lend itself to machine work? If so, what machines are available? Does it show off the material? These questions, this data, are collected and considered at this stage not as *solutions*—it is too early for that—but as possibilities that will be winnowed out later in the design process.

The outcome was a decision to work within the English Arts and Crafts Movement and, in particular, to take advantage of the visual possibilities inherent in frame-and-panel construction. The sketches on p. 71 show some of the wealth of variations.

Drawings—Do you have to be able to draw to design? The answer has to be no, but drawing is the fastest way you can express and analyze visual ideas of form and space, both to yourself and your client. It's like a language. When you use sketches to converse with yourself, you don't yet know where the conversation will lead and at times, you watch the ideas develop as though you were an onlooker.

Anyone who has the wish can learn to draw. The muscular skill required to write your name is far more complex than that needed to draw a straight line. A great deal of our reluctance to work on the drawing board is that it is such a merciless medium. It's like expecting to pick out a tune on a piano when we have no knowledge of the instrument. We become quickly frustrated and embarrassed, yet we all have to begin somewhere and my own experience reminds me of what the feeling is like. Classes in perspective, life or plant drawings are all useful. But even without classes, we are all capable of drawing squares, triangles and circles, which are the basic elements of all furniture forms.

The bed required dozens of sketches. These were done quickly, often in succession as I developed various ideas. Don't be afraid to experiment. Draw an orthographic view, photocopy it, vary the sizes, trace the various parts then move the elements around. Do everything you can to get your collection of shapes fitting together in a harmony that appeals to you. Check your progress against your initial list of data to make sure you aren't straying from your design brief. Sleep on it and have a look the next day.

Deliberations—Solutions begin to evolve from the work on the drawing board. For the bed's headboard, I decided to treat the frame and panel in a manner that would lift it out of the traditional mold. It occurred to me that if the headboard was held in place by the top and bottom frame member, then by using a dry mortise-and-tenon joint between the headboard and post, the whole board could be turned upside down and back to front, presenting four different faces of the headboard.

I wanted two looks from the headboard. Both had to come from the same form—one when it was made of exotic material, and the other when it was made of a hardwood. The material I had in mind was English brown oak, and to create the focus, I decided to use ebonized ash for the frames. For a more prosaic look, I wanted the same form to look good when made totally of cherry. To accommodate orders for different bed widths, the center panels would be made wider or narrower. In this way, the sizes and proportions of all else remained the same.

I decided not to have a footboard. This way, attention would be focused on the headboard, and the blankets would be more visible. The legs needed to be sufficiently large to hold the bed up and define the corners, but no more. Some sketches developed initial ideas about the form of the legs. I wanted the connecting frame or rails to be low-key. Certainly, I didn't want large rails going round the base of the bed. I have always imagined knocking into these and being the recipient of some colorful bruises as a result.

Before sketches can be refined into working drawings, real sizes must be decided upon. I planned for a standard-size mattress with 1 in. to 1½ in. between mattress and frame to allow for sheets and blankets. A list of the standard bed sizes is given on the facing page. The height of the mattress within the bed frame should be worked out so that the headboard is positioned correctly. It's very easy to design the whole thing then put the box spring and mattress in place only to discover that when the pillows are placed on the bed they practically obliterate the headboard. Also, the headboard must retain the pillows and not let them slip under its the bottom edge.

Other considerations came into play. We had in mind multiples: the bed had to be producible by machine woodworking methods using what I had available—tablesaw, bandsaw, jointer and planer. Moldings and other treatments could come from the router, so only a small number of jigs had to be made. One virtue of this minimal manufacturing technique is that if you select your materials well, you can offer what appears to be quite a range of product. In fact, it's all made the same way, just detailed and finished differently.

The dry mortise and tenon connecting the end rail to the bedposts allows the headboard to be flipped, and also allows the bed to be knocked down for packing and transport. Obviously, the rails have to be firmly connected to the legs when the bed is set up. I used a bed bolt and captive nut in the rail end. But for the side rails on the production model of this bed, I decided to use a U-bolt system instead, which is stronger and easier to install. Details of this construction are shown on the facing page. Since I didn't want a show-wood rail around the bed, and since I wanted it to be softened in some way, a torsion box was the solution. Made with ½-in. medium density fiberboard, they are light in weight but very robust looking. The outside core strips are large enough to receive a large radius. The U-bolts are captive in a groove routed into a solid block at each end of the torsion-box/rail. The rail itself is wrapped with ½-in. foam or Kapoc batting and covered with cloth. My preference was black silk for the ebonized frame and neutral brown cloth for the cherry.

The holes made in the legs have to accept a socket wrench, thus they need a plug or some form of cover once the bed has been assembled. This illustrates how the design process occasionally folds back upon itself—because now a round of research into plugs and covers is called for. If you find yourself having to research major stuff at this stage, however, you have probably skimped on the necessary work at the beginning.

Solid stuff—No matter how accomplished any of us are as a draftsman, the point comes when we reach the end of what we can usefully do at the drawing board. We need to see how our ideas translate into the real thing by making a scale model or a full-scale mock-up. I prefer a mock-up that, although full size in its parts, needs only to be fastened together quickly—hot-melt glue works well—in such a way that half of it is completed. This half is then placed against a mirror so that the whole image can be looked at and evaluated. At this stage you need to concentrate on form and how shapes interrelate, not on wood grain, so a wood such as poplar will do. It is a good idea to spray paint your mock-up white and review it purely in terms of shapes and negative space.

Beyond this point, further design research is really a function of quantities. If large numbers of the item are to be made, one or more mock-ups need to be constructed, and jigging and production methods tested. Such was not the case here, so we went right to a prototype, which is shown at the beginning of this article. No matter how much you try to get it right the first time, there are improvements that can be made. It requires that you never close the doors on your thinking and never become so obsessed with your efforts that you can't consider changes. □

Ian Kirby is a designer, author and educator. He operates Kirby Studios in Cumming, Ga.

An Outdoor Lounger
Build your way to a better tan

by Brian Tinius

The author's inclined tanning lounge is designed for standard-size pads and has wheels for mobility. Its curved top slats and spline-joined frame are made with three different jigs.

I grew up in Seattle, Wash., where anything accidentally left outside would be in no condition to return indoors after only a week. Memories of rusting little tractors and rotted Lincoln logs have kept my furniture designs strictly indoor affairs. Here in Southern California, the climate is more forgiving, although smog, humidity and temperature fluctuations can also be hard on outdoor furniture. So, when I was asked to create some work for a sculpture garden in the nearby Santa Monica mountains, I very hesitantly accepted. Well, a coffee table is hardly meant for a garden setting, so I took on the challenge of designing a piece of outdoor furniture that would be simple, straightforward and could stand up to the elements.

I decided to build a lounge chair that reflects the Southern California obsession with being trim and tan, so my design had to be physically light and visually lean. After doing a few sketches, I came up with a design that could best be described as an inclined tanning lounger, or what I came to call a "sun sled." I wanted the top to have a look of lightness, so I tapered the ends of each slat, rounded the edges of the bottom frame and added wheels for mobility. I also designed the top so a standard 25-in. by 80-in. lounge pad could be used.

I chose maple for the project because it's strong, takes a good finish and is relatively inexpensive. It took me about two hours of searching through the stack at the local hardwood store to locate the clear stock I needed. Most of the 4/4 boards had to be more than 10¼ in. wide to accommodate the radius of each crescent-shaped slat. When I got the wood back to the shop, I made a mat board template of a slat and laid out all the pieces for the top,

avoiding knotholes and splits. I marked out all the slats I needed, plus a few extra pieces for tests and mistakes, then trimmed all the slats to their finished length.

Since the project calls for a lot of repetitive operations, like cutting the curves for the top and sawing the spline joints in the frame, I designed several jigs that would allow me to get the work done quickly and accurately. The jig I used for bandsawing the top curves consists of a subbase attached to the bandsaw table, plus a pivoting carrier of ½-in. plywood (figure 1) cut to the overall width of the top and 1 in. longer than the 15-in. radius of the curve. A 3-in.-wide fence made of hardwood is screwed down to the plywood from the top, with its working edge 4⅞ in. from the pivot hole and parallel to the line of cut. With the fence in this position, the outside curves on the center slats are cut, then set aside. Before the remaining slats can be cut, the jig's fence must be moved 1⅛ in. toward the blade. To hold down the slats, I used quick-action clamps made by De-Sta-Co (350 Midland Ave., Detroit, Mich. 48203, catalog #217-U).

Next, I taper all the curved slats on their bottom outer edges. By saving the inside radius cuts for later, a straight edge remains on each piece to align it to a wedge-shaped tapering jig (figure 2) that supports and guides it through bandsaw rough-cutting and planer trimming operations. The jig is basically a 9-in. by 24-in. plywood box with a 6° slope. Since the maximum thickness my bandsaw will cut is 6 in., the pieces must extend 5½ in. beyond the end of the jig to clear the blade guides (facing page, center). To grasp and register each piece on the wedge jig, I screw on a piece of the scrap from the outside radius cuts and a stop strip. Using a hold-down clamp to secure the work, place the jig on edge, with the wider end nearest the blade so that the straight edge of the workpiece is down and the underside faces out. The bandsaw's fence is set to trim away a thin wedge from the end of each board.

After all tapers are rough-cut on one end, the bandsaw's fence is moved to the opposite side of the blade and the taper is sawn in the other end. Since the wedge jig must be flipped over to adapt to the new position of the fence, the stop assembly and clamp must also be repositioned (figure 2) to keep the straight edge of the workpiece down on the table. After first doing a test piece, I cut the second taper the same way I did the first.

I use the same wedge jig to trim the tapers with the stop and clamp setup moved down to the lower position, as shown in the bottom photo. I lay the taper flat on the planer bed and trim the ends down, a little at a time, until it's ⅜ in. thick and the taper runs in about 3¾ in. from the end. Make certain that the metal clamp clears the cutterhead before you begin, and keep the jig flat as you pull the jig through after it stops feeding forward. Also, if the rollers in your planer are set farther apart than the length of the taper, the work may have to be hand-fed, so be sure to do a test piece first. Several alternative methods for cutting the tapers are practical: you can use a panel-raising bit on a shaper, an angle jig with a router, or even a drawknife and block plane or belt sander.

After both ends have been tapered, the inside radii are cut on all but the two center pieces, using the same jig employed for the outsides. Simply move the fence toward the blade 3 in.

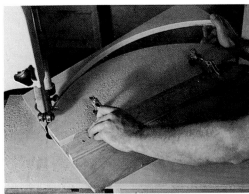

With work held securely by quick-action clamps, Tinius' radius jig bandsaws curves for the top slats quickly and accurately.

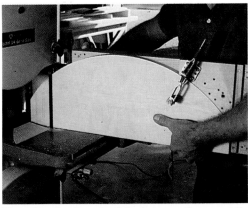

Tapering jig does double duty: author uses jig on edge to rough-cut taper on the bandsaw, then repositions fence and flips jig over.

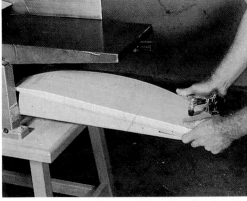

Jig passes through the planer for final trimming. Be sure to shut off the planer and pull the jig through after it stops feeding forward.

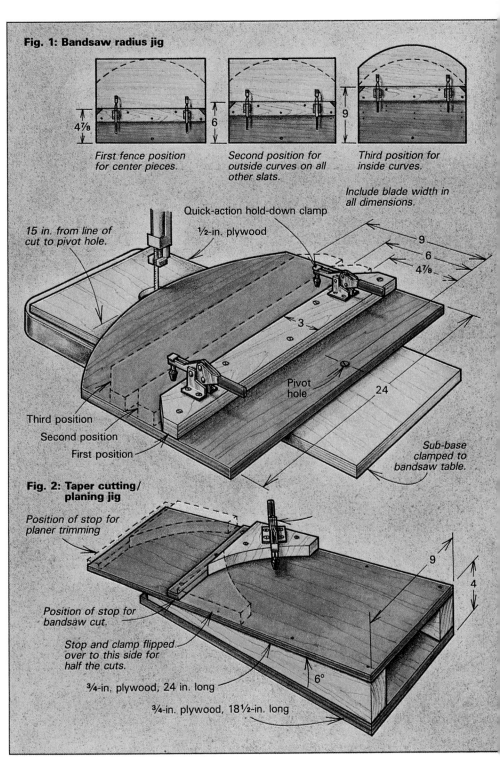

Fig. 1: Bandsaw radius jig

4⅞ — First fence position for center pieces.

6 — Second position for outside curves on all other slats.

9 — Third position for inside curves.

Include blade width in all dimensions.

15 in. from line of cut to pivot hole.

Quick-action hold-down clamp

½-in. plywood

9
6
4⅞

3

Pivot hole

24

Third position
Second position
First position

Sub-base clamped to bandsaw table.

Fig. 2: Taper cutting/ planing jig

Position of stop for planer trimming

Position of stop for bandsaw cut.

Stop and clamp flipped over to this side for half the cuts.

¾-in. plywood, 24 in. long

¾-in. plywood, 18½-in. long

9
4
6°

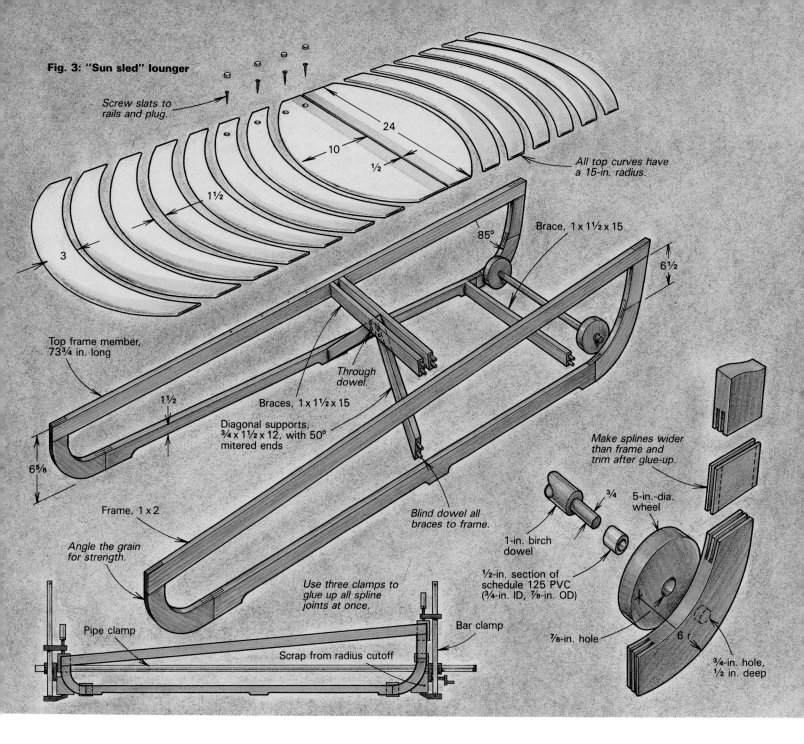

Fig. 3: "Sun sled" lounger

Screw slats to rails and plug.

All top curves have a 15-in. radius.

24

10

1/2

1 1/2

3

85°

Brace, 1 x 1 1/2 x 15

6 1/2

Top frame member, 73 3/4 in. long

1 1/2

Through dowel.

Braces, 1 x 1 1/2 x 15

Diagonal supports, 3/4 x 1 1/2 x 12, with 50° mitered ends

Make splines wider than frame and trim after glue-up.

6 5/8

Frame, 1 x 2

Angle the grain for strength.

Blind dowel all braces to frame.

3/4

5-in.-dia. wheel

1-in. birch dowel

1/2-in. section of schedule 125 PVC (3/4-in. ID, 7/8-in. OD)

Use three clamps to glue up all spline joints at once.

Pipe clamp

Bar clamp

7/8-in. hole

6 r

Scrap from radius cutoff

3/4-in. hole, 1/2 in. deep

(plus the thickness of the blade), clamp down the work and proceed. I sand off the sawmarks with a rubber sanding block and 80- or 100-grit paper and, at the same time, ease the sharp arrises. The pieces are now ready to be finish-sanded and have their top edges routed with a 3/16-in. radius round-over bit set up on a router table.

Before the radius jig is stowed away, I cut one more piece in a 1 1/2-in.-wide arc. This will be used later as a spacer to keep the slat spacing consistent when the top is laid out on the frame.

The frame assembly (figure 3) consists of 1-in. legs and rails ripped 2 in. wide, joined by a 6-in. radius at each end cut from a separate square. First, I cross-cut the top and bottom rails and the short vertical legs to length. Both ends of the rails, the top ends of the front legs and one pair of radii are cut at a 5° angle to match the slope of the sun sled. I use double-spline joints to join the leg and rail assemblies together. They're strong, attractive, simple joints that can be a colorful accent if the splines are made from a contrasting wood. Best of all, I use the same jig setup (with very few adjustment changes) to cut

the spline slots in all the pieces—curved ones included.

The sliding jig for cutting the slots uses the radial-arm saw with its head turned sideways 90° (see photo, facing page). The jig consists of a 3/4-in. piece of plywood with a stout hardwood guide on the underside of the outer edge. The guide bears against the front edge of the saw's table, and the jig holding the workpiece is moved from right to left through the stationary sawblade. A 1/8-in.-high stop is attached on the top front edge, parallel to the back edge, and a 2-in.-wide fence with hold-down clamps is attached perpendicular to the stop. The blade must be set parallel to the top of the jig to obtain a true and clean cut. The top edge of the blade is set 13/16 in. above the jig table, and the radial arm is locked down with the blade protruding 2 1/8 in. past the stop.

After making sure all the pieces are the exact same thickness, a test cut is made. *Be very careful*—if your saw is like mine, you'll have to remove the blade guard for this operation. All the frame ends, except the rails, are first slotted face-up, then flipped over and cut again face-down. Since the top rail ends are cut at an angle, a 5° wedge must be slipped between the rail and the fence. The slots at the foot end of the rail are slotted ⅝ in. deeper than the rest to accommodate the added depth needed to meet the inward curve of the slot below it. After slotting, the curved pieces are completed by cutting both inside and outside radii. I make the splines (two for each joint) from scraps.

The wheels are bandsawn from 5-in. squares; a 1-in.-diameter birch dowel is used as an axle. An inch-and-a-half on each end of the axle is reduced to ¾ in. in diameter in order to slip through the wheel and fit into the leg assembly. To reduce wear and keep out moisture, I put a 1-in.-long collar cut from ½-in. Schedule 125 thinwall PVC pipe over the end of the dowel, up to the shoulder where the wheel will be (see figure 3).

For the glue-up, I use Wilhold Plastic Resin, which has good water resistance and a set-up time that's long enough to allow me to do the assembly unassisted. I glued each leg assembly in two sessions, but it could be accomplished in one with help. The difficulty is that each joint must be clamped in both directions to obtain a nice tight joint (figure 3). After glue-up and trimming of the spines, all edges are ready to be routed with a ³⁄₁₆-in.-radius round-over bit before finish sanding.

I finish-coat the frame before I do the final assembly and dowel the diagonal supports into place. The only clear finish I've found tough enough to stand up outdoors is varnish—either spar or polyurethane. Instead of the high-gloss spar varnish usually seen on a boat's brightwork, I like a satin luster to give the lounge the softer look of natural wood. I brush on four coats of McCloskey Man O'War spar varnish, sanding lightly between each. I use the dowel holes drilled in the frame (to join the cross braces) to hang the pieces up on a board with pins, like a hat rack. After allowing a week of drying time, I assemble the rest of the frame.

The proper finishing of the top is crucial because it receives the brunt of the sun and wear. After talking to several paint salespeople, I prefer a synthetic enamel called Sintec made by Sinclair Paints (available from any Sinclair dealer, white #7500, bright yellow #7513). It's an industrial-grade product that's used on farm implements and wears well outdoors. I also use Sinclair's "best" exterior-wood primer, knowing from experience that a top finish can only be as good as the preparation that goes into the surface below it. This primer has what's called a "controlled penetration" and takes a long time to dry (24 hours, if the weather is favorable). The first time I sprayed the stuff, I applied the first coat too heavily, and had to wait three days for it to dry. Also, the overspray from the enamel is different from anything I've ever used before—it floats through the air, still wet, and leaves a white film everywhere it lands. With that experience behind me, I return to my spray schedule, spraying two prime coats on both sides of each piece plus two enamel coats in about a week's time. I also spray a couple of sun-yellow stripes on the two middle pieces.

Once the top slats dry, I'm ready for final assembly. I start by carefully positioning the straight edge of one of the middle slats on top of the rails, clamping it down temporarily. Using a drill guide, I sink pilot holes through the top into the rails below. The top piece is then unclamped and moved to the drill press, where the holes are countersunk for 1¾-in. #10 stainless steel screws. These steps are repeated as each top piece is positioned and screwed into place, one by one, using the 1½-in. crescent cut earlier as a spacer. The countersunk holes are later plugged and sanded, dabbed with primer and touched up with the synthetic enamel. You could also blind-dowel all the top pieces in place.

After I finished the sun sled, I realized that all the crescent-

After radial-arm saw's head is rotated 90° and locked in place on the rail, slotting jig slides workpiece through the ³⁄₁₆-in.-wide dado blade. Stay clear of the exposed blade while cutting the joints.

Photo: Lois Gervais

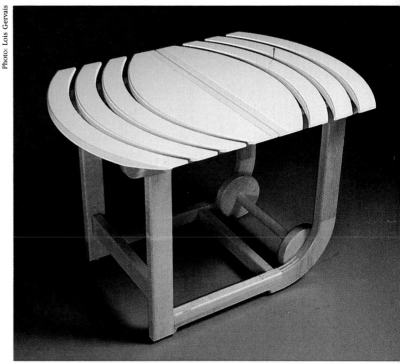

This table's top is made from the bandsawn scraps of the lounger. It's a practical and useful complement to the sun sled, especially if you make both pieces at the same time.

shaped scraps that covered the floor of my shop could be used to make the top of a small sun table. The construction uses the same jigs and processes as the lounger, so the two pieces can be efficiently built at the same time with only a few setup changes.

The inner radii for the top slats are cut on the bandsaw jig with the fence moved 2 in. (plus blade thickness) closer to the blade. The underside tapers should be about 1½ in. long, so you'll have to experiment to find a new position for the tapering jig's fence.

The table's lower frame is built essentially the same way as the sled's, except that the legs are mortised—not splined—into the top rails, and there's no need to angle-slot any of the pieces. The table has an extra stretcher in front but lacks the diagonal bracing of the lounger. When completed, it makes a fine companion piece to the sun sled. And, while lounging by the pool after a hard day at the racquet club, you'll need a place to set your drink between dips. □

Brian Tinius builds furniture of his own design in North Hollywood, Calif.

Creating a Couch

Laminated curves for multipurpose seating

by Scott Dickerson

Some time ago, a client approached me to design and make the furniture for an open, combination dining and living room. Basically, he placed the 22 ft. by 46 ft. area on my drawing board and said, "Fill it up with what we need." My solution, shown on the facing page, included the designing and making of two couches, which I'll describe here.

The primary challenge in couch design is accommodating the sizes and postures of different sitters and a variety of uses—conversation, reading, reclining, napping and so on. These demands produce conflicting requirements. Seat depth, for example, shouldn't exceed 16 in. for a small person to sit comfortably, but a large person requires a seat at least 21 in. deep to lie down on. The customary approach to these conflicts is to compromise the different uses and measurements, accepting that all people can't be accommodated equally well. I think that beginning the design process with compromise greatly diminishes the chances of success. Therefore, I begin by trying to satisfy all needs—I may conclude with compromise, but usually the level of dissatisfaction is much lower.

My first step was to measure and map the room, locating the relevant details—windows and sliding glass doors opening on a harbor view, a brick fireplace opposite the view, red oak flooring, eggshell white walls, and a spiral iron stair to the second floor. Next the clients and I discussed how they wanted to use the seating. They usually entertained small groups, occasionally a large party. The couch would be used for reading, napping, watching television, looking at the harbor and fireplace gazing. How, I asked, can I give you a good view of both the harbor and fireplace, since they are on opposite sides of the room? That's your problem, they said with a smile.

After ten days of casual consideration and a day of drawing, I decided that the only way to serve both views was with a pair of J-shaped couches placed facing each other. The encircling couches would also work well for conversation. The relatively straight section of each couch would be long enough for a person to lie down on, while the sharper curve would be a better place to sit and talk. A table in the center could hold books, snacks and beverages, or a portable television. The clients liked the plan and we agreed to proceed.

From my sketches, I prepared scale drawings. I use 100% rag vellum tracing paper printed with a faint blue ⅛-in. or ¼-in. grid (available in rolls 20 yd. long and 42 in. wide from Charrette, 31 Olympia Ave., Woburn, Mass. 01888.) The grid lines greatly simplify the enlarging of scale drawings to full size.

As I drew the seat curves in plan view, I suddenly realized that the J-shape could provide for both sitting and lying without compromise. I had assumed that the seat had to be the same depth all around the curve. Now it occurred to me that I could change the depth along the curve to suit the different postures: narrow at the tightly curved end for sitting, widening toward the other end for lying down. Sitters with different leg lengths would have a choice of places to sit comfortably. I found that a seat depth increasing from 15 in. to 24 in. would function well and produce fair curves without irregular bulges or hollows.

Next, I drew the elevation views of the end frames. The client had requested an erect and alert sitting posture, so I chose a back recline angle of 15°, as suggested in *Humanscale 1/2/3*, a useful book of ergonomic information published by MIT Press (28 Carleton St., Cambridge, Mass. 02142). Most people prefer a back with greater recline, say 20°. (If you chose a greater angle, reposition the top rail and replot its curve.) A back cushion height of 18 in. keeps them as low as possible without reducing comfort; when the sitter compresses the seat cushion a couple of inches, the cushions will reach the average sitter's shoulder blades.

The client had emphatically demanded a couch that he could rise from without a struggle. A seat height of 15 in. and very firm seat cushions makes rising much easier, but still allow the sitter's feet to reach the floor. Seats for a relaxed posture should rise slightly from back to front so the sitter doesn't slide forward, away from the support of the back cushion. I made the seat 1 in. higher in front than in back; the sitter's weight increases the angle of incline. The 1 in. difference is less noticeable at the lying end of the couch because of the greater seat depth, so someone lying down won't be tilted into the back cushions.

After establishing the essential measurements for the couch frame, I designed the cushions. The profile of support for a sitter's body is a line that curves from the back of the knee down slightly and around the buttocks, behind the sacral vertebrae and pelvis, up and forward into the lumbar vertebrae, then back around the thoracic vertebrae and ribs. The complex curvature of this profile is not provided by cushions made from flat slabs of foam of uniform compressibility, especially in the lumbar region of the back. A better support profile can be created by laminating foam blocks of different compressibilities to make a cushion core. Figure 1 shows the foam blocks I used for making the back cushion. The ILD (Indentation Load Deflection) numbers are used by the foam industry to specify foam compressibility—the lower numbers are softer than the higher numbers.

The ILD 60 foam specified for the seat is extra firm, many people would prefer a bit softer cushion, ILD 45. The back cushion is block laminated with a soft foam, ILD 27, in the sacral and thoracic areas to allow the sitter to sink farther into

From *Fine Woodworking* magazine (November 1986) 61:66-71

These couches neatly resolve several conflicting seating requirements. The pair of curved shapes allows easy conversation. Varying seat width permits both sitting and lying in comfort. Curved laminated rails carry slats that support the seat cushions (below).

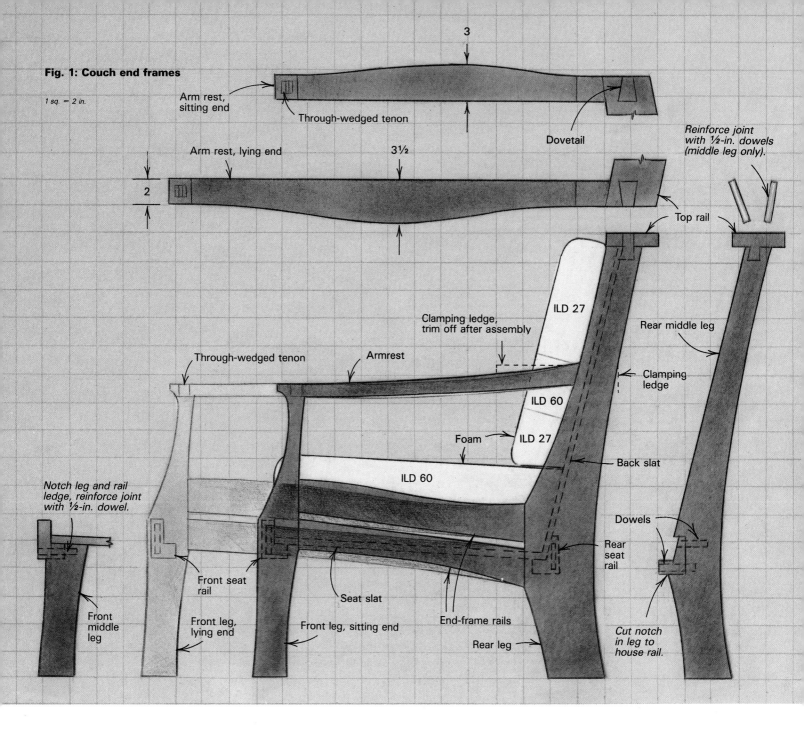

Fig. 1: Couch end frames

1 sq. = 2 in.

3

Arm rest, sitting end

Through-wedged tenon

Dovetail

Reinforce joint with ½-in. dowels (middle leg only).

Arm rest, lying end

3½

2

Top rail

Clamping ledge, trim off after assembly

ILD 27

Rear middle leg

Through-wedged tenon

Armrest

ILD 60

Clamping ledge

Foam

ILD 27

ILD 60

Back slat

Notch leg and rail ledge, reinforce joint with ½-in. dowel.

Dowels

Rear seat rail

Front middle leg

Front seat rail

Front leg, lying end

Seat slat

Front leg, sitting end

End-frame rails

Rear leg

Cut notch in leg to house rail.

the cushion. The lumbar block of ILD 60 presses support firmly into the lumbar area. The seat cushion is 6 in. thick; the back cushion 3 in. The foam core of each cushion is wrapped with polyester fiberfill to soften the surface texture of the cushion and bridge the different foams to create a smooth support curve.

Because the curvature of the support profile is provided by the foam core, the structure supporting the cushions can be flat. I use wood slats because they're resilient and durable: ash for the seat, cherry for the back to match the cherry couch frame.

The remaining end-frame design detail was locating the armrest. A sitter rarely uses couch armrests for resting arms; instead, armrests assist in rising from the seat and in keeping pillows from falling off. Proper armrest height for supporting a sitter's arm is 10 in. above the compressed cushion surface, but that would allow a pillow to slip out under the armrest, so I lowered it to 8 in.

The couch has three curved rails, glued up from thin laminates. The top rail is a flat surface 4 in. wide, which hides the junction of the back slats and top rail and visually emphasizes the curvature of the couch. The width also provides necessary

lateral stiffness. The end-frame legs, rails and armrests have simple curvilinear lines consistent with the general form of the couch. Two middle legs support the seat rails where they curve from the lying to sitting sections.

Making the couch begins with a continuation of the design process—drawing a full-size plan view on the workshop floor. The floor drawing establishes the lines of seat and back rails so clamping forms can be set along those curves for laminating.

A clear area, at least 8 ft. by 12 ft., is necessary for bending the laminate strips. The clamping forms are screwed directly to the floor, so it must be flat—the glued laminations will conform to any humps, hollows, or twists. (Plywood or particleboard will work where the floor is uneven or concrete.) I paint the floor flat white so the pencil lines will show well. With a chalkline, lay out a grid of 8-in. squares, including horizontal and vertical baselines, then plot the points to scale-up from your ⅛-scale grid drawing. Draw the inside line of each rail—it's easier to bend and clamp the laminates around a convex than a concave curve. Drive a four-penny finish nail into each point, then spring a flexi-

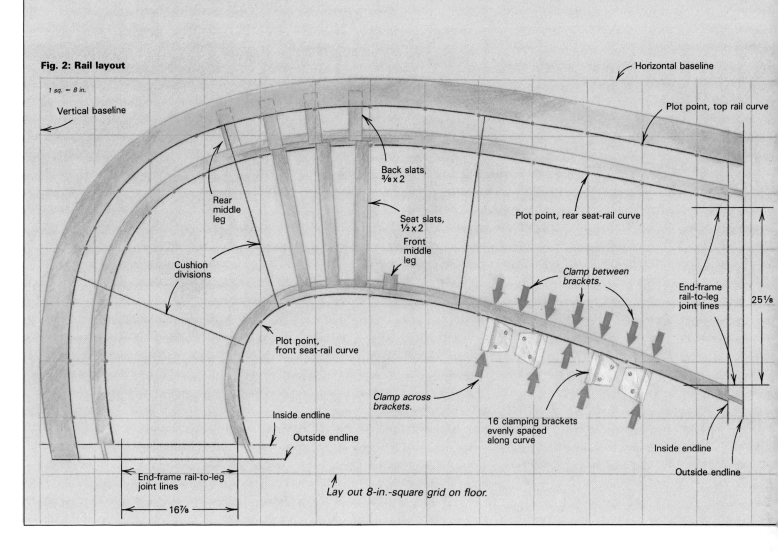

Fig. 2: Rail layout

1 sq. = 8 in.

Vertical baseline

Horizontal baseline

Plot point, top rail curve

Back slats, ³⁄₈ x 2

Rear middle leg

Seat slats, ½ x 2

Front middle leg

Plot point, rear seat-rail curve

Clamp between brackets.

End-frame rail-to-leg joint lines

25⅛

Cushion divisions

Plot point, front seat-rail curve

Clamp across brackets.

16 clamping brackets evenly spaced along curve

Inside endline

Outside endline

Inside endline

Outside endline

End-frame rail-to-leg joint lines

16⅞

Lay out 8-in.-square grid on floor.

ble batten of straight-grained pine or spruce around the nails.

The fairest curves are drawn using a batten just thin enough to bend around the curve without being permanently deformed, but thick enough to be stiff between nails. I used a ¼-in. and ½-in. batten. Where necessary, relocate the point nails and re-spring the batten until the line is fair. Make sure the final version of the line extends at least 2 in. beyond the actual rail length, for extra clamping stations to hold the laminates through the curve. Mark the inside and outside faces of each end frame, as shown in figure 2. These lines are necessary for marking the cut-off and joint lines on the completed rails.

I made 16 brackets as clamping stations and screwed them to the floor at equal intervals around each curve, in turn, for laminating (figure 3). The brackets will be closer together for the front seat rail than for the other rails, which is fortuitous since the thinner laminates required for sharper curves need closely spaced clamps. Tack a ½-in.-thick strip of wood to the floor in front of each bracket to support the laminates. This allows the faces of the clamps to be centered while saving your knuckles.

An additional clamp between each bracket is necessary for tight joints. Softwood pads between the clamp faces and laminates spread the pressure and avoid marring the lamination surface. To keep the glue that is squeezed out from sticking to the floor and brackets, I waxed everything—floor, brackets, spacer strips, and clamp blocks—with a heavy coat of paste wax.

I determined the right thickness for the laminates by bending samples of different thickness around the form. The laminate should bend easily and spring back when released, indicating that its fibers haven't been strained and, therefore, weakened. While thinner strips also passed this test, they don't make tight

glue joints between clamps. The thicknesses I used are indicated in figure 3. Measure around the brackets to find the laminate length—make them plenty long. During clamping, laminates slide around; I cut them ¼ in. wider than the rail height shown on the drawing so I could plane the rails to size.

I prefer to cut laminates for each rail from a single plank. Re-assembling them in order blends the color and grain pattern back together and makes the glue lines barely visible. I rip the strips on the tablesaw with a Forrest Custom-Line 10-in. carbide ripping blade, specially ground to produce a glueable surface without planing. I rip only the number of laminates I am planning to glue that day, since freshly worked wood surfaces glue much better. Because I work alone, I glued the back top rail in three stages—first the inside section, then the middle, which forms a ledge to support the back slats, and finally the outside. This gave me time to spread the glue and place the clamps before it dried, and made it easier to align the strips. I V-marked the top of the plank with red lumber crayon so I could re-assemble the laminates in order, and marked the centerline across the plank to match a rail centerline marked on the floor.

I've laminated with Titebond, a yellow aliphatic glue, for ten years without a joint failing or creeping. It's non-toxic, cleans up with water before curing, and sets well in the 65° temperature of my workshop. It sets up quickly, however, so you have to be very organized and move fast. I advise making a dry run to work out procedures. Distribute the clamps and their softwood pads near the brackets. Spread glue onto each surface of the laminates, except the inside and outside faces. Stack them in order and rush over to the brackets, matching the centerline on the laminates with the centerline marked on the floor. Begin setting clamps at

Fig. 3: Rail lamination

Top rail

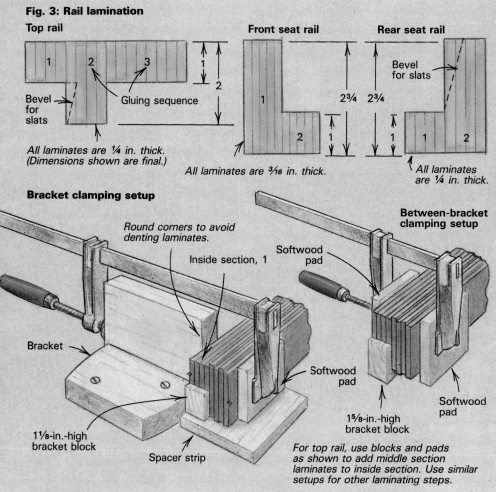

1 | 2 | 3

Bevel for slats

Gluing sequence

All laminates are ¼ in. thick.
(Dimensions shown are final.)

Front seat rail

1

2

2¾ 2¾

1 1

All laminates are ³⁄₁₆ in. thick.

Rear seat rail

Bevel for slats

1 2

All laminates are ¼ in. thick.

Bracket clamping setup

Round corners to avoid denting laminates.

Inside section, 1

Softwood pad

Bracket

Softwood pad

1⅛-in.-high bracket block

Spacer strip

Between-bracket clamping setup

Softwood pad

1⅝-in.-high bracket block

Softwood pad

For top rail, use blocks and pads as shown to add middle section laminates to inside section. Use similar setups for other laminating steps.

Fig. 4: Bevel-routing jigs

Rout bevels on the rear seat rail and top rail for cushion support slats.

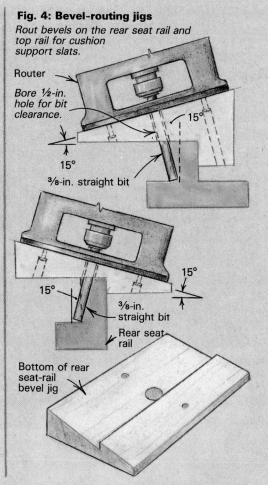

Router

Bore ½-in. hole for bit clearance.

15°

15°

³⁄₈-in. straight bit

15°

15°

15°

³⁄₈-in. straight bit

Rear seat rail

Bottom of rear seat-rail bevel jig

You will need to work fast when laminating, so lay out everything you need before spreading the glue.

Align the rails on the floor drawing and knife their ends and shoulder lines against a straightedge. Try squares help position the straightedge exactly above the end-frame lines.

Fig. 5: Mortise-and-tenon layout

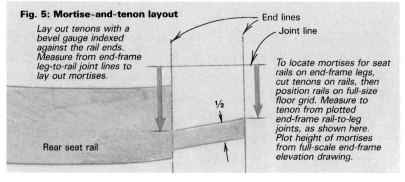

Lay out tenons with a bevel gauge indexed against the rail ends. Measure from end-frame leg-to-rail joint lines to lay out mortises.

End lines

Joint line

½

Rear seat rail

To locate mortises for seat rails on end-frame legs, cut tenons on rails, then position rails on full-size floor grid. Measure to tenon from plotted end-frame rail-to-leg joints, as shown here. Plot height of mortises from full-scale end-frame elevation drawing.

the middle. Work to one end then return to the middle and set the clamps to the other end. Don't leapfrog a bracket—the laminates won't be able to slip by each other and will gap between the clamps. After completing the bracket clamps, go back and set the clamps and pads between the brackets.

I leave the laminates in the form for eight hours at 65°, then scrape off the excess glue, joint one edge and thickness plane to 1⅛ in., which leaves some extra height to correct misalignment when joining the next section. Saw the laminates for the middle section and re-organize the gluing set-up. Blocks are necessary at each bracket to raise the inside section so it joins the upper part of the middle section, and to transfer clamping pressure between the bracket and the middle section (figure 3). The clamps between brackets require blocks for the same purpose.

After the glue has cured, I scrape the glue squeeze-out and handplane the middle laminates flush with the top edge of the inside section. Then I joint first the bottom, then the top, of the assembly to bring it to its final thickness of 2 in. Adding the final outside section is a repeat of the previous operations, except that the blocks holding up the outside laminates are not required to transfer clamp pressure, so I use them only between brackets. The block should hold the outside laminates ⅛ in. above other sections to allow for slippage. Plane the top edge of the outside section flush with the others by hand—it won't pass through the planer without twisting on the bed. I planed the uneven ledge surface with an electric block plane, working up flush to the middle laminates with a rabbet plane.

The procedure for making the front and rear seat rails is essentially the same as that for the top rail. Each of these laminations requires two steps—one to make the slat ledge, the other to add the wider apron to it. After planing the assembled seat rails to the finished height, I routed the bevels for the slats on the seat back and top rails using a jig, as shown in figure 4. It took several cuts to complete each bevel, and constant concentration to follow the curve and hold the router flat on the rail. I put the rails aside for a few days while I assembled the end frames of the couch; this allows bending stresses to settle, resulting in a more stable curve.

I drafted a full-size drawing of the elevation view of both end frames on ⅛-in. grid paper. These drawings enable exact measurements to be taken of the parts and angles of joinery. I also use them to make patterns for the parts—place carbon paper between the drawing and pieces of Marlite (⅛-in. tempered hardboard, painted white on one side). Trace the part, then bandsaw the Marlite to the pattern. The end-frame joinery is straightforward mortise and tenon. I split the end-frame rail in two, as shown in figure 1, to avoid the stress to the joint caused by the seasonal expansion and contraction of a wider rail.

To mark the length of the curved rails and the joint shoulder lines, put the three rails on the floor grid, aligned with their respective layout lines. The rails won't follow the lines exactly, but adjust the position of each rail to minimize the discrepancy. Put a few ¾-in.-thick shims under the top rail to lift it to the same level as the seat rails. Place a straightedge on top of the rails, aligned with the outside face of the end frame. Now knife a line along the straightedge—this marks the cut-off line for the rails. Repeat the procedure for the inside face of the end frame to mark the shoulder lines. Extend all the lines with knife and square on the front and back faces of the rails.

It's very important to cut off the ends of the rails true to the plane of intersection with the outside face of the end frames to provide a square-edged, flat surface for laying out the joints. The seat rails join the end frames with through tenons 2¼ in. wide

and ½ in. thick. For greatest strength, the tenon should parallel the direction of the grain of the rail; because the curvature of each rail is different, the angle of the tenons to the rail ends will differ. I used a bevel gauge against the rail end to lay out the tenons. I knifed the tenon outline on the top and bottom surfaces, then cut the tenons with a backsaw and paring chisel.

The mortise layout is complicated by the angle of entry of the tenons. Once again, a true plane is needed for lay out. I measured from the joint line between the end-frame rail and leg to lay out the mortise cheeks on both faces of the leg (figure 5). To determine the measurements, place the rail on the floor grid again, and mark the position of the tenons on the end-frame layout. The elevation drawing will give you the measurement from the ends of the legs to the mortises. After laying out, bore out the waste, guiding the bit with a bevel gauge set at the angle of the mortise, then pare the cheeks to fit with a chisel.

Before gluing the seat rails and end frames together, cut the dovetail tenon for the top rail on the back leg. It's easier to do this now while the end frame can be held in the workbench vise. I glued the seat rails and end frames together clamping a wooden handscrew clamp to the rail to provide purchase for the quick-action clamps. Gluing 120-grit sandpaper to the wooden clamp faces kept it from slipping. If the joints are well fitted, it's not necessary to apply great pressure to bring them together. Drive a pair of wedges into the tenons to lock the joint. After the glue cured, I reinforced the joints with ½-in. by 3-in. dowels, driven into holes bored into the ledges.

Lay out and cut the dovetail in the top rail, first cutting away the ledge back to the shoulder line. Before gluing the top rail in place, locate and cut the simple notch joints for the middle legs. I clamp the back leg to the seat rail and knife lines for the top notch on the rail and for the bottom notch on the leg. A similar procedure works for the front middle leg. After gluing and clamping the middle legs, I reinforce the joints with ½-in. dowels.

I cleaned off the excess glue at all the joints, rounded all the corners and edges, and sanded the couch. After three saturation-coats of Watco Danish oil, the couch was ready for slats. The 26 seat slats are straight-grained white ash, ½ in. by 2 in., distributed as evenly as possible around the flaring curve of the seat. Round their edges and oil them, then cut each to fit and attach with wood screws. The ⅜-in. by 2-in. back slats are cherry, nine at the the sitting end, twelve at the lying end. I spaced the slats evenly on the bottom rail, then used a level to plumb each slat position vertically onto the top rail. This produces slightly varied spacing on the top rail, but I prefer plumb slats to exactly equal spacing.

After a couple more wipedown and rubout oilings with Watco, the couch was ready for the upholsterer. I gave him sketches that showed the details of cushion construction—block laminating the foam, wrapping with polyester fiberfill—and discussed the job with him. The back cushions have to bend around the curve of the back rails, so we decided to use heavy-duty snaps to hold them to the slats. Dividing the back space with smaller cushions at the sitting end, progressing to wider cushions at the lying end, allows the narrower cushions to fit into the sharper curve more easily; I also liked the emphasis that size progression gave to the flare of the couch. Since it's important that the cushions fill their spaces so the slats don't show at the corners of the cushions, they should be made a bit oversize, to be compressed slightly to fit the space. □

Scott Dickerson designs and makes seating and furniture in Cape Rosier, Maine.

The author made four of the easy chairs described in this article and 14 additional pieces in a limited production run of contemporary furniture that required developing jigs for accurately and consistently making more than 375 mortise-and-tenon joints.

Making Easy Chairs
Tenoning square rails to round legs

by Ray McCarthy

Over the years, I have developed a pretty efficient system for building traditional-style furniture and contemporary cabinets. But when architect Al DeVido approached me with his design ideas for a whole house full of contemporary furniture, I had to rethink my entire operation. He wanted me to make 14 chairs of various styles, one sofa and three tables that involved 72 legs and more than 375 mortise-and-tenon joints, a mass of millwork and joinery greater than anything I had confronted before. And although DeVido designed the furniture, I was still responsible for its structural quality. In gearing up my shop and methods for this production run, I had to avoid getting hung up on the idea that the standard way is the only way. For example, traditional wisdom calls for cutting joints while pieces are square and then shaping them. But the jig system I developed made it easier to shape the stock and then chop the mortises.

In this article, I will describe the basic design and techniques I used to build an easy chair. You also can scale up the chair dimensions to build the sofa or apply the system to a table. It's a good first project for a chairmaker because you can use a single easy chair, whereas dining chairs generally require building a set. Each of the four easy chairs has four corner posts joined to side panels,

a back panel and a front rail with mortise-and-tenon joints. Flats routed on the legs using a simple jig setup give these joints the appearance of being coped. A plywood seat base, fastened to cleats, slants gently from the front rail to the back of the chair and a slatted backrest supports overstuffed cushions. The panels for the sides and backs are overlapping decorative layers of veneered plywood. Different shapes and colors were used for each panel, as can be seen in the photo above. The side and back panels are assembled before joining them to the posts.

Stock preparation—I used white ash because the design called for a light-color wood, and I wanted a more prominent grain pattern than either birch or maple. I selected $^{12}/_4$ stock for the legs and $^5/_4$ stock for the other parts and looked for pieces with consistent color and straight grain. The $^5/_4$ stock was already surfaced on two sides, and when the lumberyard offered to surface the $^{12}/_4$ stock free of charge, I jumped at the chance; however, I supervised the operation to ensure the wood was fed in the proper direction through the planer to avoid excessive tearout.

Because 3-in.-thick ash is especially prone to warping, I cut it 1-in. oversize and let it stabilize for a few days before working on

From *Fine Woodworking* magazine (December 1989) 79:74-77

the legs. The extra width was just enough to allow me to remove the bow that developed after ripping. Straightening the badly warped wood on a jointer would have taken a lot of time, so I reripped the pieces on the tablesaw with a straightening jig—a piece of ½x8x96 plywood with a strip of hardwood along the bottom that fits in the miter-gauge slot in the tablesaw. The stock butts against a fence at the back of the jig, and strips of sandpaper glued across the jig at 12-in. intervals keep the stock from sliding. The only problem was that the thickness of the jig brought the 3-in. ash above the maximum height of the sawblade. I cut the stock as high as I could, snapped off the waste and then removed the lip remaining on the top corner with a hand-held power planer. Then, I ran the straight edge against the fence to rip the stock to a rough dimension just over 2¾ in.

At first, I considered turning the legs, but then I decided a shaper would be the best way to produce the uniformly round posts required for accurate joints. I ordered three sizes of custom-made carbide quarter-round cutters for the job: one size for the sofa and easy chairs, one for the dining table and one for the dining chairs, side chairs and side tables. To end up with round legs, the thickness of the stock must be equal to the diameter of the cut, so I thickness-planed the leg stock to 2¾-in. squares. Also, I carefully adjusted the shaper to avoid undercutting or leaving any excess material. Pushing 72 pieces of heavy ash through the shaper four times each while maintaining a uniform feed rate and holding the stock tight to the table and fence was technically simple, though a bit strenuous. Next, I cut the legs to length on my radial-arm saw with a stop block and sanded them to remove cutter marks and ridges. An alternative technique would be to cut the mortises in the legs while the stock is square and then turn the legs round. However, it will take a skilled hand to get the uniformly round and straight legs possible with the shaper. And this technique will require coping the entire length of the frame sides to meet the legs.

Even though I wanted the assembled frames to appear as if they had been coped to the legs, I didn't want to go to all the trouble of cutting them to match the profile of the legs. To achieve this effect, I used a router and the jig setup shown in the photo above to cut flats on the legs to the required dimensions. Since these flats correspond in length and width to the frames to be joined to the posts, as shown in figure 3 on p. 87, the joints fit together so snugly they appear coped. The jig consists of two 1¼x2¹³⁄₁₆x40 hardwood router supports that must be true and square, two small filler strips of ½x¾x2½ hardwood, two wedges and three ¼-in. plywood stop block templates: one for the back panel, one for the side panels and one for the front rails. To cut the flats, sandwich the leg between the router supports and put a wedge under each end of the leg. Wedge up the leg at both ends until it is flush with the top of the jig, and then clamp the leg securely between the supports. Now, clamp a plywood template on top of the leg/jig sandwich to control the length of the flat to be routed and to secure the assembly to the bench. With a ¾-in. straight bit in the router, adjust the depth of cut to set the width of the flat. Make this adjustment using a scrap piece of leg stock. Begin at a shallow depth and keep increasing the depth until the flat is ⅟₁₆ in. wider than the finished thickness of the assembled frames. A flat that is slightly narrower than the rails will leave an apparent gap between the leg and rail.

After routing a flat on one side of the leg, you must make another flat at exactly 90° to the first one to ensure the chair will be square. The jig will automatically position the leg by referencing off the just-routed flat. To do this, simply rotate the leg 90° so the just-milled flat faces the inside surface of one of the side jig pieces. Place one of the small filler strips of hardwood at each end of the milled flat, between the leg and the jig piece. Adjust the leg flush with the top of the jig using the wedges and clamp the leg tight between the jig pieces. The router will cut the second flat precisely perpendicular to the first, provided the jig pieces are square.

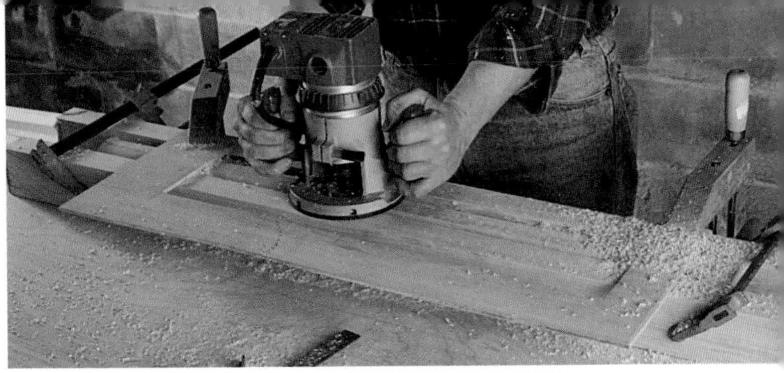

The side pieces of this jig hold the leg and provide a work surface to rout the flats that give the joints between the legs and panels a coped appearance. The flats also provide a reference surface for mortising the round legs.

Fig. 1: Mortising setup

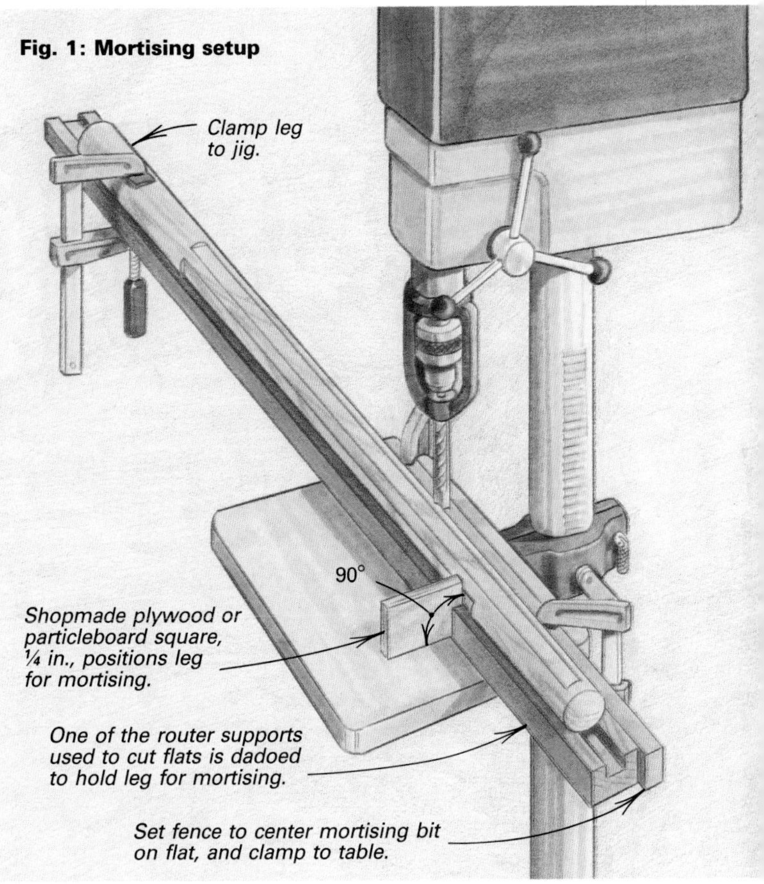
Clamp leg to jig.
90°
Shopmade plywood or particleboard square, ¼ in., positions leg for mortising.
One of the router supports used to cut flats is dadoed to hold leg for mortising.
Set fence to center mortising bit on flat, and clamp to table.

Machining the mortises—I cut the mortises with a ⅜-in. mortising-chisel bit in the drill press, but you could rout them or cut them by hand. Because a mortising bit has tapered sides, it is difficult to square the bit to the work. I first square the table to a piece of drill rod chucked in the drill press. Then, to keep the round legs from rolling during mortising, I make a cradle from one of the router supports used to cut the flats by dadoing a 1-in.-wide by ¾-in.-deep groove down the center of the piece, as shown in figure 1 above. Because the router supports have already been trued and squared, they will hold the leg square to the mortising bit. Although a V-groove can be used, I think the square corners hold better with less clamping pressure. Cutting the dado is easier too. Position the leg in the cradle for mortising by referencing from the squared-up drill-press table with the ¼-in. plywood or particleboard shopmade square, shown in figure 1. After clamping the leg to the cradle, clamp a fence to the drill-press table, centering the

Drawings: Bob La Pointe

mortising bit on the flat of the leg, and set the depth stop for 1⅛ in. Lay out the mortises as shown in figure 3 on the facing page and start drilling.

Three thousand strokes later I was done mortising the legs, but the bit left the bottoms of the mortises very rough. I cleaned these up with a chisel before thoroughly sanding the legs, starting with 120-grit paper and working up to 220-grit in an orbital sander.

With the legs finally out of the way, I began work on the rails and stiles that would make up the back and side frames of the easy chair. After jointing and planing the ⁵⁄₄ ash until it was 1¹⁄₁₆ in. thick, I ripped the rails and stiles to the dimensions shown in figure 3. When cutting the rails to length, allow an extra 1¹⁄₁₆ in. at each end for the tenons. I cut the tenon cheeks on my table-saw using a stock Delta tenoning jig, which securely holds the work even when cutting longer pieces. I then crosscut the shoulders using a stock miter gauge with a wooden fence attached. Check the tenons to be sure they don't bottom out in the mortises and allow at least ¹⁄₁₆-in. clearance on the top and bottom so you'll have a little flexibility when positioning the frames on the legs. The frames' positions are determined by the ends of the flats, not by the tenons.

To determine the length of the stiles, fit the frame rails in place on the leg, tight against the top and bottom of the flat, and then measure the length of stile and add ½ in. on each end for stub tenons. I cut the stub tenons on the tablesaw with the tenoning jig and rout the corresponding mortises in the rails with a ⅜-in. straight bit guided by a stock router-mounted fence and stop blocks.

The great strength of this chair evolves not only from the glue joints, but also from the massive rails, which are more than 5 in. wide, and the precision-mating of the mortise-and-tenon joints. It's important when dealing with these great widths, however, to observe seasonal, across-the-grain movement of the wood. I offset 3½-in.-wide mortise-and-tenon joints to connect the legs to the frames. Gluing only the mortise-and-tenon portion of the joints allows for slight expansion and contraction of the rails each year without wreaking havoc in the joints. When assembling the side frames and the back frame, be sure the shoulders of the rails are flush with the edge of the stiles, as this edge must butt evenly to the flat routed on the legs.

The rear frame requires cutting a large, angled groove into the front, bottom of the top rail to support the backrest slats before assembly. With a ⁵⁄₁₆-in. dado blade set at 10° and raised 2¼ in., position the rip fence to leave the full thickness of the rail at the bottom when the rail is run between the fence and the dado blade, as shown in figure 2 below. If you don't do this, the rail will be thinner than the stiles at the joints. You'll probably have to make

your own saw-table insert because the stock inserts don't usually allow the dado blade to be raised this high. A dado blade raised this high can be dangerous, so use a featherboard to hold the stock to the rip fence. With the rail lying face down and leaving at least a ³⁄₁₆-in.-deep groove for the backrest slats, trim the waste with a standard blade set at the same angle as the dado blade.

The veneered panels – The side and back frames have Carpathian elm burl, Honduras mahogany and white ash veneered panels that contribute to the easy chair's contemporary accent. The mahogany and ash are preveneered plywood, but I veneered the elm to ¼-in. lauan (Philippine mahogany) plywood. I bought all the plywood and veneering supplies from my local lumberyard, but veneer supplies are also available through Constantine, 2050 Eastchester Rd., Bronx, N.Y. 10461; (212) 792-1600.

I bandsawed the plywood to the various shapes, and then I belt- and disc-sanded them to nice, fair curves. The shapes do not require exacting accuracy but should have smooth, flowing lines. Using the plywood pieces as templates, cut the veneers, where needed, slightly oversized. Also cut thin strips for veneering the raw plywood edges. Although contact cement has traditionally been considered too weak and flexible for veneer work, I used it because these are purely decorative, non-wearing surfaces and I don't have the presses necessary for traditional veneer work.

I applied veneer strips to the exposed plywood edges and trimmed them with a laminate trimmer before cementing the face veneers. Next, I filed and sanded the edges of the face veneers after rough trimming them with the laminate trimmer. Before installation, I finished the veneered panels with urethane, buffed them with steel wool and waxed them. This finish provides a higher luster than the rest of the chair, which is finished with tung oil.

The side frames have two curved panels overlapped on one full-frame backup panel. I routed the inside of the side frames with a ⅜-in. ball-bearing-guided rabbeting bit set ¼ in. deep and then squared out the corners with a chisel. The full-size ash-veneered plywood background panel is screwed into the rabbet with ⅝-in. #6 flat-head screws. The two overlapping curved plywood panels are then simply contact-cemented to the front of this panel.

The rear frame uses three overlapping, curved panels with an open space at the top through which the backrest slats can be seen from the rear, as shown in the photo on p. 84. Rabbeting the rear frame was somewhat more complicated because the three panels do not close in the entire space and two layers of the plywood panels need to be rabbeted into the frame. I placed the actual panels on the frame and marked the rabbets, which are routed with a ⅜-in. ball-bearing-guided rabbeting bit. Rout the ½-in.-deep rabbet for the middle panel along the bottom rail and up the side rails to the marks. After marking for the background panel, I reset the depth of cut on the router to ¼ in. and routed the required rabbet. These panels are held in place by two battens screwed into the rear frame stiles, as shown in figure 3 on the facing page. The foreground panel is contact-cemented to the middle rabbeted panel.

Assembling the chair – After you cut the front rail and tenon each end, as shown in figure 3, glue and clamp the two front legs to the rail. Before I glued the frames to the legs, I filed slight chamfers on the corners of each frame (see figure 3) to make it easier to clamp the frames to the legs. Chamfer only the center of the rails or the chamfer will show after assembly. Now, glue and clamp the two back legs to the rear frame. When the glue dries on these units, glue the two side frames to the back unit and then glue the front unit to the sides. With everything glued and clamped,

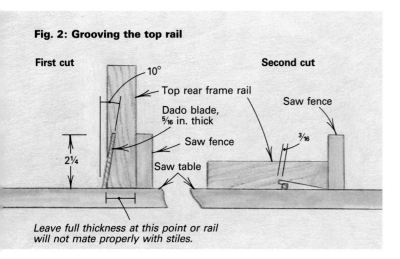

Fig. 2: Grooving the top rail

First cut

10°

Top rear frame rail

Dado blade, ⁵⁄₁₆ in. thick

Saw fence

Saw table

2¼

Second cut

Saw fence

³⁄₁₆

Leave full thickness at this point or rail will not mate properly with stiles.

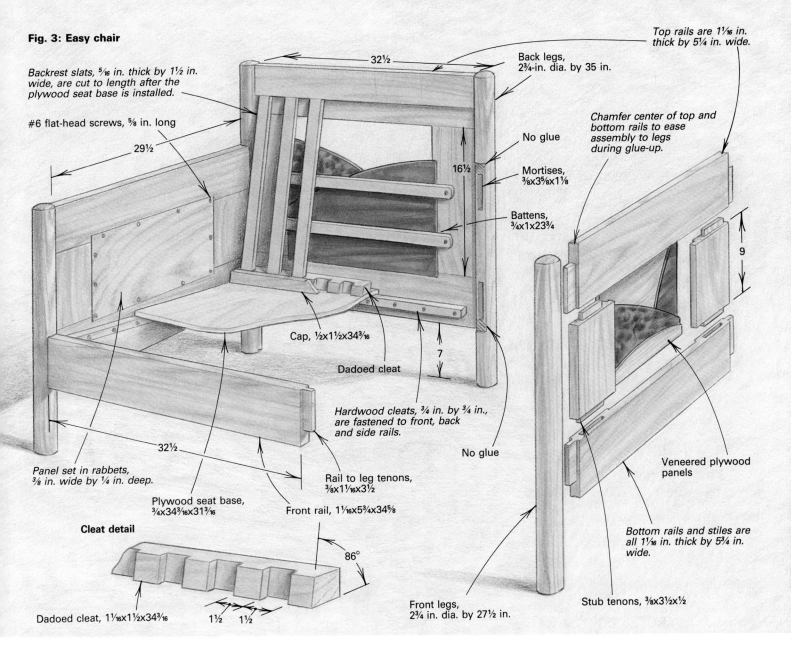

Fig. 3: Easy chair

Backrest slats, $\frac{5}{16}$ in. thick by $1\frac{1}{2}$ in. wide, are cut to length after the plywood seat base is installed.

#6 flat-head screws, $\frac{5}{8}$ in. long

29$\frac{1}{2}$

32$\frac{1}{2}$

Back legs, 2$\frac{3}{4}$-in. dia. by 35 in.

Top rails are 1$\frac{1}{16}$ in. thick by 5$\frac{1}{4}$ in. wide.

Chamfer center of top and bottom rails to ease assembly to legs during glue-up.

No glue

16$\frac{1}{2}$

Mortises, $\frac{3}{8}$x3$\frac{5}{8}$x1$\frac{1}{8}$

Battens, $\frac{3}{4}$x1x23$\frac{3}{4}$

9

Cap, $\frac{1}{2}$x1$\frac{1}{2}$x34$\frac{3}{16}$

Dadoed cleat

7

Hardwood cleats, $\frac{3}{4}$ in. by $\frac{3}{4}$ in., are fastened to front, back and side rails.

No glue

Veneered plywood panels

Panel set in rabbets, $\frac{3}{8}$ in. wide by $\frac{1}{4}$ in. deep.

32$\frac{1}{2}$

Plywood seat base, $\frac{3}{4}$x34$\frac{3}{16}$x31$\frac{3}{16}$

Front rail, 1$\frac{1}{16}$x5$\frac{3}{4}$x34$\frac{5}{8}$

Rail to leg tenons, $\frac{3}{8}$x1$\frac{1}{16}$x3$\frac{1}{2}$

Bottom rails and stiles are all 1$\frac{1}{16}$ in. thick by 5$\frac{3}{4}$ in. wide.

Cleat detail

Dadoed cleat, 1$\frac{1}{16}$x1$\frac{1}{2}$x34$\frac{3}{16}$

1$\frac{1}{2}$ 1$\frac{1}{2}$

86°

Front legs, 2$\frac{3}{4}$ in. dia. by 27$\frac{1}{2}$ in.

Stub tenons, $\frac{3}{8}$x3$\frac{1}{2}$x$\frac{1}{2}$

measure the diagonals to check for squareness and make adjustments, if necessary, by clamping diagonally on the long measure to pull the chair square.

The seat platform is $\frac{3}{4}$-in. plywood attached to $\frac{3}{4}$-in. by $\frac{3}{4}$-in. hardwood cleats that have been screwed to the bottom rails on all four sides. I fastened the front cleat so the top of the plywood is flush with the top of the rail; the back cleat is 2 in. lower. Cut the plywood to size, rounding out the corners to clear the legs. Now, temporarily place the plywood seat on the cleats and draw lines under it on the side frames to locate the side cleats. Screw the side cleats in place and then screw the plywood seat to them.

Eleven slats, spaced $1\frac{1}{2}$ in. apart, form a backrest support for the overstuffed cushion. The length of the backrest slats is determined by cutting one slightly long and trimming it until it just slips under the lip of the $\frac{5}{16}$-in. groove in the top rail of the rear frame. Then, with the slat pressed firmly against the angled cut of the groove, mark the position of the cleat that holds the bottom of the slat and determine the angle for the face of the cleat, as shown in the cleat detail in figure 3. On my chairs, this angle is about 86°, but it varied slightly from chair to chair, so be sure to measure the angle before cutting. With my radial-arm saw, I dadoed the angled face of the cleat to accept the backrest slats. Then, I glued and screwed the cleat to the plywood seat from beneath. The back-rest slats are glued into the grooved top rail with marine-grade epoxy, but float freely in the dadoes of the bottom cleat to compensate for any movement of the plywood seat. Screw a hardwood cap over the front of the dadoed cleat to hold the backrest slats in position.

I belt-sanded the slight crown on the top of the legs, first with 60-grit paper and 120-grit, and then finish-sanded with an orbital sander progressing from 120-grit through 220-grit paper. As an alternative, you might want to round over the tops of the legs with a $\frac{1}{4}$-in. or $\frac{3}{8}$-in. quarter-round bit in the router, but this must be done before the chair is assembled.

Because the success of any finish starts with the preparation of the piece, I sanded all the furniture with 120-grit through 220-grit paper before applying two coats of pure tung oil thinned to about one-half its consistency with mineral spirits. Pure tung oil is available from many marine supply stores and numerous mail-order companies, such as Garrett Wade Co. Inc., 161 Ave. of the Americas, New York, N.Y. 10013; (212) 807-1757. The overstuffed cushions were made by a local upholsterer and are not attached to the chair. □

Ray McCarthy is a professional woodworker and builds custom furniture and cabinets in Sag Harbor, N.Y.

The author grips the muslin with the palm of his hand, instead of his fingers, to stretch it smoothly and evenly over the seat. Then, he rolls the horse hair under at the edges, so that no hair hangs over the edge roll, and tacks the muslin in place.

Upholstering a Slip Seat
A traditional approach with horse-hair padding

by Don Taylor

Most experienced woodworkers consistently produce refined furniture that draws praise from friends and family. But give those same craftsmen a piece of material and they turn to all thumbs. With a little knowledge and practice, however, most woodworkers can produce a slip seat that will do justice to the finest furniture. In this article, I will describe the traditional technique of upholstering a slip seat for a chair, be it a Chippendale or a modern-style dining chair.

Recessing the slip-seat frame into the chair rails minimizes the upholstered appearance, while horse-hair padding, suspended by webbing and burlap over an open wooden frame and covered with upholstery material, provides comfortable cushioning. Horse hair was traditionally the preferred padding because it retained its

loft and stayed in place better than Spanish moss, grass or other alternatives. Although horse hair is used for restoration work, it is expensive and often difficult to work; therefore, I'll also discuss the more common method of gluing high-density foam, which is easier to work, very durable and more comfortable, to a plywood platform in the sidebar on p. 90.

The first step in upholstering any chair is to build the wooden frame to fit the chair and serve as the foundation for the seat. Interwoven jute webbing, stretched across and tacked to the top of the frame, provides the seat's main support and is the base for the padding and covering materials. Tacking burlap over the webbing prevents the horse-hair padding, which is laid on top of the burlap, from filtering through and being damaged by the webbing.

Cotton muslin, stretched and smoothed over the horse hair, is wrapped over the edge of the frame and tacked to the bottom. This is perhaps the most critical step of the operation because it determines the seat's final shape and form. Finally, cotton batting is loosely laid over the muslin to add extra softness and prevent the horse hair from uncomfortably poking through the upholstery material, which is stretched over the cotton batting, wrapped over the edge of the frame and tacked to the bottom of the seat frame.

Tools and materials—Only a few specialized tools, which are shown in the top photo at right, are needed for upholstering. A basic tool kit includes a tack hammer, upholstery shears, a webbing stretcher and a tack lifter, all of which are available from Constantine (2050 Eastchester Rd., Bronx, N.Y. 10461; 212-792-1600) for under $50. You'll also need a utility knife, a tape measure and a straightedge, such as a 54-in. upholsterer's metal straightedge, carpenter's square or T-square. A sewing machine is helpful, but not absolutely necessary.

For a traditional seat, you'll also need about 8 ft. of 3½-in.-wide red-stripe jute webbing, several pounds of curled horse hair, about 6 ft. of $\frac{5}{32}$-in. welt cord, about 4 sq. ft. each of 10-oz. burlap, cotton muslin, cotton or polyester batting, and a piece of upholstery fabric, some white chalk and some no. 2, no. 3 and no. 8 upholstery tacks or webbing nails.

Constructing the seat frame—The open seat frame is constructed from a medium-density hardwood such as soft maple or white elm. Cut the ⅞-in.-thick by 2¼-in.-wide strips to fit your chair. Mortise-and-tenon joints were traditionally used, but I believe that dowel or bisquit joints work just as well. Whatever joint you use, allow a full ⅛6-in. clearance on all sides between the seat frame and the chair rails for the upholstery fabric. Because some fabrics are thicker than others, I recommend buying the fabric before constructing the seat frame so you can make sure you leave enough space.

I make full-size poster board or cardboard templates for laying out the stock and determining the angles of the frame pieces. If you use mortises and tenons, allow extra length on the side rails for the tenons. For dowel or bisquit joints, cut the stock for a butt fit. Next, the frame is glued and clamped together. When the glue has dried, handplane or belt-sand the joints flush before you rip an 8° bevel around the top outside edge. The bevel starts on the side of the seat frame at a point even with the top of the chair rail when the frame is placed in the chair. This bevel softens the transition from upholstered seat to chair frame, and it also reduces wear on the upholstery. Sand or plane away all sharp edges and corners so they won't cut through the fabric, and then test-fit the seat frame to ensure there is enough clearance for the fabric. If the seat is tight, plane it to fit; if it's loose, tack cardboard along the edge of the seat frame to fill the gaps.

Installing webbing and padding—With either the front or back rail facing you, clamp the seat frame to your workbench. Do not cut the webbing to length until after it has been stretched and tacked in place. Center the first strip of webbing about 1 in. onto the rail that is facing away from you. Then, fold 1 in. of webbing either under or over itself to provide a strong double thickness for nailing. Next, I drive webbing nails or no. 8 upholstery tacks into the center and each outside corner of the webbing, and then drive two tacks in between, for a total of five tacks. The last two tacks are spaced farther away from the edge than the first three and are staggered to prevent splitting.

After the first end is secured, the webbing is stretched taut with the webbing stretcher, as shown in the bottom photo at right. The webbing stretcher is a block of wood with a row of protruding

Basic upholstery tools for making a slip seat include from left to right: a tack lifter, shears, tack hammer and a webbing stretcher. You will also need webbing nails, no. 8, no. 3 and no. 2 upholstery tacks, chalk, a dark marker and a measuring tape.

Stretch the webbing taut by levering the webbing stretcher against the wooden frame. Note the position of the webbing on the frame, the nailing pattern and the weave pattern of the webbing. The loose ends of webbing will be folded over and nailed with webbing nails in the same pattern as the other end.

nails that grip the webbing and a handle that levers the block against the seat frame, thereby stretching the webbing. The webbing should not be stretched so tight that it distorts the frame; it should yield just slightly under pressure. Try to stretch each band to the same tension. Drive in five equally spaced no. 3 upholstery tacks about ¾ in. from the inside edge of the seat frame to temporarily hold the strip. Cut webbing about 1 in. beyond the row of upholstery tacks so you have enough material to fold the webbing over, and then retack it through a double thickness with five webbing nails as before. This process should be repeated when a strip of webbing is added to each side of the first band. Next, weave two bands of webbing at a right angle to the three bands of webbing

After the burlap is tacked in place, install the edge roll and notch the corners to avoid build up of material. Allow the edge roll to overhang the seat frame about 1/16 in.

rail, close to the edge of the burlap, and pull the burlap toward the front corners until it is taut. Then, tack about 1½ in. from each corner of the front rail, and complete the front of the frame by spacing tacks 1 in. apart between the tacks previously installed. When the front rail is finished, do the same to the back rail. Be sure to pull the burlap taut, but don't stretch it excessively. The burlap is tacked to the side rails in the same manner as the front and back rails.

Making the edge roll—An edge roll tacked around the top outside edge of the seat frame keeps the padding in place and softens the frame edges, increasing comfort and reducing wear on the fabric. I make the edge roll by wrapping 5/32-in. welt cord with cotton muslin, burlap or even upholstery material, leaving a ½-in. flap of doubled material to one side of the roll, and machine-sewing as close as possible to the welt cord. A zipper-foot or welting-foot attachment on a sewing machine allows sewing close to the welt cord. You could also hand-sew the edge roll, or you could even apply the edge roll without sewing by driving no. 3 tacks through the flap as close to the cord as possible. Starting in the center of any side, allow the edge roll to overhang the seat frame by 1/16 in., and tack through the flap of material along the outside perimeter of the seat frame. After the first tack, pull the edge roll tight and tack about 1 in. from the corner. Fill in the space with no. 3 tacks about 1 in. apart. Cut a V-notch at the corner, bend the edge roll around it and tack close to the corner, as shown in the photo at left. Then, stretch the edge roll tight and tack about 1 in. from the next corner. Fill in the space with no. 3 tacks and repeat this procedure until you are back where you started.

running front to back, alternating over, under and over, as shown in the bottom photo on the previous page.

The next step is to cut a burlap barrier 2 in. wider and deeper than the installed webbing. Whenever installing material in upholstering, you should always work from the center, to ensure adequate material on each side for pulling and stretching and to keep the material square to the frame. After centering the burlap on the seat frame, temporarily tack the middle on all four sides; it is much easier to remove these tacks with the tack lifter if they are not driven completely home. Now, remove the tack on the front rail and turn the burlap over or under so it extends about ¼ in. beyond the edge of the webbing. Drive a tack in the center of the

The next task is to lay in the horse-hair padding. Curled hair is available in three different grades that are based on the amount of horse mane included in the mix. The cheapest is a mix of 15% horse mane and 85% hog hair, followed by a mix of 50% horse mane and 50% horse tail, while the top of the line is 100% horse mane. Retail prices range from $8 to $12 per lb., usually with a 50-lb. minimum. New England Upholstery Supply Co., 23 Sanrico Dr., Manchester, Conn. 06040; (203) 643-6773, sells horse hair at a 50-lb. minimum, as well as a full line of upholstery supplies. Your best solution might be to salvage horse hair from older furniture.

High-density foam: a convenient alternative

Upholstering with high-density polyurethane foam offers some real advantages over traditional horse hair. Foam is readily available at fabric or upholstery supply stores, reasonably priced and easier to use. In addition, cushions with foam maintain their loft and don't "sing" as horse-hair seats do when people sit on them.

Foam can be used with the open seat frame and jute webbing as before or with a solid seat platform, as shown in the photo at right. The open seat frame makes a slightly more comfortable seat, but a ½-in. or ⅝-in. plywood platform is much easier and quicker to make. In addition to the foam and platform, you will need cotton muslin, upholstery fabric, tacks and spray adhesive suitable for foam. Although cotton or polyester batting is optional with this

The extra cushioning provided by foam makes it practical and comfortable to build a slip-seat base by simply gluing high-density foam to a piece of ½-in. plywood, which is then upholstered the same way as the traditional horse-hair slip seat.

procedure, either could be used to further shape the seat.

Upholstering with foam: I cut the foam to the full size of the seat and then bandsaw a 45° bevel around the top edge. The foam can also be cut with a utility knife and metal straightedge or an electric carving knife. Cement the foam to the seat platform by spraying a 3-in. band of adhesive around the perimeter of the foam and seat platform. I find it easier to place the plywood on the foam, as shown in the photo at left. Cover the foam, which has been glued in place, with polyester batting, layering it until you reach the desired fullness. Using the techniques described in the main article, finish up the seat by installing the muslin cover and upholstery fabric. —D.T.

Also, you can check with your local upholstery shops because many times some hair will be left from a piece that's been reupholstered. The quantity of hair needed depends on the size of the seat, but an average 14-in. by 16-in. seat takes 1 lb. to 2 lbs. of hair. If you use reclaimed curled hair, pull it apart to fluff it up and restore its loft. Before putting on any horse hair, mark the centers on the bottom of the front and back seat rails to establish reference points for later installing the cotton muslin. Now, lay the horse hair evenly on top of the burlap, building up about a 3-in. layer that's somewhat thicker in the middle to give the seat a crown. Pat the hair into position with your hands, feeling for voids and low spots as you go.

Installing the cotton muslin—Once the muslin is on, it is very difficult to correct mistakes, so I take extra time here to smooth the fabric and add hair to fill voids and to shape the cushion. Cut the cotton muslin, allowing at least 2 in. extra on all sides, and mark the center on the front and back edges with a pencil. Align the center marks on the muslin with the center marks previously made on the bottom of the frame. Using no. 2 upholstery tacks, temporarily tack the muslin at the center point of the front rail of the seat frame, pull the muslin tight and tack the center of the back rail. Repeating this procedure, temporarily tack the center of the sides. I then remove the tack on the front rail, smooth the muslin from the center of the seat to the front edge to remove any slack, and retack. I find it easiest to work with the seat on edge, smoothing with one hand, holding the material in place and then retacking with the other hand, as shown in the photo on p. 88. As you pull the muslin, curl the hair under on the edges to eliminate voids and give the seat a firm edge. Pull the muslin with the palm of your hand, not just your thumb, to get smoother results, and work the fabric back and forth so no hair hangs over the edge roll. Then, pull the muslin tight to one corner of the front rail and tack it. Repeat the process on the other corner of the front rail. Following this sequence, I tack the back rail and then the side rails in position. I don't fully set any of these tacks until I have worked my way around the seat frame and have completely smoothed the muslin.

Once the muslin fits tight, with no wrinkles or voids, I drive the tack in the center of the front rail home, and tack the material every ¾ in., working from the center to the corners and pulling and smoothing material as I go. The process is repeated first for the back rail and then the side rails. Finish installing the muslin by pulling the corners at a 45° angle to the frame and holding it with a no. 2 tack, as shown in the top photo at right. Cut the excess muslin along each side of the tack to the point of the corner, fold over the material on the sides and tack before cutting away the excess material, as shown in the center photo at right. I check the seat carefully for voids or low spots in the padding and redistribute the horse hair with a sharp ice pick. Poke the ice pick carefully through the muslin, and then use the point to move the horse hair from surrounding areas into the low spots.

To improve comfort and appearance, I put a layer of cotton or polyester batting, the material used for lining quilts, over the muslin cover. Cotton batting, the traditionally used material, should be separated so only half the thickness is used. Tear cotton batting with your fingers to fit the muslin cover; however, use the seat frame as a pattern and cut polyester batting to fit. I cut the upholstery fabric with 2 in. of extra material on each side and apply it the same way as the cotton muslin, but with no. 3 upholstery tacks. Again, work from the centers to the corners, pulling and smoothing as you go. The material should be stretched tight to eliminate wrinkles, but it doesn't need to be as tight as the muslin. Less pulling will be required because the shape of the seat

To finish the corners of the seat, pull the material toward the diagonally opposite corner and tack it in place as shown above. Cut toward the corner on either side of the just-installed tack to remove any excess material.

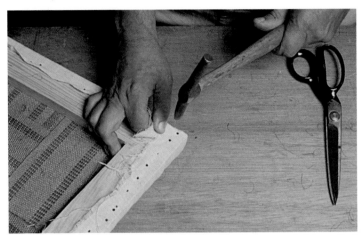

After cutting the excess material, the remaining material is pulled over the tack installed at the side of the frame toward the opposite side so that it is parallel to the front edge of the frame. Then, tack it with a no. 2 upholstery tack, as shown in the photo above.

Pull the material on the front of the frame parallel to the side of the frame and tack it. The corners of the upholstery are folded first at the sides and then at the front so the seams are visible only from the sides. A cambric cover on the bottom of the seat finishes the chair.

has already been formed, but be sure to pull the fabric evenly so that patterns or lines will be square to the seat frame. When turning the corners, I fold the sides in first and then the front, as shown in the bottom photo above, so the fold is not seen from the front of the seat.

To finish the slip seat, I apply a thin, usually black, cambric cover to the bottom of the seat frame to protect the webbing and padding from dust and dirt. The material is attached with no. 3 tacks by following the same procedure used for the burlap. □

Don Taylor is a furniture designer and owner of Taylor Furniture Manufacturing and Upholstery in Deer River, Minn.

Cold-Molded Cradle
A boatbuilding method applied to furniture

by Larry Hendricks

Resembling a truncated canoe, author's cradle was made using a boatbuilding technique called cold-molding. This cradle is made of African mahogany veneer, but teak was used for cradle shown in the construction sequence.

I first conceived of this cradle when I received a phone call from an acquaintance who wanted both a cradle for a soon-to-arrive child and a family heirloom that could be passed on to future generations. As we talked, I remembered the popular nursery rhyme in which Wynken, Blynken and Nod sail off in a wooden shoe, and the design popped full blown into my head. Sketching my idea on the back of an old envelope, the story of Moses in the bullrushes and the notion of launching an infant on a new life came to mind as the cradle took on its boat-like shape.

The boat idea suited my customer and me perfectly. I've always wanted to be a boatbuilder and the cradle project would give me an excuse to experiment with a boatbuilding method called cold-molding, a woodbending technique related to the form-laminating process described on pp. 96-100. Cold-molding differs from form lamination in one important way: instead of bending the wood by laminating many glue-coated thin strips between two forms—a male and female—the curved shape is made by wrapping strips of veneer around a mold, layer by layer, until the desired thickness is achieved. Staples temporarily hold each layer in place until the glue cures, so you don't have to struggle with mating two forms accurately or with a lot of clamps. With cold-molding, compound curves are easily

achieved and the resulting structure is so strong that internal bracing isn't needed. The process I've described here is readily adaptable for all kinds of curved furniture plus, of course, boats of all sizes, from canoes to schooners.

The photo sequence explains the order of events. As for materials, almost any veneer will do for the cradle's skin. For the project described here, I used $\frac{1}{16}$-in.-thick teak, which is fairly straight-grained. Highly figured burl could be used, but the veneer must be thinner in order to lay flat. I used three layers of veneer for the cradle body, and five for the ends. Because it has good gap-filling properties, epoxy is the best adhesive for cold-molding, though plastic resin or yellow glue will also do. I used the West System epoxy, available from Gougeon Brothers, 706 Martin St., Bay City, Mich. 48706. A word about safety: all epoxies are strong irritants. Some people are more sensitive than others. I'm not affected by the resin so I'm working barehanded in the photos. I strongly recommend, however, that you use the protective gloves Gougeon sells.

Larry Hendricks makes furniture in Warren, Conn. For more on cold-molding, refer to issues No. 61, 64, and 65 of WoodenBoat Magazine, *P.O. Box 78, Brooklin, Maine 04616.*

From *Fine Woodworking* magazine (March 1986) 57:74-77

1

2

Before molding begins, the mold must be built. Mine consists of nine particle-board patterns called stations, each a cross section of the cradle shape at a point along its length (figure 1). The stations are secured by a removable strongback that holds them vertical and parallel to each other. Pine strips, called ribbands, are nailed into grooves in each station to provide support when the veneer is molded. Before laying veneer, carefully sight the ribbands for fairness of curve. Plane or sand away humps, and shim flat spots. The body plan in the drawing gives a general idea of the cradle's shape, but you can alter it to suit yourself. To define shape precisely, boatbuilders use a technique called lofting. It's too complex to explain here, but a book on the subject is *Lofting* by Alan Eaitses, available from *Wooden-Boat* (address at left). The finished cradle must be removable from the mold, or vice versa. Like a canoe, my cradle has tumble home—that is, the hull rises above the waterline to a maximum width or beam, then sharply tucks in to a narrower beam. To provide an escape route for the form, I made it in three sections (**1**) so it can be broken down inside the cradle and removed when molding is done. The three sections are held together by two false ends doweled into the end stations, as shown photo **2** and in figure 1. Before starting, coat the mold with paste wax so the epoxy won't stick to it.

Fig. 1: Cradle construction

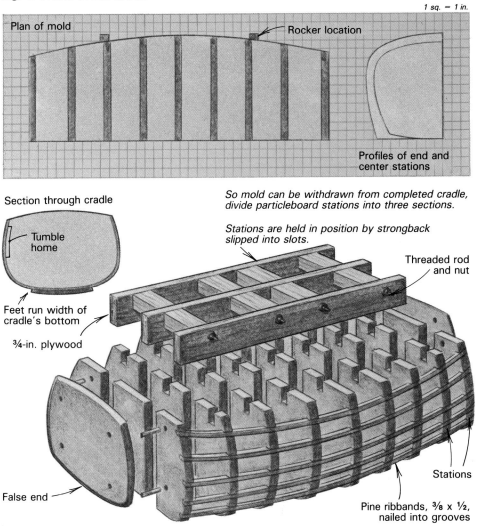

1 sq. = 1 in.

Plan of mold

Rocker location

Profiles of end and center stations

Section through cradle

Tumble home

Feet run width of cradle's bottom

¾-in. plywood

So mold can be withdrawn from completed cradle, divide particleboard stations into three sections.

Stations are held in position by strongback slipped into slots.

Threaded rod and nut

Stations

False end

Pine ribbands, ⅜ x ½, nailed into grooves

3

4

5

6

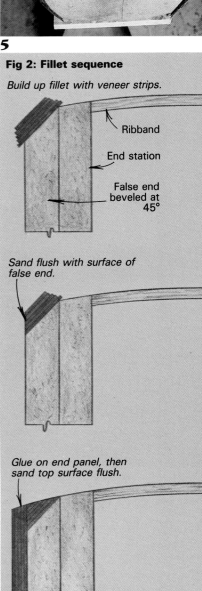

Fig 2: Fillet sequence

Build up fillet with veneer strips.

Ribband

End station

False end beveled at 45°

Sand flush with surface of false end.

Glue on end panel, then sand top surface flush.

There is no joinery in the cradle—epoxy holds it all together. Because the joint between the end panels and body is only ⁵⁄₁₆ in. wide, it should be reinforced with fillets, which also form a smooth transition between the sides and end panels on the inside of the cradle. To form the fillets, I build up strips of veneer about 1 in. wide (**3**). The first fillet layer is stapled to the form's false ends, subsequent strips (four or five layers will be needed)

are staggered to overlap butt joints in the lower fillet strips. Remove the staples before adding a new fillet layer. Once the glue cures, sand the fillet flush, as shown in photo **4** and figure 2.

I make the end panels next by gluing up an oversized blank consisting of five layers of veneer, alternating grain direction 90° for each layer (**5**). A veneer press is handy for this, but I placed the stacks of epoxied veneer between two plywood backing boards

and piled 175 lb. of concrete blocks on top. Waxed paper between the backing boards and each end-panel sandwich keeps them from sticking together. Bandsaw the end panels a bit oversize, then glue in place, spreading epoxy carefully on the fillet, not on the form's false end. Once the epoxy has cured, sand or rasp the end panels to the shape of the mold, being careful not to remove too much material (**6**). Keep the shape as fair and smooth as possible.

7

8

9

10

11

Begin molding in the middle of the form and work toward both edges. At this point the strips aren't glued edge-to-edge, but only where they land at the fillet/end panel juncture. Begin by wrapping a 3-in.-wide piece of veneer (jointed straight on both edges) diagonally around the form (**7**). When the strip is positioned properly, staple it first in the center then work toward the ends, stapling where necessary to make the strip conform to the mold. My staple gun has adjustable tension, which I set at light pressure to leave the staples proud for later removal. Or, you could use a small piece of cardboard under each staple. Measure and cut another strip for each side of the center strip (**8**). Only one edge need be jointed; the other will be scribed to the contour of the first strip using a technique boatbuilders call spiling. There are many ways to spile, but the method I use is to drive a ⁵⁄₁₆-in. staple in the new strip near the middle of the mold. The strip being spiled should be positioned so its edge just touches the previous strip at the center of its length. Working toward both ends, I use a small bullnose plane to trim the new strip's overlapping edge to a tight fit. The first and third layers of veneer must be tightly spiled, since they will form the inside and outside the cradle.

After the first layer is completed and cured, the second is laid diagonally in the opposite direction (**9**), again starting in the center. Spiling needn't be as accurate here since this layer will be visible only at the cradle ends. As you lay up this layer, mark a pencil line showing roughly where the strip will go and remove the first layer's staples only from this area. Spile, apply epoxy to the back of the strip and inside the pencil line, then staple.

When the second layer has cured, remove all the staples and scrape or sand the surface smooth and fair. Trim off the rough ends of strips at both end panels and what will become the cradle's top edge, or gunwale. Later, when molding is completed, this line (the cradle's sheer) can be sawn and worked fair with a rasp or sandpaper. For appearance, I lay the third layer lengthwise, but it could be laid diagonally opposite to the second. Spile very carefully because the third layer is the most visible. To prevent marring, I use cardboard under the staples, and a lead weight helps hold things down while I plane the edges (**10**). When the glue has cured, remove all staples and sand or scrape to a smooth finish. If the surface is not fair enough to your eye, don't hesitate to add another layer. After finish sanding, add rockers to the bottom, then break down the form to remove it from the cradle (**11**). The inside will be rough from the staple holes, so scrape and sand thoroughly, then fill with an epoxy-sawdust mixture. I finished my cradle with polyurethane on the inside and tung oil on the outside.   □

Form Laminating Curved Carcases

Glued-up layers look like solid wood

by Anthony Giachetti

Each curved side of Giachetti's French walnut butterfly cabinet was made by gluing up resawn plies in a curved, two-part form then edge-gluing four 5-in.-wide curved sections into a panel. Lamello plates join the carcase components.

From *Fine Woodworking* magazine (September 1985) 54:40-45

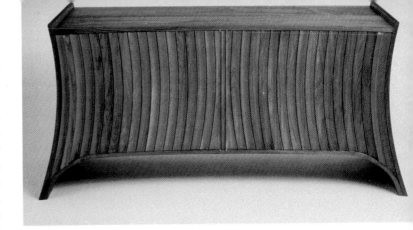

I started making curvilinear furniture because I was no longer excited with my straight-line casework. Curved elements now form the basis for almost all of my furniture designs. I like the dynamic springlike energy that curved sides impart to my sideboards, desks and blanket chests. The sides appear to be bent from single, wide pieces of solid wood, but they're actually made up of several narrow sections, each form-laminated to the desired curve, then edge-glued to form a panel. Form laminating is a process of gluing up thin strips of wood by clamping them into or around a curved form. When the laminates are resawn from one board and reassembled in the same order, glue lines are barely visible.

Form laminating may not be for everybody. Resawing and surfacing the laminates is time consuming and wastes a lot of wood. Working up curved side panels can take the better part of a week. But it has its advantages, as I discovered the hard way. For my first attempt at curved sides—a jewelry case—I simply bandsawed the curve from thick rosewood, planning to edge-glue two 6-in.-wide pieces to make a 12-in.-wide panel. It wasn't long after sawing that the pieces began to cup badly, the result of a rapid change in moisture content in the now exposed interior of each board. Weak short grain, another problem with bandsawn curves, is also solved by form laminating because the grain follows the curve.

Form laminating also has several advantages over steam bending. Species that are almost impossible to steam bend, such as teak, rosewood and mahogany, can be bent by laminating. Even a fairly small radius can be achieved by using thin laminates. Springback, the tendency of bent wood to return to its original shape when removed from the mold, is both less severe and more predictable with form laminating than it is with steam-bent solid wood.

My designs often start as a sketch scribbled on the back of an envelope or a scrap of wood. Once the idea is firmly established, I make scale drawings and finally, full-size drawings on heavy tracing paper, working out all the joinery details and the relationships between curved and straight parts (see box, p. 100). Full-size drawings force the designer to confront aesthetic and technical problems that may not be apparent in a sketch. Is the curve graceful or comical? Are good joints possible at the angles that the curved members join the other wood elements? Such problems should be solved on paper.

I start the full-scale drawing with the curved side. I draw uniform-radius curves with trammel points mounted on a long stick, adding the thickness of the lamination to the radius to draw the outside line of the curve. For more complex curves, I draw one line by bending a length of thin, straight-grained wood or a flexible plastic spline. Next, I mark off the parallel line with a compass and the arc method shown in figure 1.

Once the curvature of the cabinet side and its position in a vertical plane have been established, I add the remaining structural elements. If the cabinet is symmetrical I draw only to the center line. Approximate dimensions for the top, side and bottom panels can be taken from this drawing but, because the actual curve of the panel may differ, you'll need to trace the panel on the drawing then redraw the angles and joints based on the new shape.

Almost any wood can be form bent if the laminations are thin enough. I design curves and select wood for the best appearance, then worry about the bending afterward, although the gluing ability of the wood is an important consideration. A beginner

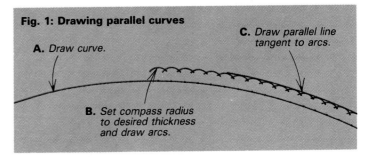

Curved door slats (top and facing page) are tongue-and-grooved without glue and pinned through sliding-dovetail battens. Blanket chest (above) has form-bent sides, veneered-plywood front and back. Carcase details are shown on pp. 100-101.

Fig. 1: Drawing parallel curves

A. Draw curve.

C. Draw parallel line tangent to arcs.

B. Set compass radius to desired thickness and draw arcs.

would do well to start with straight-grained walnut rather than oily woods, like teak or rosewood, that are often difficult to glue. (Thickness planing or sanding oily wood immediately before gluing helps overcome these problems.)

In general, light-colored woods more readily show glue lines; highly-figured woods are difficult to resaw accurately and impossible to thickness without an abrasive surfacer. I prefer to reserve showy figure for the tops of my furniture.

To determine the number of laminates you'll need you must consider wood species, the degree of curvature and the amount of springback deemed acceptable. To minimize springback, I don't recommend using fewer than four plies. For a 30-in.-long, ¾-in.-thick panel that deflects 2 in. or 3 in., I'll typically use five plies. Tight curves and hard-to-bend woods require thinner laminates, but overestimating the number of laminates is costly in both wood and time. Test-bending a few assemblies will save time in the long run.

Springback is a direct function of the number of laminates. With two plies, springback will be approximately 33% of the initial radius of the form. With five plies, springback drops to

Photos ©1983, 1984 Stephen Rubicam Photography

A pivot-block fence (top) permits feed-angle changes to correct bandsaw-blade drift. A face vise is convenient for initial clamping of two-part forms (center). Pipe clamps are applied once the vise is closed and the clamped form is removed from the vise to dry. The edges are squared up on the tablesaw (bottom).

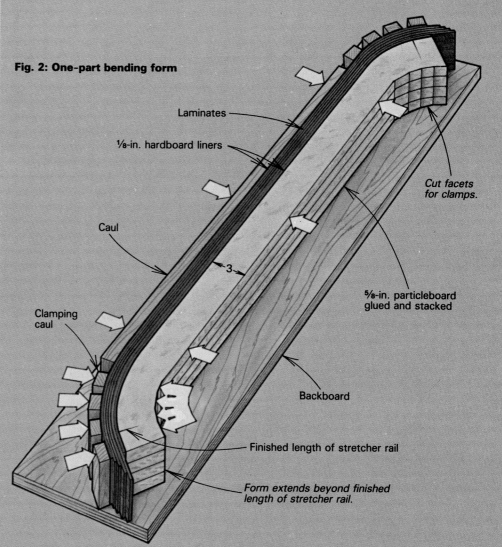

Fig. 2: One-part bending form

Laminates

1/8-in. hardboard liners

Caul

Clamping caul

3

Cut facets for clamps.

5/8-in. particleboard glued and stacked

Backboard

Finished length of stretcher rail

Form extends beyond finished length of stretcher rail.

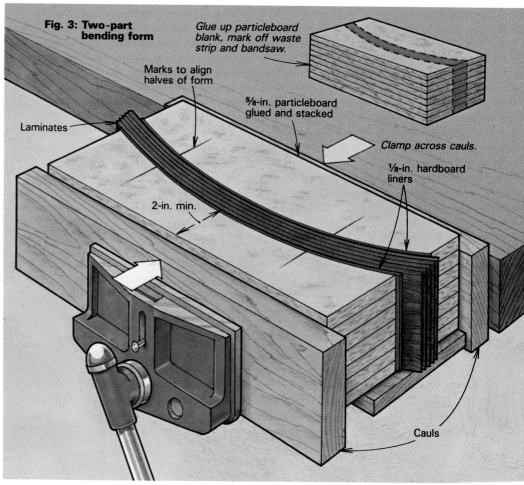

Fig. 3: Two-part bending form

Glue up particleboard blank, mark off waste strip and bandsaw.

Marks to align halves of form

5/8-in. particleboard glued and stacked

Laminates

Clamp across cauls.

1/8-in. hardboard liners

2-in. min.

Cauls

4%. The formula for determining springback is $100 (1/n^2 - 1)$, where n equals the number of laminates.

I resaw all the laminates in each assembly from one board then reassemble the plies in the same order. This looks good and minimizes cupping and twisting in the glued-up piece. The only exception is when I bookmatch adjacent sections in the glued-up panel, and even then I keep most of the plies in the same sequence.

For a five-ply, ¾-in.-thick assembly, I start with a dressed board at least 1½ in. thick to allow for saw kerfs, thicknessing the laminates, and an extra ply or two as insurance against mistakes. The board should be 3 in. longer than the finished length, measured along the curve, to allow for the planer sniping the ends of the laminates and to ensure a smooth curve through the ends of the piece. To avoid problems with warping, I rarely resaw boards wider than 7 in.

Resawing can be done on any properly tuned bandsaw as long as the blade is sharp and well-tensioned and the guides are set to close tolerances. I use a ½-in., 4 tooth-per-inch skip-tooth blade and a pivot block fence, which allows any drift in the blade to be quickly corrected by adjusting the angle of the feed (top photo, facing page). Joint the board before each cut and scribe a guideline along the entire length of the top edge, ¹⁄₁₆ in. over the finished laminate thickness.

When thickness planing pieces ¼ in. or thinner, run the stock through on a piece of ¾-in. hardwood plywood, a little longer and wider than the stock to be planed. To minimize tearout, reduce the planer feed rate, if possible, or angle the workpiece into the cutterhead to obtain a skew cut. Even a superbly tuned planer may completely destroy thin pieces of wavy-grained wood, so you may want to surface them on an abrasive surfacer. Many millwork shops rent time on their abrasive surfacers at reasonable rates. A finished grit of 60 or 80 will be fine for gluing.

When designing a bending form, the most important consideration is even distribution of clamping pressure. Pressure should be as nearly perpendicular to the curves as possible. I make both one-part and two-part forms, and each type has certain advantages.

For curved cabinet sides I usually make a two-part form as shown in figure 2, facing page. This type of form distributes pressure evenly across wide laminates, 4 in. or more, that are bent into relatively shallow curves. For narrow laminations or complex bends, I make a simple one-part form, also shown in figure 2, that allows me to get clamps all around a complex curve while maintaining clamping pressure at right angles to the curve. On the other hand, clamping pressure isn't as evenly distributed and it's possible to end up with dents in the finished lamination.

I make my forms of ⅝-in. particleboard and yellow glue. These solid forms work well for laminations up to 7 in. wide. Wider laminations usually require ribbed forms.

For a two-part form, I glue up a particleboard blank then bandsaw it into two pieces. While gluing the blank, keep the layers in line with cauls, then trim the two long clamping edges parallel and square to the faces using either the bandsaw or the tablesaw. Transfer the curve from the full-scale drawing to tracing paper, allowing for the ⅛-in.-thick hardboard liners that flank the laminates. To compensate for springback, modify the curve on the tracing paper by flexing a plastic spline into a tighter curve and tracing around it. Transfer the modified curve directly onto the form blank. Position the curve so that the

clamping pressure will be as nearly perpendicular to as much of the curve as possible. To make two or more identical forms, I make a thin, flexible template from ⅛-in. hardboard. By pulling the template into a tighter curve before tracing onto the form, I can compensate for springback.

Before cutting out the waste strip, where the laminations will go, I mark the form so that the two sections can be lined up accurately during glue-up. I bandsaw the waste with a sharp blade, just enough to negotiate the curve. This ensures the straightest possible tracking through the thickness of the form. I cut to the waste side of the line, leaving no margin for cleanup—the hardboard liners will even out minor irregularities.

One-part forms are much simpler to make. I just bandsaw the male curve from a particleboard blank, relieve the back side for the clamps, then screw the form to a backboard for support. Faceting the back side of a curve prevents the clamps from sliding around.

Before gluing-up, I lay out all the laminate bundles and arrange them to get the best possible grain match in the finished panel. I mark the outside laminates in each section with "out" and "up" to ensure that the bundle goes into the form in the correct way.

Glue for laminating must be strong enough to withstand the tendency of each lamination to return to it's original shape. White glues (polyvinyl acetate) are flexible when dry and particularly susceptible to cold creep. Yellow glues (aliphatic resin) are somewhat more resistant, but resorcinol and urea formaldehyde (plastic resin) glues are most resistant to creep. These types also set slowly enough to allow time for glue application and clamping. Urac 185, a modified urea formaldehyde (available from Nelson Paints, P.O. Box 907, Iron Mountain, Mich. 49801) has given me good results and has the added advantage of having medium-brown color. Resorcinol's dark color makes it unsuitable for light-colored woods. With either of these adhesives, a shop temperature of 65°F must be maintained during the entire eight- to ten-hour curing period.

During glue-up, it's important to work quickly, but in an orderly way. Clamps and forms should be ready for use. To make glue cleanup easier, wax the forms and the hardboard liners with paste wax. I find it convenient to use my face vise, as shown in the center photo on the facing page, to hold the two-part forms while putting on the clamps.

I apply the glue to all surfaces with a 3-in.-wide hard rubber roller, available from photographic supply houses. Small drops of squeeze-out should be expected. Large rivers of squeeze-out indicate too much glue and result in a nightmarish cleanup job.

Once the glue is applied, I slip the assembled laminates into the form, align them, close the vise, then apply one or two bar clamps to each side of the form near the center point. When applying clamps, always start at the center and work toward the ends. Once the clamps are on I remove the form from the vise and let the glue cure overnight.

After removing the assembly from the form I clean up one edge with a scraper then joint it with the convex curve against the jointer fence. I'm after a straight edge, not necessarily a square edge—I rely on the tablesaw to produce square edges for gluing. I use a 60-tooth carbide rip blade with collars on either side to reduce blade wobble. With the convex side down and the jointed edge against the fence, I trim the glue off the other edge. Then I trim the jointed edge to achieve squareness. The stock must contact the table right next to the saw blade. A slow but constant rate of feed yields best results.

With only one form, it takes four days to glue up four sections

Joinery on a curve

Making curved panels takes a long time, so to keep the project economically viable I need an efficient way to join the carcase. Plate joinery is fast, strong and well suited for curved casework. Plate joinery requires a hand-held plunge-cutting machine that cuts a slot in each of the pieces to be joined. An eye-shaped, compressed-beech plate slips into the slots, expands when glue is applied, and locks tight in about 15 minutes. During this time, the joints can be adjusted about ⅛ in. for proper alignment of the parts.

As an alternative, I'd suggest a loose spline joint, but I don't recommend dowels for attaching curved sides. Dowel holes must match up exactly and this kind of accuracy isn't feasible when working with curves. The spline would allow some leeway to adjust parts during assembly.

My Lamello machine has an adjustable fence that makes slotting the angled ends of the top and bottom panels easy. To cut the corresponding slots in the case sides, all I need to guide the Lamello is a straightedge clamped against the inside face of the panel. Both sets of slots are cut perpendicular to the line of the joint, not parallel to the top of the case.

I build two basic types of carcases. The first type has structural top and bottom panels joined to the curved sides. The ½-in. to ⅝-in.-thick vertical interior panels are plate jointed to the top and bottom panels. On these verticals, I hang drawers, shelves or whatever the design calls for.

To assemble the case, first I glue the verticals to the bottom panel, with the top panel dry-clamped to the verticals, to ensure squareness. When these joints have dried, I glue the top to the verticals at the same time that I attach the curved sides. Because of the angles involved, the joints between the top, bottom and curved sides won't slip together unless the top can be lifted up slightly.

Attaching the curved sides is a hectic

Carcase construction

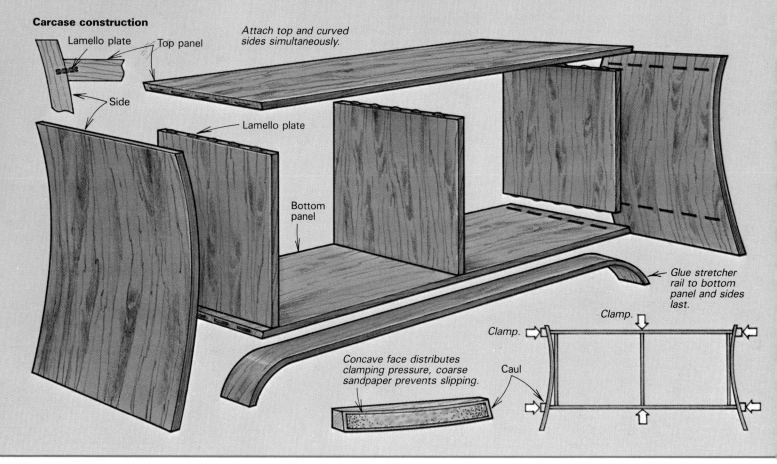

I build two basic types of carcases. The first type has structural top and bottom panels joined to the curved sides.

Labels in illustration: Lamello plate; Top panel; Attach top and curved sides simultaneously.; Side; Lamello plate; Bottom panel; Glue stretcher rail to bottom panel and sides last.; Concave face distributes clamping pressure, coarse sandpaper prevents slipping.; Caul; Clamp.; Clamp.

Edge gluing curved sections into a panel is best done on two sawhorses. Waxed cauls clamped across the panel ensure proper section alignment and keep the panel from bowing.

for one curved panel: I make four forms, reducing laminating time to two days. If I use the forms a second or third time, the investment in form-making is well worth it. An expensive alternative is to use a radio-frequency or dielectric gluing machine, which works in principle like a microwave oven and cures water-based glues in a few seconds.

The bent sections are now ready to be glued into panels. I set them in order on two sawhorses, convex side down. This arrangement provides room for clamping cauls, critical for proper joint alignment—it's too easy to sand through a laminate trying to correct misaligned surfaces. These waxed cauls run across the width of the panel and help keep the panel from bowing under the pressure of the bar clamps.

I make a dry trial-assembly to check the joints and wax the surfaces adjacent to them. Waxing eliminates the possibility of part of the assembly process that requires planning and an extra pair of hands. I use four cauls to distribute clamping pressure across the width of the side panels. One face of each caul is ripped at an angle and planed slightly convex from end to end so that pressure will be distributed from the center of the panel to the edges. Coarse sandpaper glued to the cauls keeps them from slipping.

Once the cabinet has been assembled, I glue the stretcher rail to the underside of the bottom.

I use a different construction for my blanket chests. The front and back panels are ½-in. Baltic birch plywood veneered on both sides. I bandsaw the panels about ½ in. oversize in length and width, and

trim them to final shape with a straight bit in my pin router. A portable router with a straight bit and rub collar would do as well. Guide it against a ¼-in. hardboard template made by tracing the curved sides and stretcher profile on the hardboard then bandsawing to shape. I set the router bit to cut about ⅓ of the panel thickness from each side, which leaves a tongue in the middle. The tongue fits in grooves in the curved sides and stretcher rails.

To assemble, glue the stretcher rails to the front and back panels. Plate join the bottom panel to the front and back and glue the bottom panel to the stretcher rails. Plate join the bottom to the curved sides and glue the front and back panels to the sides. —A.G.

Blanket-chest bottom panel and stretcher rail detail shows Lamello plate slots.

Blanket-chest construction

Cut groove on tablesaw to receive tongue on panels.

Hinged lid

Back panel

Front panel

Stretcher rail

Plate join foot to side and stretcher rail.

½-in. birch ply with ³⁄₃₂-in. veneer both sides

Bottom

Trim panel from each side with router to leave tongue.

Plate join bottom to front and rear panels. Glue bottom to stretcher rails.

tearing out wood while scraping off glue. Yellow glue would work fine for edge gluing, but I use urea formaldehyde glue here as well, for no better reason than consistency.

When the glue is dry, I trim the joints flush with a compass plane or a scraper. The convex surface must be perfectly straight where the horizontal members join it—I lay a straightedge across the width of the panel to check. Make any corrections with a low-angle block plane by planing across the grain.

I rip the panel to just over finished dimension then compare it to the curve on the full-scale drawing. If, as is often the case, the panel curve differs from the drawing, I redraw the curve to match the panel before going any further.

I've made a sliding cutoff jig for crosscutting curved panels on the tablesaw. It is simply a large piece of veneer-core plywood with two hardwood strips on the bottom that ride in the

sawtable's miter-gauge grooves. A wooden fence across the front edge of the plywood keeps the stock square to the blade. I place the panel convex side down on the jig, with one end blocked up so that the end I'm going to crosscut rests on the jig next to the line of cut. To determine the blade angle, I represent the saw table on the full-scale drawing by drawing a tangent line at the cut-off point, another line to represent the cut, then measure the angle between the lines with a protractor. For a smooth cut, a panel hold-down helps. For panels that are wider than the 26-in. capacity of my sliding table, I resort to cross cutting with a Skilsaw guided along a fence clamped to the work. □

Anthony Giachetti is a furniture designer/maker in East Boothbay, Maine.

Guide blocks and full-size templates ensure accurate joinery and simplify the construction of the curved drawer fronts used in this desk. Each drawer is made up of four layers of 3/32-in.-thick maple and a 5/32-in.-thick layer of pear wood.

Drawers with Curved Fronts

Templates and guide blocks simplify the joinery

by Paul Harrell

Most of my ideas for furniture involve curves, and this eventually leads me to make curved drawer fronts. These drawers seem intimidating, but actually they are not much more difficult to build than standard drawers. It's a little more work to form-laminate a curved drawer front and to cut joints at angles other than 90°, but the template method I'll describe here simplifies the process. This template technique can be applied to drawers with simple convex or concave fronts, as with the desk shown above, or adapted to the serpentine drawers found in some period casework.

In order to concentrate on getting a pleasing shape without worrying about measurements and angles, I work with templates whenever possible. Here I began with a full-size Masonite template of the top. I drew and redrew the curved front edge until I liked the shape. After sawing that curve, I refined the profile with a plane and spokeshave. Then I worked directly from this

master template to size the parts of the desk (drawer dividers and pedestal). After milling out the parts for the basic carcase, I assembled the case and used the desk itself as a guide for making templates of the drawers and their fronts, as shown in figure 1 on the next page.

Because this article deals primarily with building drawer fronts, I'll only discuss the ways in which curved drawers differ from standard ones. I recommend James Krenov's *The Fine Art of Cabinetmaking* (Van Nostrand Reinhold Co., New York, 1977) and *Fine Woodworking on Boxes, Carcases, and Drawers* (The Taunton Press, Newtown, Conn., 1985) as excellent references on drawer construction. The lamination techniques for making curved drawer fronts are pretty conventional, but I would like to add a few points.

First, make sure the form is well-faired with no flat or high spots, because any defects in the form will be mirrored in the drawer fronts. To allow for springback of the lamination, the radi-

From *Fine Woodworking* magazine (July 1988) 71:50-55

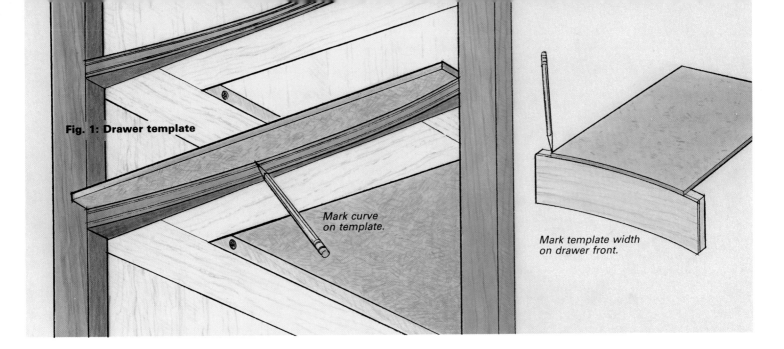

Fig. 1: Drawer template

Mark curve on template.

Mark template width on drawer front.

us of the form's curve should be slightly smaller than the drawer template. The form can't have any wind from end to end. Wind is a disaster in a drawer front: One side of the drawer will angle up as it leaves the carcase and the other side will go down, causing the drawer to twist and bind. I always check the form with winding sticks and do a test lamination.

Since it's impossible to gauge springback precisely, I make the outside lamination slightly thicker than the rest to allow for slight adjustments after assembly. This outer layer can be of a different wood. For my desk, I had only a small piece of pear with the grain and color I wanted, so I sawed this into 5/32-in.-thick layers for the drawer faces. The inner four layers are 3/32-in.-thick maple. The layers are glued together and clamped down to a form to create the shape. The front is removed from the form after the glue has dried and is left to cure and stabilize for a week before the joints are cut. The air must freely circulate around the curing fronts; they may warp if left flat on a bench.

Cutting the parts—When the drawer fronts are dry, joint the bottom edge. The convex side should ride against the jointer fence as you push each drawer front through in an arc. Next, by carefully feeding the fronts through the tablesaw, convex side down, rip each to a width that allows for a snug fit in the carcase opening. Later, when the drawer is fitted, you can plane off some wood to allow for shrinking and swelling. As I rip each drawer front, I rip a pair of drawer sides to the same width. I like to use very thin stock for the sides (about 5/16 in.), because it makes a finer-looking drawer. To keep the thin sides from warping, I use quartersawn stock, which I resaw, sticker and stack well in advance so it will have time to acclimate to the shop's humidity. I suggest you saw a few extra drawersides so you can discard any that warp.

Each front must next be crosscut to length so its ends are parallel to the run of the drawer. The drawer sides must be crosscut at an angle where they meet the fronts. This is where the next template comes into play. Instead of puzzling out the angles, I make a Masonite or plywood template that precisely matches the size and shape of the drawer. To make the template, I first rip a piece of 1/4-in.-thick tempered Masonite slightly longer than the drawer's depth to a tight fit in the drawer opening. The template should slide without any side play. Mark out the front curve directly on the template, then bandsaw it. Decide on the drawer's length, allowing room for stops if you decide to use them, and trim the template accordingly, as shown in figure 1.

To prevent rocking, a curved drawer front must be held in a cradle clamped to a miter gauge or jig when being crosscut. A test cut is made near the line that marks the front's end. If the line and the cut are parallel, the line is split on the waste side; if they are not parallel, the front is shimmed with masking tape until the line is parallel to the sawblade.

If you've built the carcase carefully, you should need only one template, because the radius or direction of the curve doesn't change across the desk. I check the template in each opening to make sure. I don't worry if there are very slight variations; they can be faired out during final fitting.

Next, I position the template on a drawer front with the curves aligned, as shown in figure 1, then mark the final length on the front with a knife. To crosscut the fronts, I use a cradle clamped to my tablesaw's crosscut jig, as shown in the photo above. With a drawer front resting on the cradle's support blocks, I stand a try square on the jig and shift the blocks until the scribed mark on the front's edge is perpendicular with the jig's surface. I mark the blocks' positions, remove the front and nail the blocks to the cradle. I unclamp the cradle and move it into cutting position.

Because springback and differences in laminate thickness may cause slight variations from front to front, I first make a test cut outside the scribed line. If this cut is parallel with the line, I make a final cut, splitting the line on the waste side. If the test cut is off, I shim one side of the front by putting a piece or two of masking tape on one of the blocks and then make another test cut. I do

Pivoting drawers

by Mark Webster

Drawers don't necessarily have to slide in a straight line; they can just as easily swing open, like a door. The drawing at right shows how I used a pivoting drawer in a tight spot. If the center drawer were conventional, its travel would be blocked by the neighboring drawers. The pivoting drawer can swing open freely. Since the drawer's pivot rod is concealed, the drawer appears no different than its neighbors.

The first step is to draw a full-size top view of the casepiece and sketch in the position of the pivoting drawer, dividers and adjacent drawers. To determine the size and shape of the pivoting drawer, use its pivot point as center and draw an arc back from the front into the case. This arc represents the back of the curved drawer side. To avoid a clumsy look, the thickness of the curved side shouldn't be much thicker than a standard drawer side. You can either laminate the curved side or bandsaw it from solid stock. The drawer here was so small and light that its curved side didn't require great strength, so I bandsawed it from a woodblock. If the drawer had been larger, the side would have needed to be stronger and stiffer, so I would have bent-laminated (see main article) the side to avoid weak short-grain areas found on the sawn sides.

Next, make a full-size Masonite pattern of the pivoting drawer. Tape the casepiece drawing to a sheet of plywood, position the drawer pattern on it and bore a small hole on the pivot point. Using a screw or nail as the pivot rod, test-pivot the drawer pattern. Note that the front, left side of the drawer rubs against the drawer divider next to it. Carve clearance for this from the divider before installing the pivoting drawer.

Mark the block from the drawer template and saw out the curved side, leaving its back flat to add extra strength during assembly. Bandsaw off this flat after the drawer is assembled. Square up the side's ends and cut two flats on its inside face perpendicular to the ends to act as bearing surfaces for the drawer joints. I bandsaw the inside curve, clean it up with a spokeshave and sand it smooth.

The drawer has half-blind dovetails on the corner that's visible when the drawer is open and finger joints on the

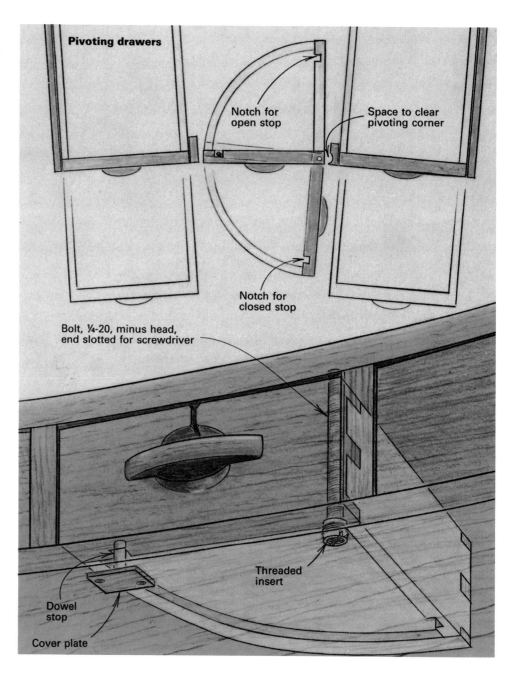

Pivoting drawers

Notch for open stop

Space to clear pivoting corner

Notch for closed stop

Bolt, ¼-20, minus head, end slotted for screwdriver

Threaded insert

Dowel stop

Cover plate

two corners that don't show. I cut the drawer-bottom groove in the front and sides with a slotting cutter on the router table. I use a straight fence for the grooves in the two straight pieces and a convex fence for the curved side.

I didn't use exotic hardware for the pivoting mechanism (see the drawing above). The pivot rod is a ¼-20 bolt, minus the head, set in a threaded insert. If the drawer is to swing smoothly, the three holes that affect the drawer's swing must be bored accurately. The threaded insert hole in the drawer frame, the hole in the desktop for the

pivot rod and the pivot-rod hole in the drawer front should all be bored on the drill press to ensure they are perpendicular to their respective surfaces. A brad-point bit works best to drill these holes because it drifts less than standard twist drills.

Finally, you need to test-fit the drawer and plane or sand it where necessary. Don't install the dowel stop and the cover plate until the drawer is swinging smoothly. □

Mark Webster is an amateur woodworker in Porterville, Calif.

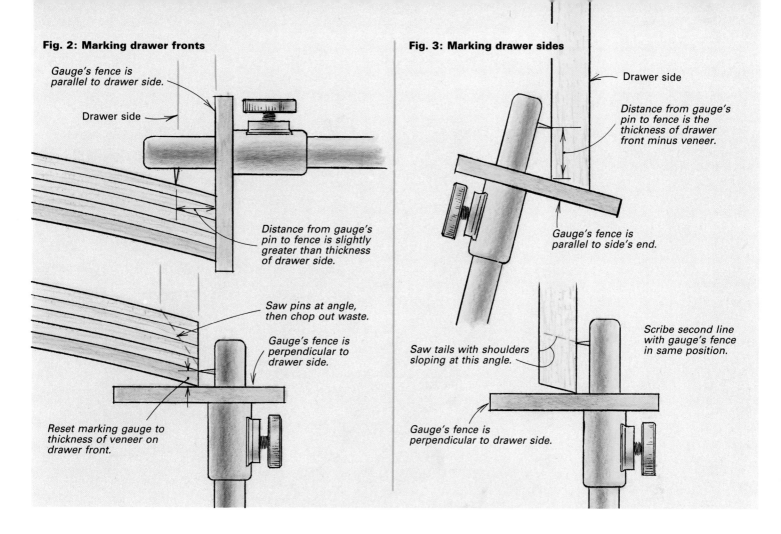

Fig. 2: Marking drawer fronts

Gauge's fence is parallel to drawer side.

Drawer side

Distance from gauge's pin to fence is slightly greater than thickness of drawer side.

Saw pins at angle, then chop out waste.

Gauge's fence is perpendicular to drawer side.

Reset marking gauge to thickness of veneer on drawer front.

Fig. 3: Marking drawer sides

Drawer side

Distance from gauge's pin to fence is the thickness of drawer front minus veneer.

Gauge's fence is parallel to side's end.

Saw tails with shoulders sloping at this angle.

Scribe second line with gauge's fence in same position.

Gauge's fence is perpendicular to drawer side.

this until the cut is parallel with the line. I cut all the drawer fronts on one side of the jig, then move the cradle to the opposite side to make the second cut. Splitting the line on the waste side leaves about a millimeter (.04 in.) of excess width to be planed off during final fitting.

The angles on the drawer sides can also be marked from the template, then sawn on the tablesaw with a miter gauge and with the arbor tilted. You can also transfer this angle with a bevel gauge. After cutting one side, I double-check the angle by locating the front and side in proper position on the template; the two pieces should butt tightly. I don't cut the sides to length until I dovetail the front corners, assemble the front and sides and check them against the template. If everything lines up, I mark out and crosscut the drawer sides. Conventional through dovetails join the drawer back to the sides.

Angled dovetails–Cutting dovetails on curved and angled drawer parts is not very different from standard dovetail joinery: You just have to work to the angled shoulder lines. To lay out the angled shoulders, I scribe around the front's ends with a marking gauge (see figure 2 above), then mark out the pins as usual with a sliding bevel gauge and pencil. Saw the pins, as you would standard half-blind pins, on a diagonal from scribe line to scribe line. When you're chopping out the waste, set the chisel on the scribe line and cut down with the chisel parallel to the ends of the front. To secure the front when I chop the pins, I clamp the front on a piece of glued-up particleboard bandsawn to its outer curve (see the photo at right). A piece of fine sandpaper glued to the plywood creates an anti-slip surface.

I also clamp a guide block to the workpiece to guide the chisel. The block, a scrap crosscut at the same time as the sides, is clamped so its angled face is parallel to the front's ends. When

The author leans the chisel against an angled guide block while chopping waste from the pins in the drawer's front. The front is clamped on a piece of glued-up particleboard bandsawn to match the curve of the front. Sandpaper glued to the block stops the front from slipping.

the pins are finished, I lay a drawer side down on the bench, then scribe the tails from the pins. A marking gauge set to the pin depth, as shown in figure 3 above, scribes the line for the depth of the tails.

When sawing the tails, angle the saw so the cut ends on the scribed lines. To chop out the waste, the chisel is again butted against the guide block. Chop halfway through the side, then flip the side over. Finish chopping with the guide block turned upside down so its face is again parallel with the side's end.

Assembly and fitting–I dry-assemble the parts, and if the drawer doesn't match the template, I hold opposite corners of the drawer and gently rack it until everything lines up. This is a run-through for what you'll have to do to square up the drawer

Fig. 4: Curved front desk

Top view

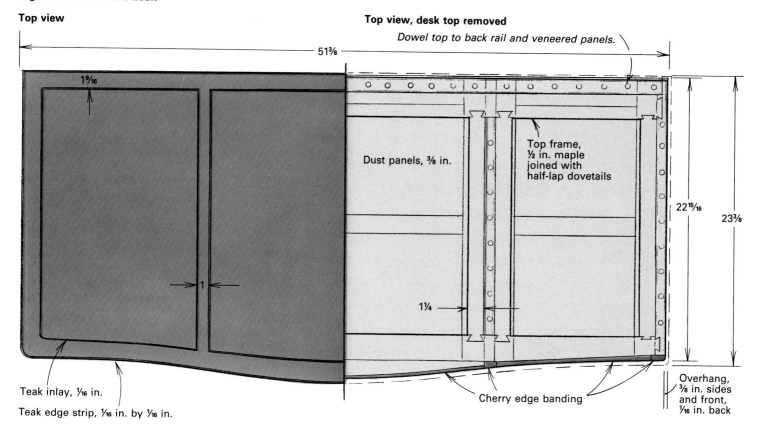

51³⁄₈

1⁹⁄₁₆

1

Teak inlay, ¹⁄₁₆ in.

Teak edge strip, ¹⁄₁₆ in. by ¹⁄₁₆ in.

Top view, desk top removed

Dowel top to back rail and veneered panels.

Dust panels, ³⁄₈ in.

Top frame, ½ in. maple joined with half-lap dovetails

1¼

22¹⁵⁄₁₆

23³⁄₈

Cherry edge banding

Overhang, ³⁄₈ in. sides and front, ¹⁄₁₆ in. back

Front view

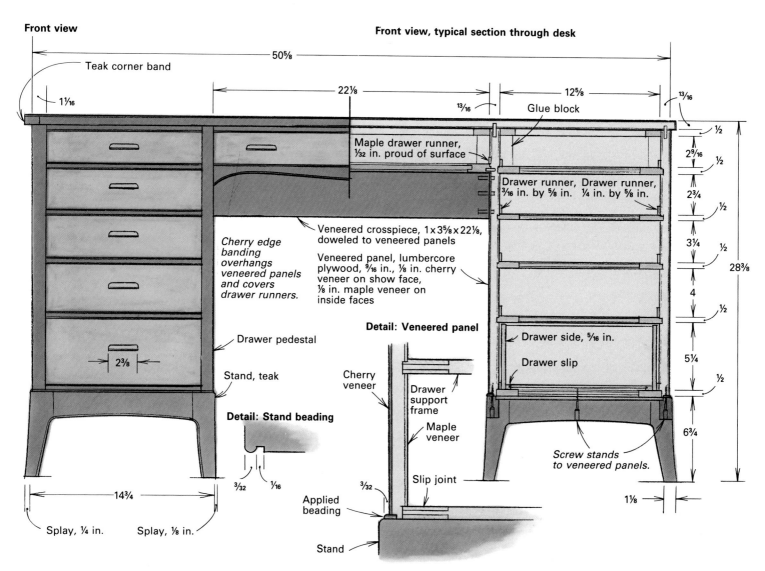

Teak corner band

1¹⁄₁₆

2³⁄₈

14¾

Splay, ¼ in.   Splay, ⅛ in.

Detail: Stand beading

³⁄₃₂   ¹⁄₁₆

Cherry edge banding overhangs veneered panels and covers drawer runners.

Drawer pedestal

Stand, teak

Front view, typical section through desk

50⅝

22⅛

¹³⁄₁₆

12⅝

¹³⁄₁₆

Glue block

Maple drawer runner, ¹⁄₃₂ in. proud of surface

Veneered crosspiece, 1 x 3⅝ x 22⅛, doweled to veneered panels

Veneered panel, lumbercore plywood, ⁹⁄₁₆ in., ⅛ in. cherry veneer on show face, ⅛ in. maple veneer on inside faces

Detail: Veneered panel

Cherry veneer

Drawer support frame

Maple veneer

³⁄₃₂   Slip joint

Applied beading

Stand

Drawer runner, ³⁄₁₆ in. by ⅝ in.   Drawer runner, ¼ in. by ⅝ in.

Drawer side, ⁵⁄₁₆ in.

Drawer slip

Screw stands to veneered panels.

½

2⁹⁄₁₆

½

2¾

½

3¼

½

4

½

5¼

½

28⅜

6¾

1⅛

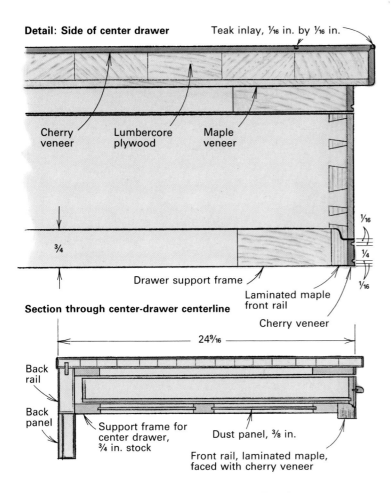

Detail: Side of center drawer   Teak inlay, 1/16 in. by 1/16 in.

Cherry veneer

Lumbercore plywood

Maple veneer

3/4

1/16

1/4

1/16

Drawer support frame

Laminated maple front rail

Cherry veneer

Section through center-drawer centerline

24 9/16

Back rail

Back panel

Support frame for center drawer, 3/4 in. stock

Dust panel, 3/8 in.

Front rail, laminated maple, faced with cherry veneer

End view, section through center of drawer pedestal

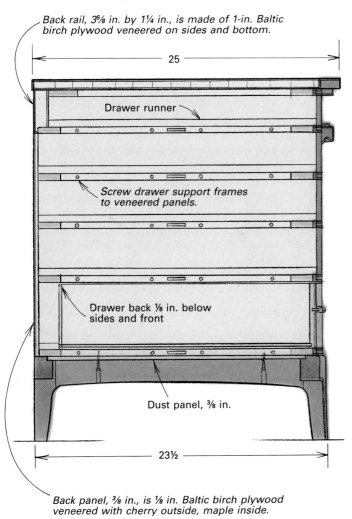

Back rail, 3 5/8 in. by 1 1/4 in., is made of 1-in. Baltic birch plywood veneered on sides and bottom.

25

Drawer runner

Screw drawer support frames to veneered panels.

Drawer back 1/8 in. below sides and front

Dust panel, 3/8 in.

23 1/2

Back panel, 3/8 in., is 1/8 in. Baltic birch plywood veneered with cherry outside, maple inside.

After the glue joints have dried, the drawers are supported on a piece of slotted plywood clamped to the benchtop, then planed to fit. Each drawer is test-fitted and judiciously planed until it slides smoothly. The bottoms are slid in place after the drawers are fitted.

during glue-up. After disassembling the drawer, I round its inside edges with a small plane, and rout grooves or glue on grooved slips for the bottom. The bottom groove on the front is cut on a shaper or router table using a three-wing slot cutter. If the inside curve of the front is convex—as with the drawer shown here—the router table or shaper should have a straight fence. If the drawer front curves in the other direction, the fence must be convex so the cutter can follow the curve.

After assembly, I plane the top and bottom edges of the drawer flush, then take a few passes on each side to clean up the dovetails. If the drawer sticks when opening, I remove it and plane any burnished areas until the fit is just right.

When the drawer slides smoothly in its opening, I cut and fit the solid-maple bottom (long grain running side to side). I try the drawer once more with the bottom in place and make any minor corrections with a finely set plane. The drawer should run smoothly all the way in and out without side-to-side play. Finally, I plane off the sharp outside corners and lightly wax the outside and bottom surfaces of the drawer sides with paraffin.

When all the drawers are fitted in the case, I fair the fronts with a compass plane and scraper. The bandsawn and carved pulls are attached to the drawers with a loose tenon. To avoid mortising the small pulls, I cut a row of mortises in the edge of a long board, then bandsaw the pulls. I mate each pull to the drawer by holding a piece of 220-grit sandpaper on the front and sliding the pull back and forth until it fits. ☐

Paul Harrell is a graduate of the College of the Redwoods' woodworking program, Ft. Bragg, Calif. He builds furniture and lives in Chapel Hill, N.C.

Designing Computer Furniture

Considering components and user comfort

by Sandor Nagyszalanczy

Fig. 1: Computer workstation ergonomics

Dimensions, designed to accommodate body sizes from men in the 95th percentile to women in the 5th percentile, and general dimensional guidelines are adopted by permission from the "American National Standards for Human Factors Engineering of Visual Display Terminal Workstations," published by The Human Factors Society Inc., copyright 1988.

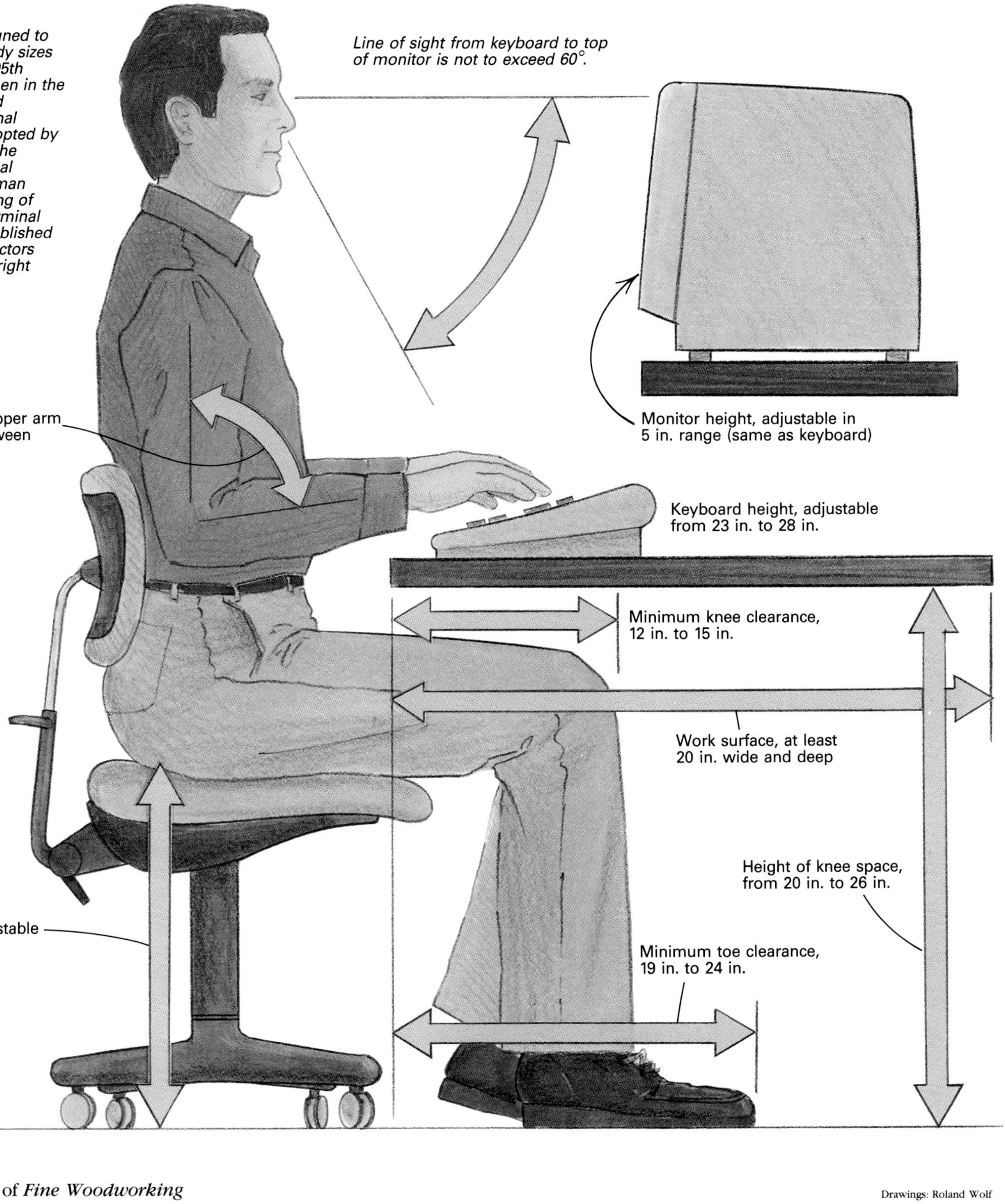

Line of sight from keyboard to top of monitor is not to exceed 60°.

Monitor height, adjustable in 5 in. range (same as keyboard)

Angle between upper arm and forearm, between 70° and 135°

Keyboard height, adjustable from 23 in. to 28 in.

Minimum knee clearance, 12 in. to 15 in.

Work surface, at least 20 in. wide and deep

Height of knee space, from 20 in. to 26 in.

Seat height, adjustable from 16 to 20 in.

Minimum toe clearance, 19 in. to 24 in.

Drawings: Roland Wolf

Photo: Terry Heffernan/Light Language

Whether we like them or not, computers have become integral parts of our lives, and they're here to stay. Computers handle our finances, connect our phone calls and teach our children. And while we can't ignore computers, few people seem concerned about furniture for them. Some folks think any object can be transformed into a piece of computer furniture just by setting a computer on it. I've seen one digitally possessed person pecking away on a keyboard set on an old orange crate, watching a monitor propped up on the floor by a carton of cigarettes—Neanderthal furnishings for high-tech tools.

Fortunately, more suitable furnishings for computers do exist. There are many commercially available workstations made from metals and plastics. However, the warmth of wood provides a pleasant contrast to the high-tech austerity of computer components, and many people are willing to pay for well-designed, custom-built units to harmonize with other furniture pieces in their homes and offices. In researching this article, I visited with more than a dozen cabinetmakers and furnituremakers who built pieces to house personal computer systems. While the work pictured here and other pieces I saw generally were attractive and well built, I was surprised at the small amount of wooden computer furniture being built, considering the proliferation of computers.

Part of the reason may be complexity: Though not nearly as complex as microchips and computer software, designing a good piece of computer furniture can be as demanding as developing the most sophisticated desk or cabinet. A well-designed computer workstation—the modern equivalent of a desk—needs to fulfill an impressive set of requirements. The equipment itself has specific needs: Components must be accessible to a seated worker, and they must be well ventilated and easily wired together. In addition, the workstation must accommodate a comfortable seat. Most workstations also serve as regular desks for paperwork. In an office in which several persons share the same computer equipment, a workstation must be flexible enough to be adapted to different people, as well as provide room for future additions to the computer system.

These diverse requirements don't mean you have to be an engineer or a magician to build a first-class workstation that's functionally and ergonomically suited to your needs. There are few restrictions on the construction methods or joinery; workstations don't require special abilities outside the realm of basic woodworking skills. This article will outline how to design and build a piece of computer furniture, as well as provide general dimensions for a typical workstation. A description of the most common computer components and hints on accommodating them in your furniture piece are provided in the sidebar on pp. 111-113. First, let's examine a few different kinds of furnishings that can function as computer workstations.

Types of computer furniture—While many people think computer furniture should look as if it came off the bridge of the *Starship Enterprise,* a functional workstation actually may resemble a conventional piece of furniture. Practically any desk, hutch or cabinet can be adapted to fit the needs of a computer user and to harmonize with the rest of the furniture in the room. For instance, the "Motus" workstation, shown in the top photo at right, designed and built by Emeryville, Cal., furnituremaker Dean Santner, is based on the modular furniture seen in modern offices: The workstation has ample surface area for computer components or paperwork (and file space), it's adjustable to fit different-size people and it can be expanded with optional work surfaces, shelves or accessories.

But computer furniture doesn't necessarily have to be part of a true workstation made for full-time computing; the furniture may be used to hide the computer most of the time. Cabinetmaker Frank Klausz of Pluckemin, N.J., built a computer cabinet for executives

Dean Santner uses mahogany lumbercore plywood covered with plastic laminate for the surfaces and shelves in his "Motus" modular furniture system. The leg columns, which are painted with a tough acrylic finish, allow the height of each work surface to be adjusted independently for user comfort.

Frank Klausz does the final drawer adjustment on a computer cabinet he designed for an executive office. The mahogany cabinet has bi-fold doors that conceal a pull-out keyboard and a two-tier printer drawer that has one slot at the front for loading paper, and another slot at the rear for paper to feed up to the printer.

who don't require full-time computer access. It's designed to match the existing furniture in an executive's office and to hide the keyboard and printer behind bi-fold doors, allowing them to be pulled out when needed (shown in the bottom photo, above). In many situations, a computer is only an incidental part of the furnishing. Furniture designer/craftsman Glenn Gauvry, who owns a company called Heartwood in Philadelphia, Pa., says he isn't commissioned to build computer workstations as often as he's asked to accommodate computers in the desks and cabinets he has always built. When I visited Heartwood, its employees were working on a reception desk for a hotel built in what Gauvry described as "cleaned-up Victorian" style. The desk's counter had a recessed cubby in the top to house a computer monitor and keyboard, so a clerk could easily check room reservations.

Work surfaces, storage and lighting—While a workstation may be just a single, flat table, Dean Santner says that a more functional computer workstation should have three separate levels: one to hold the monitor at eye level, one for the keyboard at a comfortable typing height and one for a regular writing surface. Despite a computer's electronic medium, computer work always involves paperwork as well. Therefore, a good workstation needs to function as a regular desk, if only to provide places to put copy while typing. If you are

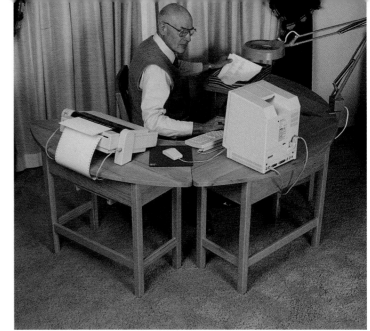

This computer workstation, built from cherry wood by Hugh Foster, features a retractable keyboard drawer, a raised shelf for two monitors, a drawer for floppy discs and two mechanical-arm lamps on wooden bases that can be moved to give light where needed.

E.D. Groves sits at his workstation built from solid oak. A swivel chair and the round design of the top allow the user to reach all work surfaces easily. Each of the three segments has a hinged top that lifts up for loading paper or supplies.

going to use a rolling "mouse"-type computer control, there should also be some flat space at desk height near the keyboard.

In addition to filing drawers for documents and other papers, the workstation must include a safe, clean place to store floppy discs and prevent their magnetic messages from being scrambled. Many computer-desk makers prefer drawers with built-in dividers to organize floppy discs. Just be sure to find out what size discs fit the computer before making the drawer; discs are typically either 3⁹/₁₆ in. by 3¾ in. or 5¼ in. square. For paper storage, a regular file drawer is useful, as well as a pencil drawer for assorted office supplies.

Lighting is a particularly tough issue with computer workstations: The trick is to keep glare off the monitor screen, yet have plenty of light available for illuminating the keyboard or writing surface. In offices with ambient light or with desks located near windows, glare can become a real problem. Monitors can be fitted with anti-glare filters over the screen (see monitor section of sidebar) or perhaps a recessed compartment can be designed into the workstation to shield the screen.

Another solution to lighting problems is to outfit the workstation with one or more adjustable lamps that can provide lighting only where it's needed. Any adjustable desk lamp is capable of giving this kind of task lighting, but architect's mechanical-arm lamps are popular because of their long reach and wide range of adjustability. Hugh Foster of Manitowoc, Wis., employs a pair of these lamps on his cherry computer desk, shown in the left photo, above. The lamp stems fit into holes in round wooden bases, which allow the lamps to be set up wherever needed. Santner's modular workstations have special fittings that will hold an architect's lamp. These fittings are designed to mount anywhere on the leg columns.

Dimensions and adjustability—Like chairs and other furniture that must provide user comforts, workstations must be designed ergonomically, which means taking into account factors such as how far the user can reach comfortably to open drawers and operate components, and what are comfortable heights for keyboards and writing surfaces. E.D. Groves, a retired professor of vocational education and technology at Mississippi State University in Starkville, Miss., tackled the problem of putting all computer components within reach (as well as within view) by making a circular workstation, shown in the above photo at right. Groves' workstation

is made up of three segments, which allow portability and flexibility in arranging the workstation to suit the user's individual needs.

Work surfaces must be at comfortable heights, so tailor them to fit your needs or the comfort of your client. For instance, to find the best keyboard height for his workstation, Foster sat down at his partially completed desk and measured where the keyboard felt comfortable, something he's concerned with since he's a professional writer. His rule of thumb is "the closer the keyboard is to your lap, the faster you'll type." If you're designing a workstation that must accommodate a range of different-size people, you may want to take a more scientific approach. The ergonomics of computer workstations have been studied by The Human Factors Society, which sells a book called "American National Standards for Human Factors Engineering of Visual Display Terminal Workstations" (available from The Human Factors Society Inc., Box 1369, Santa Monica, Cal. 90406; 213-394-1811). While the book goes into great depth on specific issues, like what kinds of casters are most efficient for workstation chairs, the book shows a few critical dimensions to use as a starting place in workstation design: keyboard height, knee space, monitor height, size of work surface area, and seat height and angle. A drawing that includes both general guidelines for determining dimensions and a range of dimensions designed to fit most people can be found in figure 1 on p. 108.

Santner, who has built workstations for hundreds of different clients over the past 10 years, takes exception to the idea of plotting workstation dimensions from an ergonomic chart. He says, "When you try to create a single, rigid design that'll fit anybody, you're bound to miss-fit almost everybody." Santner's solution to the dimensions dilemma is adjustability: The leg columns on his modular workstations are drilled with adjustment holes that allow the user to change the height of all work surfaces independently, at increments of ⅝ in. up or down. This allows the keyboard, monitor and writing surface to be optimally located. Interestingly enough, laws in Europe already mandate adjustability in workstations, and many people expect similar laws to be passed in the U.S.

Adjustability is also an important consideration when enclosing computer components in cabinets or cubbies or on multiple shelves. This is because component sizes aren't standardized—even for the same kinds of components (you encounter a similar dilemma building a stereo cabinet). Adjustable shelves allow you to tailor spaces to existing component sizes, as well as add many new components and accessories in the future.

Construction and materials—The kinds of construction techniques for building a computer workstation are as limitless as they are for building most furniture. Popular systems include plywood carcases, solid-wood frame-and-panel constructions, or veneer- or plastic-laminate-covered particleboard. The main concern is strength; computer components can be extremely heavy: CPUs, monitors (especially some of the newer, large-screen models) and laser printers can weigh 35 lbs. to 75 lbs. or more. Workstation tops, drawers and shelves must support this weight, as well as the weight of someone who may sit or lean on the piece. For instance, if the component is placed on a shelf, the span should be short—about 24 in. maximum for ¾ stock—or the shelf should be reinforced with battens glued to the underside. Otherwise, the shelf may sag or even break. If you want to gain greater strength in shelves or carcases without having to build a workstation that weighs as much as a Sherman tank, you can use torsion-box or honeycomb-core panel construction. By gluing two outer skins of plywood or medium-density fiberboard over a thin inner lattice, the resulting panels will be strong and rigid, yet very lightweight. Because cabinet backs are often left off workstations, for ventilation or access to wiring, it's a good idea to add glue blocks or bracing on the inside carcase corners to prevent the case from racking. As an alternative, cabinetmaker Klausz used a pegboard back on his computer cabinets, like the one shown in the bottom photo on p. 109. The pegboard prevents racking while the holes allow ventilation.

Joinery for workstations depends mostly on the materials and the design; Foster used mortise and tenons and dovetails to join the frame members on his solid-wood computer desk. However, exposed dovetails would be inappropriate in a modern-style, laminate-covered desk, in which biscuit joints or dowels are most commonly employed. Drawer construction depends on the materials and the load the drawer will carry. Like regular file drawers, pull outs or drawers meant for heavy components should be mounted on full-extension metal drawer slides rated to carry at least as much weight as the components. For keyboard trays, choose drawer slides that will lock in the extended position. Accuride series 3037 full-extension slides and series 322 slides, for heavy drawers and pull-out shelves, as well as series 2008 keyboard-tray slides are available from The Woodworkers' Store, 21801 Industrial Blvd., Rogers, Minn. 55374; (612) 428-2199.

Finishes—Work surfaces should be finished to withstand abrasion, so treat these as you would any other desktop, applying several coats of a durable finish. While traditional lacquers and varnishes are acceptable, finishes like catalyzed lacquers and polyurethane are even more wear-resistant. Some makers have even resorted to "industrial-strength" finishes: Gauvry's Philadelphia, Pa., shop was commissioned to build a set of computer cabinets for an insurance company and chose a paint called "Plextone" as a finish. Though the product was originally designed for auto luggage compartments, Plextone can be sprayed with regular spray equipment modified to handle the viscous mixture. Gauvry sprays the Plextone on the carcase surfaces, as well as the rounded-over edges of his cabinets. It is highly resistant to abrasion, and is also anti-static—an added benefit when working with floppy discs that can be ruined by a single jolt of static electricity. (Plextone is available in 5-gal. cans from the Plextone Co., 2141 McCarter Highway, Newark, N.J. 07104; 201-484-4443.) Plastic-laminate surfaces are easy to keep clean, and are popular for office furniture that doesn't get much maintenance. Santner's workstation has plastic laminate applied over lumber-core hardwood plywood, which he uses because it's stronger than regular veneer plywood. Both sides of each panel are covered to prevent warping, the same reason you should veneer both sides of any panel.

Seating—Since practically all computer work is done while seated, the choice of the chair used with a workstation is as important as the rest of the setup. While workstation seating is the subject of an entire article in itself, it's important to choose a computer chair that's truly comfortable: Compared to a regular dining chair used during a two-hour meal, a computer chair used in an office situation must keep the user comfortable all day long. Design-wise, this is no small feat.

I talked to Richard Schultz, a freelance contract furniture designer in Barto, Pa., about workstation seating he's designed for the contract furniture industry. Schultz says that an individual's own definition of comfort changes during the course of a workday, and the chair should, ideally, adjust to accommodate a range of different seating positions. On many modern office chairs, a host of levers and knobs allows adjustment of height, angle, rotation and even firmness. Contrary to a high-tech approach, Schultz says a rocking chair might be a good solution to allay fatigue at the workstation. That strikes me as a nice balance; front-porch comfort on the edge of the technological frontier. □

Sandor Nagyszalanczy is associate editor for Fine Woodworking.

Accommodating computer components

The components of a typical personal computer system are a CPU (central processing unit), one or more computer disc drives, a monitor or CRT (cathode-ray tube), a keyboard and a printer. The CPU, a metal box that contains the computer's central "brain," is connected to all the other components. The system's one or more disc drives load and store information on magnetic floppy discs. The monitor is similar to a television set and displays the words, numbers or graphics being processed by the computer. The keyboard resembles a typewriter keyboard: In addition to the usual letters and numbers found on a typewriter keyboard, a computer keyboard has a cursor (a flashing spot on the screen that shows you where the characters you type will be entered) and function keys that let you control various computer operations. A printer produces paper copies of your on-screen work.

Computer accessories commonly found in a simple home/office computer system include a mouse, a palm-size control unit that rolls on a flat surface, controls the cursor and performs some other keyboard functions; a power strip, an extension cord with multiple outlets designed to protect equipment from electrical surges and to provide a convenient central location for switching everything on and off; a modem, a device that allows computers to transmit information over phone lines; and a "hard" disc drive, which, like a floppy disc drive, stores information.

On the next pages are descriptions of the characteristics of individual computer components you should consider before designing any piece of computer furniture. In addition, a discussion on wiring and ventilation is provided.

Photo: Sean Sprauge

Covered in bandsawn and slip-matched Honduras mahogany veneer, the executive desk by David Welter features a pivoting drawer, that swings around to hide the keyboard and make the desktop an uninterrupted surface. The far end of the cabinet has a compartment that houses the computer's central processing unit (CPU).

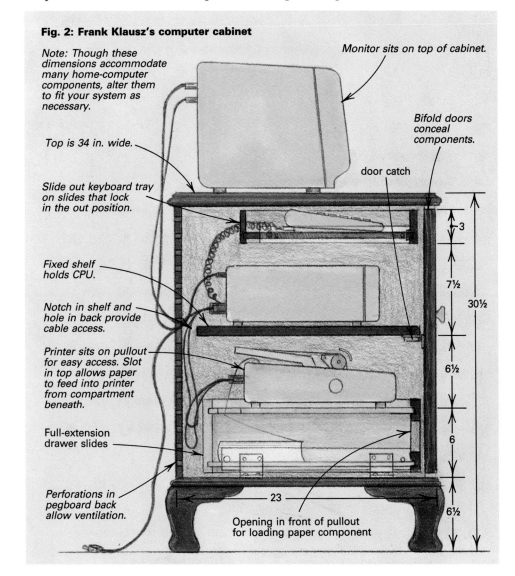

Fig. 2: Frank Klausz's computer cabinet

Note: Though these dimensions accommodate many home-computer components, alter them to fit your system as necessary.

Monitor sits on top of cabinet.

Bifold doors conceal components.

Top is 34 in. wide.

door catch

Slide out keyboard tray on slides that lock in the out position.

Fixed shelf holds CPU.

Notch in shelf and hole in back provide cable access.

Printer sits on pullout for easy access. Slot in top allows paper to feed into printer from compartment beneath.

Full-extension drawer slides

Perforations in pegboard back allow ventilation.

Opening in front of pullout for loading paper component

3
7½
30½
6½
6
6½
23

Keyboard: Unlike a regular typewriter, a computer's keyboard is most often a detached, separate unit that connects to the CPU via a coiled cord. The keyboard can be used on your lap or on a table or desktop. However, typing with the keyboard too high can be uncomfortable and can even lead to wrist problems, like carpal tunnel syndrome. Many computer desks employ a pull-out drawer or tray that's mounted under the desktop. This lowers the keyboard and allows it to be rolled out of the way when not in use. David Welter, a cabinetmaker and instructor at the College of the Redwoods in Ft. Bragg, Cal., designed a more novel way to hide a keyboard in his computer desk, which is shown in the photo at left. Mounted to a pivoting tray, the keyboard flips over when not in use to return the desktop to an uninterrupted surface. Aside from the addition of a keyboard tray and a compartment for computer components, Welter's executive desk is a typical desk. Welter's reasoning behind designing a hide-away keyboard is that an executive uses a computer occasionally.

CPU: The CPU location depends partially on whether it also houses the system's disc drive. Most home-system CPUs have at least one drive that's accessed through a slot on the front. This should be accessible to the user since discs need to be inserted and taken out often. The CPU can rest flat on a desktop or shelf, or can be enclosed in a cabinet or drawer; in any instance, it can be mounted either horizontally or vertically (check the computer's manual before doing the latter). If the CPU sits in a tight space, make sure there's clearance at the unit's intake and exhaust ports for ventilation, as well as clearance to get at the unit's on-off switch (you can also plug the CPU into a power strip, described later). Also, your design should permit the CPU to be removable, both for service and for access to the plugs and wiring on its back or side panels.

Monitor: A computer monitor should sit on the workstation so that the top of the screen is at or below eye level, with the viewing angle between monitor and keyboard not exceeding 60° (see figure 1 on p. 108. Many people put the monitor on top of the CPU, but this isn't always an attractive or a functionally desirable arrangement. If you provide a special shelf for the monitor, you also free up space below the screen for paperwork. Computer monitors are often deeper than regular TV sets of the same screen size; so make the shelf deep enough to hold the monitor without too much overhang. If the monitor is enclosed in a hutch or wall unit, leave at least a couple of inches of space around the monitor for ventilation. Extra clearance at the top also allows the monitor to be used on top of a tilting-and-pivoting monitor stand, a device that allows the user to position the screen for the best glare-free viewing. Monitor stands, as well as copy stands, anti-glare screens and other accessories, are available from Misco, One Misco Plaza, Holmdel, N.J. 07733; (201) 946-3500.

Printer: In offices, several individual computers may be connected to a single printer, housed in its own stand. A home computer setup, on the other hand, usually has a printer directly connected to the CPU. Printers will work on any flat surface, but can be fitted into all manners of compartments, drawers and pullouts. Because printers are noisy, some people prefer to enclose them entirely inside a cabinet or drawer. Cabinetmaker Frank Klausz's computer cabinet, shown in the bottom photo on p. 109 and in figure 2 on the facing page, features a pull-out printer drawer with a built-in paper compartment. Phil Smith, a Long Beach, Cal., woodworker and contractor, built a hinged cover on a printer stand he was commissioned to build to reduce the printer's noise. The cover had a slot at the back for the paper to exit, and was lined inside with thin, dense-cell foam (available as sleeping pads from outdoor supply stores) to muffle the printer's noise.

But before deciding to enclose the printer, you should consider how the printer will be used. Printers that are manually fed or are only used to print a few sheets at a time may be located on a desktop or shelf, within easy view and reach. If the printer uses a continuous paper-feed mechanism, the cabinet should provide a way for the paper to enter and exit the machine without jamming. If the printer is in the middle of a table or large desk, you can cut a slot in the surface and feed the paper up from a storage area underneath the work surface.

Disc drives and accessories: Even a simple computer system may incorporate extra drives or accessories, and you may wish to plan extra shelves, compartments or drawers to accommodate them now or as they are added in the future. Unlike regular disc drives, the memory-powerful hard drives don't use removable discs, and don't need to be located within close reach. Hard drives can be housed practically anywhere in the workstation, and can be remotely switched on and off from a separate power strip. Most other accessories can be housed on shelves, in little cubbies or in a single hutch or pullout. Some of these accessories (or peripherals as they're known) need easy access; so again, locate them within reach.

Wiring: Besides the usual AC-power cords, computer systems involve a series of cables

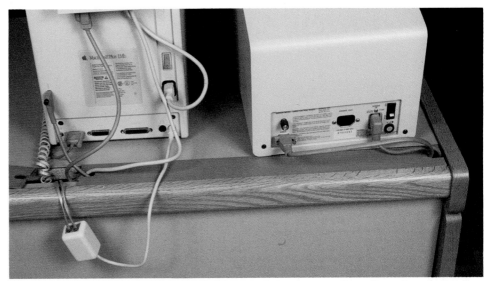

Bill and Jim Kochman's computer workstation is a prototype for a line of computer furniture the brothers were considering manufacturing in their partially automated cabinet shop. A removable plastic strip at the back of the top reveals a raceway for computer cables, which allows a user full access to the cables while keeping them neatly hidden.

connecting all the components. While wiring a computer system usually isn't more complex than wiring a stereo system, there are several points to consider. Computer cables tend to be thicker than stereo wires, and their clutter can be just as unsightly. Therefore, a well-designed workstation should provide some way of containing these cables, yet allow the cables to be easily removed and rerouted if components are added, serviced or relocated. Two different approaches to wire management can be seen in the workstations designed by cabinetmakers Bill and Jim Kochman, of Kochman Woodworking in Stoughton, Mass., and Emeryville, Cal., furniture designer/builder Dean Santner. The Kochmans provide access to the cables by creating a wire trough or raceway fit along the back edge of the desktop. The raceway is concealed by a removable cover, as shown in the photo at the top of this page. Santner's modular workstation holds the wires in hook-and-loop fasteners suspended underneath its shelves and work surface. Both of the systems allow wiring to be changed instantly.

Where wires pass through tops or carcases, holes or slots must be made large enough to pass not only the cables, but end connectors as well. Proportional to cable thickness, these holes can be surprisingly large. One computer-desk maker told me he had to painstakingly remove a 50-pin connector from the end of a cable, then solder all 50 wire connections back on because he failed to make a large enough opening to pass the connector. But instead of leaving gaping holes in your workstation, you can buy wire grommets, which reduce holes and slots down to wire-size openings. Wire grommets, as well as plugs for as-yet-unused holes, are available from Doug Mockett & Co., Box 3333, Manhattan

Beach, Cal. 90266; (213) 318-2491. Also, when sizing compartments for components, leave enough room for protruding connectors, plus extra clearance for cables that must turn a corner before being routed through a raceway or passage hole.

Ventilation: All computer components (except keyboards) need ventilation. If they're enclosed inside a cabinet, consider leaving the cabinet's back or bottom open to avoid obstructing the component's cooling vents. Though a CPU can create a fair amount of heat, the unit's built-in fan will usually cool it, provided you leave an opening in the case or drawer at least equal in size to the component's ventilation port. If you are in doubt or if the unit seems to get too hot inside the cabinet, you can always install a "muffin" fan (a 3-in. muffin fan is available from Radio Shack, part #273242). This is a small, flat AC-power exhaust fan that mounts over a hole in the cabinet and circulates cooling air.

Unlike other sensitive electronic gear, most computer components aren't particularly susceptible to dust problems in the average home or office environment. Unless you want to close a workstation with doors or with a tambour roll top to keep out kids, to ensure security or to cut down on visual clutter, there's no reason the components can't sit out in the open.
    —S.N.

EDITOR'S NOTE:
Relatively few woodworkers today are building computer furniture, but as computers proliferate, hopefully we'll see a boom in computer furnishings as well. If you've designed a piece you're pleased with, send a slide or transparency along with a description to: *Fine Woodworking* magazine, The Taunton Press, 63 S. Main St., Newtown, Conn. 06470. We'll consider the best submissions for future publication.

Two-Door Credenza

A case of dowels, dovetails and tenons

by John McAlevey

Most of my furniture designs begin as simple sketches. I draw on a regular basis, sometimes entire pieces, other times just certain curves or details. When finished, I date the drawings and stack them with drawings from previous sessions. Then, when I need ideas, I rip through the stack.

The two-door credenza shown here began that way. I was asked to build the credenza as a companion piece to a South American mahogany conference table I had made for a law firm's library. When I dug out my first drawings of the table, the rough sketches showed how I had experimented with slight curves, plain round edges and large overhangs as I designed. I knew the credenza would need similar curves and an overhanging top for it to relate visually to the table.

I like to plan all my joinery and construction details before I even touch the wood. After rough-sketching the credenza, for example, I made a complete set of working drawings, including joinery details. Since this credenza has a top that overhangs the sides, I couldn't use dovetails, my usual method for casework, to join the corners. I knew I could have added an applied top to overhang the dovetailed case, but this seemed a waste of wood. Stub tenons would have worked, but they seemed a waste of time.

So, I began to rethink my ideas on joinery. Why not mix traditional joints, like dovetails and mortises and tenons, with production-oriented joints, like dowels or plate joints? These joinery combinations would save time while maintaining the structural integrity of the piece. For example, I planned to dowel the top to the case, and to have a frame-and-panel back. The back would sit in rabbets in the sides of the case, but I did not wish to rabbet it into the top for two reasons. First, I thought it would put unnecessary racking strain on the dowel joints, and second, I wanted to overlap the top at the back a little bit, and thought that a rabbet here would look unattractive. The solution was a dovetailed back stretcher to which I could screw the back. Through mortises and wedged tenons could fasten the bottom stretchers to the sides, as well as add a nice design feature. I could simply plate-join the bottom panel to the sides to keep this joint tight, and then use cabinetmaker's buttons, as shown in the detail on the facing page, to fasten the bottom panel to the stretchers.

Since the conference table was made of South American mahogany, I used mahogany to build the credenza. I like the wood's grain and color. There are few knots and checks, and little sapwood. I view wood's figure as a beautiful landscape, and as I cut it into parts and edge-match pieces, I try to get the grain to reflect the abstract view of a hilly countryside.

For this project, I cut the door's two center stiles from the same board so the grain would match across the gap. I prepared the stock for all parts shown in the drawing at once and labeled each piece so I could keep track of the grain patterns and orientations. I milled the slab sides and the credenza top from 6/4 stock and the bottom panel, stretchers, doors and back panel from 4/4 stock.

Building the carcase – The squarer a carcase is, the easier the pieces will fall into place, the better the glue joints will hold and the less time it will take to build and fit doors and panels. I follow a logical order in doing joinery, beginning with the joints that will govern how square the rest of the carcase will be.

Here's an overview of the process: When building the credenza, I cut the through mortises in the sides and then cut tenons in the mating stretchers. The large shoulders on the tenons make these joints easiest to square. After cutting the tenons, I ripped slots inside the stretchers for the cabinetmaker's buttons. Then, after dry-assembling the sides and stretchers, I cut the bottom to size, routed the rabbet for the back and dovetailed the blind stretcher across the top.

I used my mortising machine as a horizontal borer to dowel the sides. Normally, I do mortises on this machine as well, but the sides were too heavy and awkward to clamp to the machine. It was easier to cut them with my plunge router. I installed the stock fence guide and an Inca, $\frac{3}{8}$-in. slot mortise miller bit (available from Precision Woodwork Machines, Mount Tabor Avenue, Danby Vil-

Photo: Timothy Savaro. Photoworks

Combining traditional and production joining techniques allowed the author to build this credenza economically while maximizing structural integrity.

From *Fine Woodworking* magazine (July 1988) 71:42-45

Fig. 1: Credenza

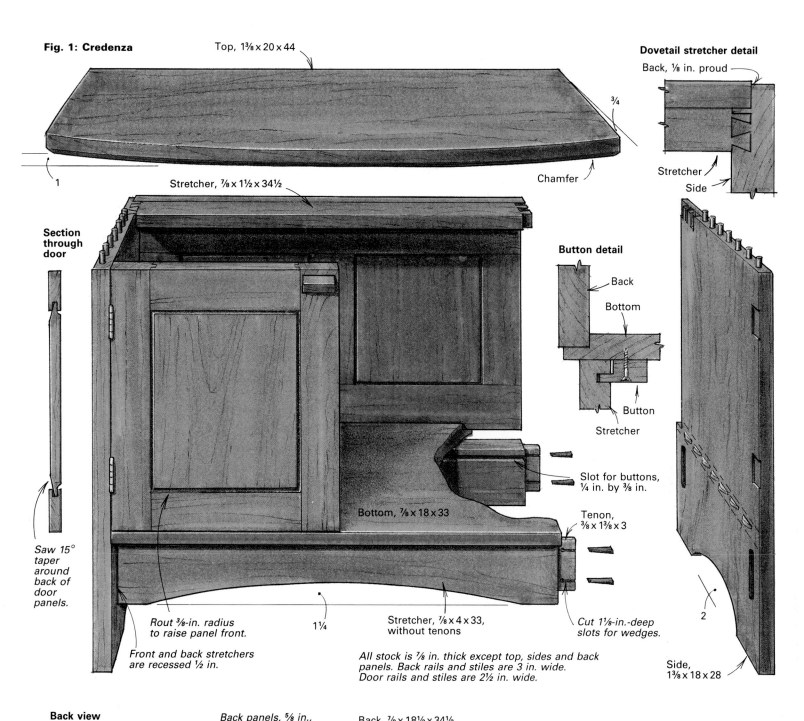

Top, 1⅜ x 20 x 44

¾

Chamfer

1

Dovetail stretcher detail

Back, ⅛ in. proud

Stretcher

Side

Stretcher, ⅞ x 1½ x 34½

Section through door

Saw 15° taper around back of door panels.

Rout ⅜-in. radius to raise panel front.

Front and back stretchers are recessed ½ in.

1¼

Button detail

Back

Bottom

Button

Stretcher

Slot for buttons, ¼ in. by ⅜ in.

Bottom, ⅞ x 18 x 33

Stretcher, ⅞ x 4 x 33, without tenons

Tenon, ⅜ x 1⅜ x 3

Cut 1⅛-in.-deep slots for wedges.

2

Side, 1⅜ x 18 x 28

All stock is ⅞ in. thick except top, sides and back panels. Back rails and stiles are 3 in. wide. Door rails and stiles are 2½ in. wide.

Back view

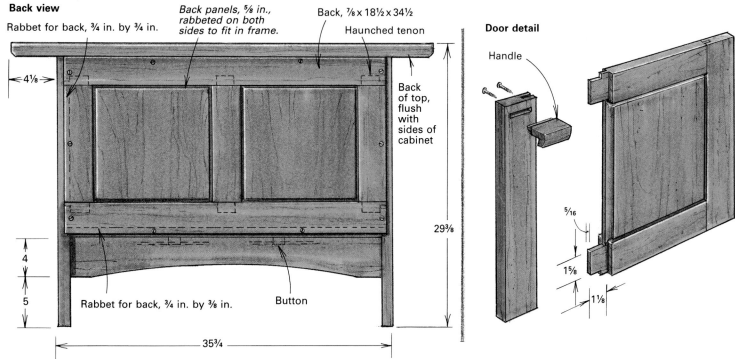

Rabbet for back, ¾ in. by ¾ in.

4⅛

Back panels, ⅝ in., rabbeted on both sides to fit in frame.

Back, ⅞ x 18½ x 34½

Haunched tenon

Back of top, flush with sides of cabinet

29⅜

4

5

Rabbet for back, ¾ in. by ⅜ in.

Button

35¾

Door detail

Handle

5/16

1⅝

1⅛

A temporary glue-up stick attaches over the dowels at the top to keep the sides from toeing in or out as glue dries.

lage, Vt. 05739; 802-293-5195) in my router. The Inca bit plunges deeper than a spiral-flute end-mill bit and leaves a cleaner mortise.

I began by carefully marking the mortise location, then clamping a scrap of poplar underneath to prevent tearout. Next, I ran the router fence along the edge of the wood and plunge-routed the mortise from the outside in three or four passes, bringing the bit to the marked edge of the mortise.

I cut the tenons on my tablesaw, first crosscutting the shoulders, then standing the piece on end in a tenoning jig to cut the cheeks. I filed the tenon cheeks round to match the radius of the mortises instead of chopping the mortises square to match the tenons. It's not necessary to match the radii exactly. The tenons will expand slightly to fill the mortises as you drive the wedges in. To accept the wedges, I handsawed two slots down each tenon to a depth of ¼ in. from the shoulders. I then drilled ¹⁄₁₆-in.-dia. holes in the bottom of each slot to prevent splitting and to permit the slot to open fully during wedging. To give contrast to the joint, I made rosewood wedges, 1 in. long, tapering down from about ³⁄₃₂ in. to a featheredge.

Next, I routed rabbets on the inside edges of the sides and on the bottom panel so I could fit the back. I cut the rabbet with a spiral end-mill bit and the same fence I used to rout the side mortises. Because the rabbet in the bottom panel goes all the way across, I routed it first. The rabbets in the sides are stopped flush with the rabbet in the bottom panel. Rather than measuring to locate the bottom of the rabbets in the sides, I assembled the sides to the stretchers and placed the rabbeted bottom panel in the carcase. Then, I marked a line on each side flush with the rabbet in the bottom panel. After disassembling the carcase, I routed the rabbets just short of the lines. To achieve the neatest joint where the rabbets met, I planned to wait until the carcase was glued to square up the ends of each rabbet with a chisel.

Before blind-dovetailing the stretcher, I reassembled and squared the carcase. I then measured between the two sides and added another 1½ in. to determine the total length of the stretcher. The extra 1½ in. is for ¾-in. dovetails at both ends. I ripped the stretcher 1½ in. wide, then crosscut it to length before cutting one full and one half dovetail pin at each end of the stretcher, as shown in the detail in figure 1. The purpose of the half-pin, of course, is to avoid undercutting the rabbet for the back. I cut the pins on my bandsaw, then marked matching sockets in the sides while holding the back of the stretcher flush with the back of each rabbet. I then sawed and chopped the waste from the sockets and test-fit the stretcher in place.

Next, I rested the bottom panel on the stretchers and lightly clamped the sides to be sure that the length of the bottom was correct. With all the parts lined up, I marked the edges of the bottom panel and the side. These marks would be the reference points for laying out the plate joints. With the case disassembled,

I used the standard 90° fence on my plate joiner to cut the kerfs in the ends of the bottom panel. To cut matching kerfs in the sides, I removed the stock fence from my plate joiner and used a board clamped to the case side as a fence.

These plate joints deserve careful layout and precise cutting, because the case bottom must align with the tops of the stretchers. If things don't work out exactly, there are two cures: You can plane down the tops of the stretchers, or you can reshape the tenons slightly so the wedges will drive the stretchers up.

If you don't have a plate joiner, substitute ¼-in. by ¾-in. wooden splines for the plates. Dry-assemble as above, then mark the location for the splines. After disassembly, clamp a straightedge on the side as a fence and rout a ¼-in.-wide by ⅜-in.-deep slot in the side, stopping 1 in. short of the front and back edges. Rout the other side, and then rout matching slots in the ends of the bottom panel.

The next step is to lay out and bandsaw the curves in the stretchers, sides and top. Drawing the gentle curves is easy when using spline weights and a spline. (For more information on splines, see the sidebar on the facing page.) These curves are not necessarily segments of a circle, but can be varied to complement the overall design. Along the same lines, I prefer not to use standard router-bit profiles when rounding edges. On the underside of the top, for example, although I began with a chamfering bit and pilot bearing, I finished the job with files, planes and scrapers. This allowed me to maintain the feeling of the top's curve in the edge profile. Before glue-up, I finish-sanded the pieces on my stroke sander.

Gluing up the cabinet—The final glue-up of a cabinet can be one of those all-at-once procedures where everything goes very right or very wrong. I planned to slow things down a bit by gluing the cabinet in two steps: first the sides, stretchers and bottom panel, with the top being applied only after the other parts had dried. Gluing up in two steps would not only let me check for square twice, it would also allow me enough time to apply glue carefully, thus reducing squeeze-out.

In order for step one to work, though, I had to come up with a way to keep the sides from toeing in or out at the top-front corners as the glue dried. As a solution, I fashioned a temporary glue-up stick to fasten between the sides (see the photo above, left). I drilled dowel holes in the sides to accommodate the top, then placed dowels in the first hole of each side. I then drilled holes in the glue-up stick at each end and slipped the stick over the two dowels. The holes in the stick must be carefully spaced to hold the sides square: If the holes are not far enough apart, the sides will toe in; if they're too far apart, they'll toe out.

When gluing up, it's important to drive the wedges into the through tenons before the glue sets. After the glue dries, remove the clamps and glue-up stick. Before going to step two of the glue-up, dowel holes must be drilled in the top. To mark the locations for the holes, place dowel centers in the holes in the sides. Locate the top on the centers so that it overlaps the corners at the front and the back equally. Press down hard enough for the centers to mark the top, then bore at each mark. After drilling the holes in the top, glue the dowels in place and clamp the top to the carcase.

Making the doors and back panel—You don't often see a cabinet with a frame-and-panel back anymore, but I decided to install a finished back for two reasons. First, it added versatility to the credenza. Having an attractive back means the piece can be used away from the wall. Second, since the credenza has no

Laying out curves

A lot of my furniture has curved edges, which lend a subtle simplicity to my designs. But drawing large, smooth curves can be difficult. I solved this problem when I learned about splines and spline weights architects often use. They are available from Charrette, 31 Olympia Ave., P.O. Box 4010, Woburn, Mass. 01888; (617) 935-6010 or (212) 683-8822 in New York.

The spline is nothing more than a 5/16-in.-wide strip of clear plastic. Spline weights are cast, felt-bottom weights with hooks in their ends to hold the spline. Pulling or pushing on the spline after each end is hooked in a spline weight bends the spline in a smooth arc, which can then be easily followed by a pencil.

Each spline weight costs about $14. Four splines are available in lengths of 23½ in., 35½ in., 47 in. and 59 in. They range in price from $3 to $7.

Because splining shallow curves requires very little bending, you can substitute a narrow strip of oak for the plastic spline. That's what I did to mark the credenza's top.

To lay out the curved edge in the front of the credenza, as I'm doing in

The author uses his spline weights and an oak spline to lay out the curve in the top front of the credenza.

the photo at left, I marked a line at midpoint along the front edge of the top. Next, I penciled marks ¾ in. back from the front edge on each side and placed the spline weights near those marks. I put each end of my oak spline under a spline-weight hook, placed a finger on the spline at the point where I had marked the center, and then pulled the spline to the edge. While doing this, I moved each spline weight so the ends of the spline lined up with the marks on each side. With everything aligned, I ran my pencil along the spline to transfer the curve to the top.

With minor variations, I used this same procedure to mark all the curves on the edges of the credenza. For instance, because I wanted the curves in the sides of the top to arc more heavily toward the front, I pulled the front spline weight back to tighten the radius in front and pushed the rear spline weight forward to open up the radius in the back. To make the tighter concave curve at the bottom of each side, I used a short plastic spline and pushed it away from the edge to form the arc.   *–J.M.*

---

drawers or shelves, you're likely to see the inside of the back when the doors are open, unless the credenza is chock-full.

The stile-and-rail frames for the doors and back are of standard haunched mortise-and-tenon construction. To raise the door panels, I sharply radiused the edges in the front of each panel with a ⅜-in.-radius cove bit in a router mounted in my tablesaw extension. I stood the panel vertically and guided it against the tablesaw fence. Because the edge was fairly thick, and my cuts were shallow, I didn't take the trouble to use an extra-high fence, which would have provided more support and made the work much safer and easier.

I also raised the backs of the door panels slightly. I set the tablesaw blade to 15° and again held the panel vertically against the fence. I made the panels in the back from ⅝-in. stock. Instead of raising these, I rabbeted the edges to create a centered tongue to fit the frame. After scraping and sanding, I gave each panel one coat of Watco oil, front and back, to keep it from adhering to its frame during glue-up.

Finishing the credenza—Because I sanded the carcase pieces on my stroke sander before glue-up, the only sanding left to do was on the frames of the doors and back. Machine-sanding certain components gives them a sanded-to-death look. I find this to be especially true of the frames surrounding raised panels, because there are so many lines that must remain parallel or square to each other. As such, I spent a lot of time scraping and hand-sanding the door frames to give them crisp, sharp lines.

Once that was done, I mortised the doors and sides for the brass butt hinges, made and installed door handles and fastened

the panel on the back with brass flat-head wood screws. To keep the doors closed, I installed simple magnetic catches to the underside of the top.

I agonized over where to put the door handles. If I mounted them at midpoint on the stiles, they would balance the look of the credenza but would obstruct the beautiful figure that continued across the door gap. I finally decided to tuck the handles up under the top where they would be unobtrusive and easy to reach without bending down. To make the handles, I roughed a long blank on my tablesaw, cut the handles to length, then smoothed the surfaces with files and block plane. In the past, I had simply mortised this sort of handle in place, but I found the tenons on the handles occasionally broke off. So, on this credenza, in addition to mortising the handles, I fastened them with screws from the back.

I never put less than three coats of oil on a piece I've made, but there are times when I apply many more: It all depends on how long the piece hangs around the shop. I apply the first coat of oil and let it dry for a few days. Between subsequent coats, I rub down the wood with 0000 steel wool. Before delivery, I apply a coat of Watco satin wax.

There's a secret advantage to using Watco oil and wax. Clients will be bound to call me some day complaining of a scratch, expecting me to drive to their home or office to make a repair. It's certainly easier to explain that they can not only do the repair themselves with products available at any hardware store, but they can also maintain the finish with ease. □

John McAlevey designs and builds furniture in Franklin, N.H.

Building a Nightstand
A small table with an oriental flair

by Gary Rogowski

A nightstand shouldn't be so plain that it puts you to sleep. I designed the cherry nightstand in the photo below as part of a bedroom set, but I think the resulting table stands alone quite nicely. The cloud-rise pattern on its rails along with the rosewood pull on the drawer give the nightstand a look reminiscent of Chinese furniture. The basic design can be adapted for an end table, but keep in mind that if you change proportions in one area, other dimensions will need to change as well.

Since it was designed as a nightstand, the first parameter for establishing dimensions was the 20-in. height of the bed's mattress, to which the stand would be a partner. I decided on a height of 23 in., and then proportioned the stand's width and depth to complement this height and allow enough space on top for a lamp, book and cup. The flaring legs add visual weight to the base of the nightstand, while the cloud-rise pattern on the rails softens this effect and lightens the load. The rails are inset from the legs to provide depth and shadow

Photo: Jim Piper

Although designed as a nightstand, this little cherry table would serve just as well as an end table alongside a couch or chair in any room in the house.

play, and the overhanging top is beveled to give the entire piece definition and a certain oriental grace. The rosewood drawer pull is the final touch and gives the stand its own personal character.

The nightstand is constructed following the same methods I use for larger cabinets or chests. The carcase frames are joined with haunched tenons in routed mortises and the panels that fill these frames are glued up from solid cherry. The bottom shelf and the nightstand's top, which are also solid wood, are mounted as shown in the drawing to allow for seasonal expansion and contraction. The drawer parts are all joined with sliding dovetails and the ¼-in. plywood bottom is slid into grooves in the sides and front and screwed to the bottom of the drawer's back. Although simple in design, the nightstand is a challenge to build because of its joinery and details.

Joining the carcase – The nightstand requires about 4 bd. ft. of ⁸⁄₄ cherry for the legs and about 18 bd. ft. of ⁴⁄₄ cherry for everything else including the drawer parts. I mill the parts for the entire piece about ⅛ in. oversize and let them sit for about a week in the shop, so they can warp or cup if they're going to, before final dimensioning. The 1½-in. by 2¼-in. legs are then milled and crosscut to length, and all the mortises and panel grooves are routed in them before the outside face is tapered. Similarly, the rails are milled to size and the tenons tablesawn on their ends before the cloud-rise pattern is bandsawn. The top rails, drawer glide rails and side panels can be milled now as well. The panels are only ⅜ in. thick, so I resaw them from full ⁴⁄₄ stock and sticker them so the interior and exterior moisture contents can equalize for a few days before I glue up the book-matched boards. The nightstand's ¾-in. top and its bottom shelf can be glued up somewhat oversize at this time.

I use a plunge router with a ⅜-in.-dia. bit to cut all the mortises, and then chisel the ends of the mortises square to accept the square tenons. You could round the tenons to fit the radius of the router bit instead, but on a joint this small I figure the more gluing surface the better. The mortises should be about ¹⁄₁₆-in. deeper than the tenons to ensure the tenons don't bottom out and to provide space for excess glue. When the mortises are complete, cut the tenons on the ends of the rails on the tablesaw. First, cut the shoulders with the rail flat on the table and the miter gauge set to 90°. Then, make a simple tenoning jig to hold the rail vertically as you run it along the rip fence and trim the tenons to fit the mortises. Finally, bandsaw the tenon to create the haunch. I'm partial to haunched tenons because the haunch allows the tenon to run full width to resist twisting, while the main portion of the tenon can extend deeply into the leg or stile without weakening this member.

The top rails above the drawer in the front and back of the

From *Fine Woodworking* magazine (January 1990) 80:88-91

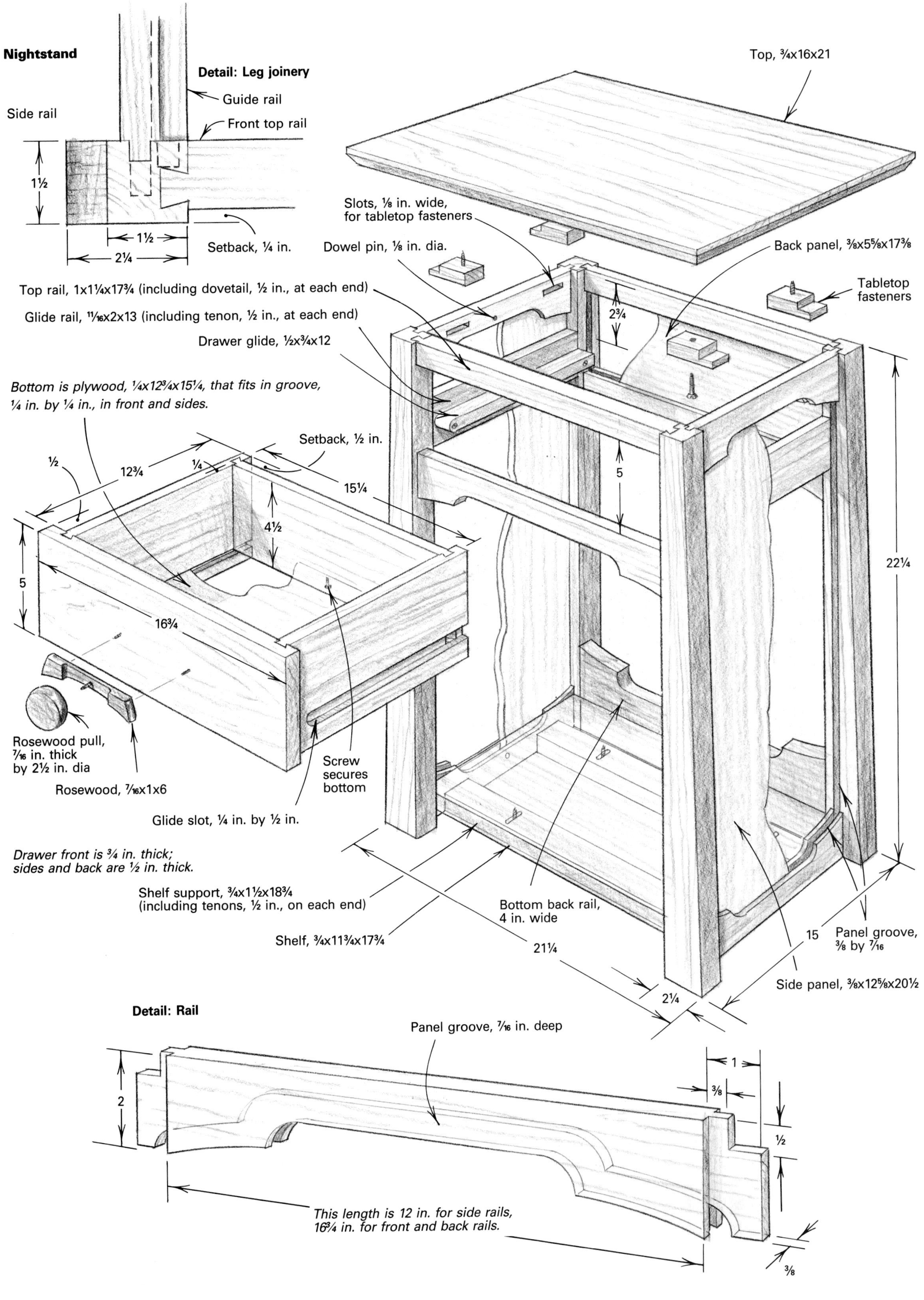
Nightstand
Detail: Leg joinery
Guide rail
Side rail
Front top rail
1½
1½
2¼
Setback, ¼ in.
Top, ¾x16x21
Slots, ⅛ in. wide, for tabletop fasteners
Dowel pin, ⅛ in. dia.
Back panel, ⅜x5⅝x17⅜
Tabletop fasteners
Top rail, 1x1¼x17¾ (including dovetail, ½ in., at each end)
Glide rail, 11⁄16x2x13 (including tenon, ½ in., at each end)
Drawer glide, ½x¾x12
2¾
Bottom is plywood, ¼x12¾x15¼, that fits in groove, ¼ in. by ¼ in., in front and sides.
Setback, ½ in.
½
12¾
¼
15¼
4½
5
5
16¾
22¼
Rosewood pull, 7⁄16 in. thick by 2½ in. dia
Rosewood, 7⁄16x1x6
Screw secures bottom
Glide slot, ¼ in. by ½ in.
Drawer front is ¾ in. thick; sides and back are ½ in. thick.
Shelf support, ¾x1½x18¾ (including tenons, ½ in., on each end)
Shelf, ¾x11¾x17¾
Bottom back rail, 4 in. wide
21¼
2¼
15
Panel groove, ⅜ by 7⁄16
Side panel, ⅜x12⅝x20½
Detail: Rail
Panel groove, 7⁄16 in. deep
2
1
⅜
½
⅜
This length is 12 in. for side rails, 16¾ in. for front and back rails.

Drawing: Roland Wolf

With the side frame clamped to the workbench, Rogowski routs the panel groove with a bearing-guided slotting bit. A ½-in.-thick board is laid atop the shaped rail to fill the setback between the inside surfaces of the rail and leg, providing a consistent surface for the router base.

nightstand are dovetailed into the top of the legs. I cut these dove-tail-shape mortises and tenons with a dovetail bit on my router table. The mortises are cut first, and then the fence is moved over so it exposes only a small portion of the bit to cut the tenon on the ends of the top rails (see the top and center photos on the facing page showing drawer construction).

When all the mortises and tenons are cut, dry-assemble the frame to check for fit and to see that the tenon shoulders pull up tightly. Disassemble the parts and fine-tune the tenons if necessary. At this time you can also shape the rails. Because the same cloud-rise pattern is repeated at the end of each rail throughout the piece, I make a full-size template from ¼-in.-thick Masonite and use it to draw the shape on the rails. I bandsaw just outside this line, attach the template to each rail with double-stick tape and trim to the template with a flush-trim bit on my router table. I stop just short of the end of the curves to prevent tearout and finish up with very light cuts with the router. Clean up the final shape and remove the router marks with a spokeshave or file and then sand the curves smooth.

Next, dry-assemble the legs and the shaped side rails to form the side frames. However, leave out the drawer glide rails because they'll be in the way as you rout the panel groove on the internal edges of the frames. Clamp the frame to the workbench and use a ¼-in. slotting bit to cut a ⁷⁄₁₆-in.-deep groove centered in the edge of the rails. The bearing of the slotting bit follows the curve of the rails but you'll need to place a ½-in.-thick board on the rails, as shown in the photo above, to bring the rail's surface flush with the legs. The panel is ⅜ in. thick, so I reset the bit's depth and make two passes to cut a ⅜-in.-wide groove. Repeat this procedure to rout the groove on the back legs and rails for the small back panel that covers the drawer opening. After the panel grooves are cut, disassemble the frames and draw the taper on the out-side surface of each leg. Then, bandsaw close to the line and clean up the face on the jointer.

Making the panels and gluing up the carcase—Now, turn your attention to the panels. Glue up the side panels and cut them and the back panel at least 1 in. longer and wider than the inside di-mensions of their respective frames. After the glue is dry, plane the panels ⅜ in. thick. Then, lay the appropriate frame on its panel and

trace around the inside edge of the frame to define the panel's shape. Add ⁵⁄₁₆ in. around the entire perimeter of this line so the panel will fit into the groove, and then bandsaw the panels to size. I check the fit of the panels in the grooves and handplane the panels to fit snugly. Then, I finish-sand them and apply the first of three coats of a mixture of equal parts Danish oil and polyure-thane varnish. I wait a day in between coats and finish both sides of the panels the same. Prefinishing the panels ensures that no unfinished wood peeks free of the frame if the panel shrinks dur-ing an especially dry season. It's also much easier to wipe on and rub out the finish before assembly.

After the third coat of finish on the panels is dry, you're ready to assemble the side frames. Use just a little glue on the tenons to prevent excess squeeze-out onto the legs or panels, and brush a more liberal coat of glue into the mortises, especially at the mouth of the joint. Don't forget to glue in the drawer glide rails. After the frame is glued up and clamped, check to see that it's flat and hasn't been twisted out of shape by clamping pressure. When the frame is dry, pin the panels in place with ⅛-in.-dia. dowels drilled from the inside of the top and bottom rails and centered in the middle of the panel (see the drawing on the previous page). These dowels keep the panels centered and prevent them from rattling too much if they shrink in dry weather.

The front and back rails can now be glued into the side frames to form the carcase. In order to simplify the glue-up as much as possible, set aside the dovetailed top rails and back panel. It's not necessary to glue these parts in place at this time because the pan-el can be slid in place and the rails glued into their mortises after the rest of the carcase is glued up. I get the clamps ready, one for each of the rails that I'm gluing in place, plus a couple extra to square up the clamped-up carcase if necessary. Because it's diffi-cult to clamp to the tapered legs, bandsaw angled clamping blocks and tape them to the tapered surfaces so the clamps won't slip.

Lay one of the side panels flat on the workbench with the mor-tises up, and glue the front and back rails that are below the drawer, the back bottom rail and the shelf support rails into their mortises. Then, with the other side panel laying on the bench with its mortises up, spread glue and fit all the tenons of the five rails into their mor-tises, and force the joints home with bar or pipe clamps. Then, place the nightstand upright on a reliably flat surface and, if all four legs don't make contact, clamp diagonally across the front and back of the carcase frame to square them up. Test-fit the top rails into the dove-tail mortises to see that the carcase hasn't been distorted out of square in the horizontal plane by uneven clamping pressure. Now, you can insert the back panel and glue in the top rails.

With the base of the stand assembled, the top of the stand and the bottom shelf can be ripped and crosscut to size. I rout slots in the upper side rails with a ⅛-in. slotting bit for the tabletop fasten-ers that hold the solid top in place. The bit's depth must be set properly so the fasteners will hold without too much strain or slop, so I first cut a practice piece to check this setting. I bevel the edges of the top, as shown in the drawing, and then I apply three coats of my oil/varnish mix to the glued-up carcase frame and to the top and the bottom shelf. When the finish dries, I fasten the top and the bottom shelf in place.

Constructing the drawer—One of the nice things about using sliding dovetails to join the drawer sides to the front, is that I can use the same setups to join the back of the drawer to the sides. The secret to a good-fitting sliding dovetail is accurately milling the parts. The drawer sides and back must all be the same thick-ness and their ends and edges must be square with the planed faces. I use a ¾-in.-thick front with ½-in.-thick sides and back. Rip the drawer parts $\frac{1}{16}$ in. over their finished width so any chip out resulting from routing the dovetails can be jointed smooth. Crosscut the back a little long so you can cut it to fit after you've routed its mortises in the sides. Before routing, carefully hand-sand all surfaces with a sanding block because surface-sanding the mortised parts after routing them will spoil the fit of the dovetails' shoulders.

The top and center photos at right show the two setups for routing the mating parts. Before routing the dovetail mortises, I like to rout or dado $\frac{1}{4}$-in.-wide slots centered where the mortises will be so the dovetail bit doesn't have to remove so much wood in a single pass. Then I rout the mortises with the fence set for a $\frac{1}{2}$-in. setback. I hold a scrap block in front of and behind the drawer part to reduce the possibility of the bit tearing out the edge as it enters or exits the cut.

After cutting the mortises, unclamp one end of the fence and move it into the spinning bit so it cuts into the fence. When only a small portion of the side of the bit is exposed, as shown in the center photo at right, reclamp the fence. I've found that I get the best fit by lowering the bit just a hair when I cut the tenons. However, to avoid a chance of lowering the bit too much and losing all reference to the original height, you can use a thin paper shim under the ends of the workpieces as you cut the male portion of the dovetails. To set the fence for a snug-fitting dovetail, make a test pass on both sides of an off-cut from the drawer sides that has been sanded to the same thickness as the drawer parts. The test dovetail should slide into the mortise without excessive pressure, but without any slop. When you've got the fit just right, cut the tails on the front ends of the sides, and then slide them into the mortises in the drawer front and measure between the sides to get an exact measurement for the length of the back. Trim the back to length and rout the tails on both ends. Now, joint the edges of the parts to remove sawmarks or chip out, and rout the grooves for the drawer glides in the sides. Finally, rout the bottom grooves in the sides and front, and rip the back piece narrow enough that the bottom will slide beneath it.

I shellac my drawer parts on all sides, except the drawer face, before gluing them together, taking care not to get any finish into the joints. Shellac is a quick finish to apply and by adding a few drops of your favorite scent, the drawer will smell much sweeter than an oil-finished drawer. The outer face of the drawer front is finished with the same oil and varnish mixture used on the rest of the nightstand.

When gluing up the drawer, spread glue only in the mortises to avoid excessive squeeze-out. Begin by gluing the sides into the front one at a time with the drawer front standing right-side up near the edge of the bench, as shown in the bottom photo at right. Start the dovetail into the mortise and then press it home with a bar clamp spanning from beneath the bench to the top of the drawer side. Keep the side moving once you start or it will freeze up and you'll need a great deal of force to break it free. Have a piece of $\frac{1}{4}$-in. plywood handy to check the alignment of the bottom grooves. When both sides are in place, turn the drawer around and clamp the back into the side mortises. Then, slide the bottom into the side grooves and screw it to the bottom of the back.

The two drawer glides are screwed to the drawer glide rail, as shown in the drawing on p. 119. The glides must be about $\frac{3}{4}$ in. wide to span the $\frac{1}{2}$-in. setback between the rails and the drawer sides, plus extend into the $\frac{1}{4}$-in.-deep grooves in the drawer sides. To install the glides, predrill and countersink screw holes in them and then, with the glides in the side grooves, slide the drawer into the carcase. Pull the drawer out little by little while holding the back end of the glide against the drawer glide rail from below, and screw the glides to the rails as you go. Then, wax the glides and grooves for a smooth, sliding action.

I always save designing my drawer pulls for last because I like to

In the photo above, the author cuts the dovetail mortise on the drawer front. He holds a scrap block against the workpiece to prevent chip out and as he proceeds through the cut, he moves the scrap to the back edge. A $\frac{1}{4}$-in.-deep groove, visible on the free end of the workpiece, is cut to remove most of the waste from the mortises prior to a single pass with the dovetail bit. In the photo below, the dovetail tenon on a drawer side is being cut. The fence has been moved to cover most of the bit, leaving just enough of it exposed to result in the right size tail after making a pass on each side of the workpiece.

The sliding dovetails on the drawer sides are pressed into the mortises in the drawer front with a clamp, as shown above. Then, the drawer is reversed and the back is pressed into the side mortises.

see the completed piece from all directions and play with a number of options. I make models in cardboard or alder and paint them black, to provide contrast, and then try them on the drawer face until I find a design that is complementary to the piece and easy to handle. The drawer pull for the nightstand is made of rosewood and screwed to the drawer face from inside the drawer with brass oval-head screws and finish washers. ☐

Gary Rogowski designs and builds furniture in Portland, Ore. This summer he will be teaching a course on stool building at Anderson Ranch Arts Center, Box 5598, Snowmass Village, Colo. 81615; (303) 923-3181.

Blanket Chest

Dovetails and wooden hinge are easier than they look

by John Dunham

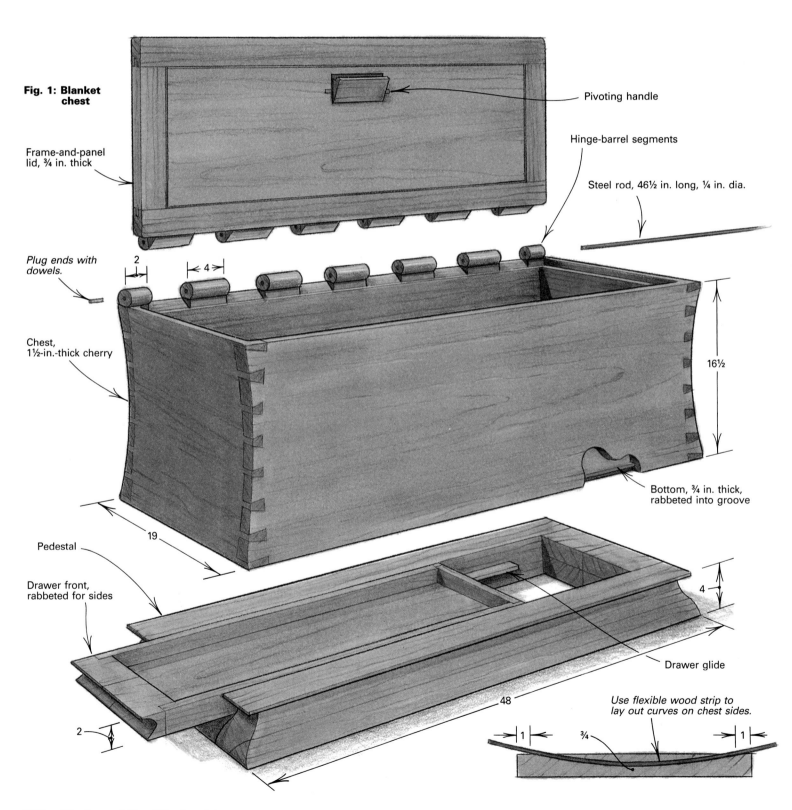

Fig. 1: Blanket chest

Pivoting handle

Hinge-barrel segments

Steel rod, 46½ in. long, ¼ in. dia.

Frame-and-panel lid, ¾ in. thick

Plug ends with dowels.

2

4

Chest, 1½-in.-thick cherry

16½

Bottom, ¾ in. thick, rabbeted into groove

19

Pedestal

Drawer front, rabbeted for sides

Drawer glide

4

2

48

Use flexible wood strip to lay out curves on chest sides.

1   ¾   1

From *Fine Woodworking* magazine (March 1989) 75:48-51

When people see my blanket chest, the first thing they notice is the curved sides, which appear to require some especially complicated dovetails. Next they notice the hinge and wonder if a metal hinge can really be replaced by wood. When they try to test it, they can't find the handle. If they're bold, they reach for the rectangular cutout in the lid and are startled when a handle pops up at the touch of a finger. They are usually so caught up in these obvious details that they miss what I think is the real surprise: the drawer hidden in the base.

I designed the chest pictured at right nearly 20 years ago when I was a graduate student in furniture design at Virginia Commonwealth University in Richmond. It remained one of a kind for a long time, but in the last few years, I've built several on commission. In the process, I've worked out a way to rough out the curves on the sides quickly by running them perpendicularly across a tablesaw molding head. And, I've learned to cut the dovetails after the curves are roughed out, to avoid chipping them out when I cut cross-grain with the molding head. By reproducing the chest, I've been able to streamline the hinge construction so it is simple and straightforward.

I've seen a lot of wooden hinges, both at craft shows and in the pages of *Fine Woodworking*. Most of them, although clever, are difficult to make, requiring intricate router jigs; or, they are bulky, somewhat fragile fittings out of scale with the box or piece of furniture they're attached to. This wooden version of a piano hinge, however, is strong, easy to build and designed as an integral part of the chest. The 13 turned hinge segments are alternately glued onto the back frame piece of the frame-and-panel lid and the back edge of the chest after these two overlapping parts have been notched to mesh with each other. I use a ¼-in.-dia. steel rod for a hinge pin instead of a long dowel, to eliminate the squeak of wood against wood.

It's the combination of these features that challenge the builder and ultimately please the owner of this blanket chest. If you decide to tackle this project, you'll need about 52 bd. ft. of 8/4 cherry for the chest, base and hinge, and 8 bd. ft. of ¾-in. stock for the lid.

The chest—Begin by gluing up about 36 bd. ft. of the 8/4 cherry for the front, back and sides, then plane these parts to 1½ in. thick. The front and back will finish up 48 in. by 16½ in.; the two sides, 19 in. by 16½ in. To lay out the curves on the outside surfaces, draw a symmetrical arch on the endgrain of one of the side pieces by bending a thin strip of wood across it and drawing along its arch, as shown in figure 1 on the facing page. The curve should begin about 1 in. from each edge and peak in the middle at just under ¾ in. The 1 in. at the ends allows room for final shaping to achieve a continuous curve from top to bottom.

You could cove the sides by running them diagonally across a regular sawblade, taking small cuts and raising the blade until you've removed most of the waste. However, my molding-head method, shown in the lower photo this page, speeds up the process considerably. To make the cove cut, I clamp a wooden fence to the saw table 8¼ in. from the center of the arbor and perpendicular to the blade. I replace the blade with a three-cutter molding head with ½-in.-radius cutters and set the blade to take only a ¼-in.-deep cut. I run an edge of each of the pieces against the fence so they go over the spinning cutterhead perpendicular to it. Then I flip the pieces around and run them through again, with the opposite edge on the fence. I raise the cutter and repeat the process until I've cut an arch within ⅓₂ in. of the line. I move the fence about ½ in. farther from the cutter, lower the cutter so it takes only a ¼-in.-deep cut and repeat the process at the new fence setting. I keep moving the fence and adjusting the cutter until the curve is roughed out. The rotation of the molding head helps keep the work against the clamped fence, and the sharpened arch of the cutters allows easy crossfeeding. As with any power-tool operation, *think safety*. Make sure your hands are well away from the cutter, and don't force too deep a cut in a single pass: I recommend a maximum ¼ in. per pass. I smooth the slightly fluted surface of the roughed-out curves with a round-bottom plane before assembling the chest.

The dovetails look tricky because of the curved sides. Actually they're regular dovetails, but they can only be laid out on the flat insides of the parts. First, lay out the pins on the inside surface of the ends. I use a 9° angle for the five pins with a half pin at each end. Saw them out with a handsaw or bandsaw as you normally would. To prevent chipping when chiseling out the waste, I back up the curved side with a soft woodblock bandsawn to match the curve. The tails are scribed from the pins onto the inside of the sides and cut in the same manner. When they've been fitted so all four sides pull tightly together, dry-clamp the chest and mark the pins and tails where they extend past the curves of the adjacent side. Take the chest apart and trim these ends on the bandsaw. At this time, dado each of the four carcase pieces for the bottom, ⅜ in. wide, ½ in. deep and ⅜ in. from the bottom edge, with a router or tablesaw. Stop the dadoes about ¾ in. from each end, or they'll show on the outside of the completed chest. The ¾-in. plywood bottom is rabbeted all around its bottom surface so it fits into the dado. Then the chest is glued up.

Because the lid is a flush fit, you'll need to cut a ¾-in.-deep rabbet around the inside of the chest's top edge. The rabbet is ¾ in.

Photo: Anthony Cosentino

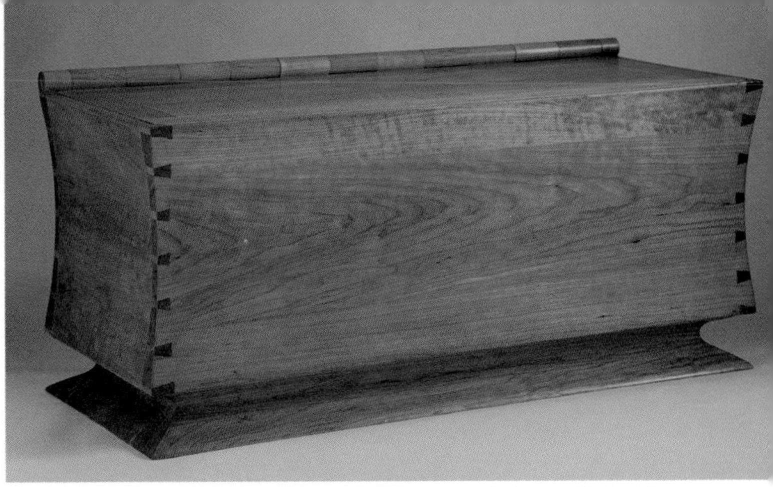

This cherry blanket chest features curved and dovetailed sides, a wood piano hinge, a pivoting flush handle and a drawer hidden in the deeply coved pedestal base.

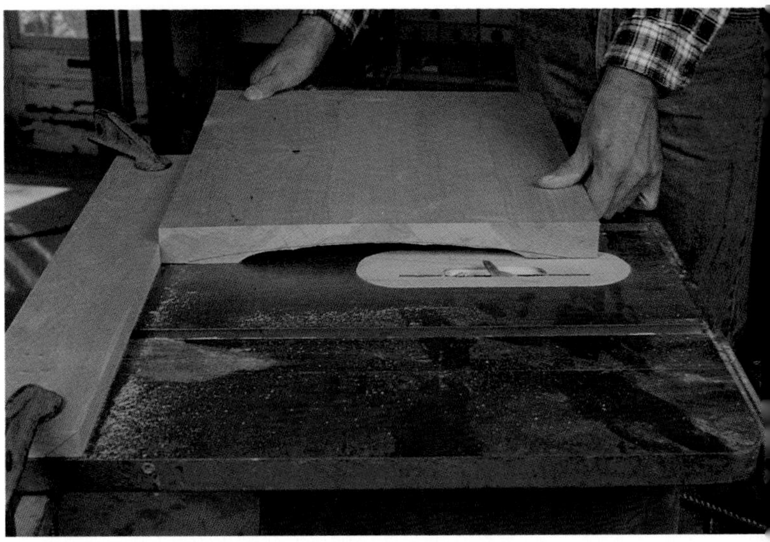

Dunham speedily roughs out the curved sides by running the work perpendicularly across a molding head fitted with ½-in.-radius cutters. To remove the waste up to his layout line, he adjusts the cutter height and the clamped fence, and runs opposite edges of the piece against the fence.

Drawings: Kathleen Creston

Fig. 2: Pivoting handle

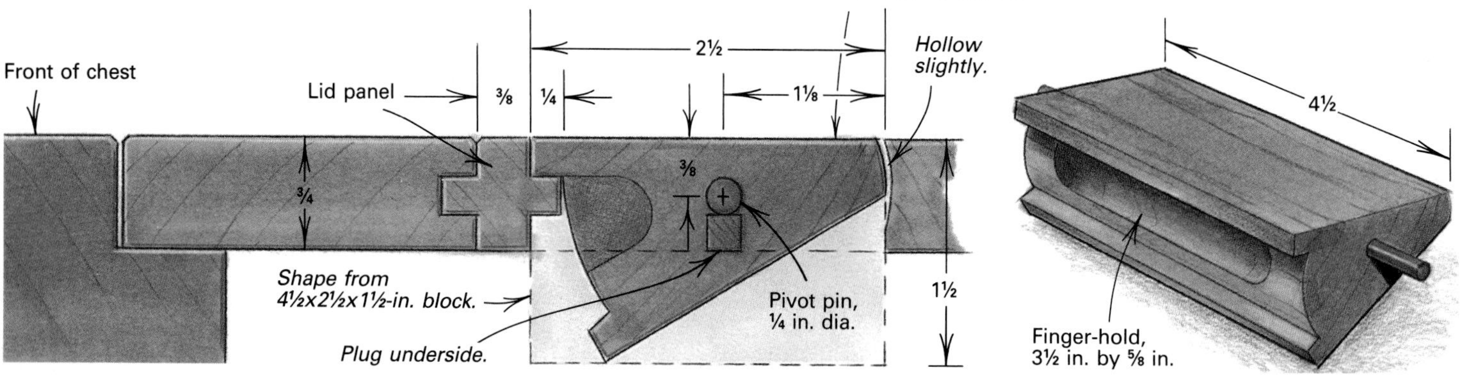
Press here to pivot handle.
Front of chest
Lid panel
3/8
1/4
2½
1⅛
Hollow slightly.
3/8
3/4
Shape from 4½x2½x1½-in. block.
Plug underside.
Pivot pin, ¼ in. dia.
1½
4½
Finger-hold, 3½ in. by ⅝ in.

Fig. 3: Notches for hinge

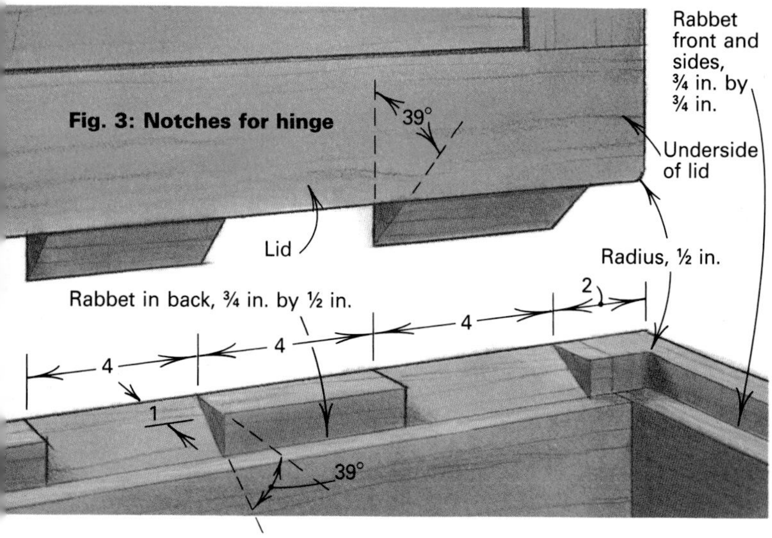
Rabbet front and sides, ¾ in. by ¾ in.
39°
Underside of lid
Lid
Radius, ½ in.
Rabbet in back, ¾ in. by ½ in.
2
4
4
4
1
39°

by ¾ in. on the front and ends, but it's only ½ in. wide along the back, to accommodate the hinge. I cut the rabbet in several passes with a ½-in.-dia. straight, carbide router bit and a fence clamped to the base of the router that runs along the outside of the chest. I stop the rabbet when I get close to the corners. After all the straight runs are done, I take the fence off the base and remove most of the waste left in the corners freehand with the router. I use a gouge to clean out these corners to a smooth ½-in. radius. Sanding completes the chest. I prefer to sand by hand: It's quieter, and besides, these curved surfaces don't match platens of any electric sanders I know of. I begin with 60-grit sandpaper that has a heavy-duty cloth backing and sand to 120 grit. Later, when I apply the oil finish, I wet-sand with 220 grit.

The chest's frame-and-panel lid is made from ¾-in.-thick solid stock. The frame parts are 2½ in. wide, joined with mortises and ¾-in.-long tenons that I cut on the tablesaw. The ¾-in.-thick solid panel is rabbeted from both sides on the tablesaw to leave a tongue that fits into grooves in the frame. Because the back frame piece gets notched to become part of the hinge, it and the front piece run full length, with the side pieces fitting between them. Size the parts so the assembled lid will fit into the rabbet in the top of the carcase, with its back edge extending flush with the *outside* of the carcase back. However, don't glue the lid together until the hinge is completed, because the hinge work is so much easier when the frame is apart. Round the front corners of the frame to fit into the ½-in. radius of the chest's rabbet, then dry-clamp the lid together and check its fit on the chest. Take the lid apart to install the handle in the panel and to do the hinge work.

Figure 2, above, shows how the wedge-shape, pivoting handle fits into the cutout in the lid's panel. It's best to make the cutout first and fit the handle to it. Begin by drawing a 2¼-in. by 4½-in. rectangle, centered lengthwise and ⅝ in. from the panel's front edge. Drill a hole in one corner of this rectangle and insert a saber or coping sawblade to saw the rectangle out. With a block clamped to your router base as a fence, cut a ¼-in. by ¼-in. rabbet along the front edge of the cutout on both sides of the panel to create a lip that acts as a stop for the handle in both its open and closed positions. Hollow out the back surface of the rectangular cutout with a gouge to allow clearance for the handle to pivot.

The handle is made as shown in figure 2. Cut out the basic wedge shape on the tablesaw, but leave the piece long so it's easier and safer to handle when making the finger hole. Hollow out the finger hole ⅝ in. deep by drilling a series of holes with a ⅝-in.-dia. Forstner bit and cleaning up the bottom with a gouge or on a router table with a ⅝-in.-dia. core-box bit. Crosscut the handle to length, and drill through the handle for a ¼-in.-dia. steel pivot pin. Chisel two slots, ½ in. by ¼ in., in the bottom of the lid panel to receive the pin. Sand the handle until it fits snugly but pivots easily, then set it aside. The handle isn't installed until after the lid is glued up and both the handle and the lid are finish-sanded. Then, you'll plug the pivot slots by gluing in wooden blocks trimmed for a snug fit.

The hinge—Now you're ready to bevel and notch the chest's back edge and the lid's back frame piece so they will mesh and swing past each other, making the hinge. On the top back edge of the carcase, lay out for the 4-in. hinge segments, starting and ending with 2-in. lengths. Draw a line with a combination square across the top edge and down to the bottom of the rabbet. Saw and chisel out every other segment, beginning with the first 4-in. segment on each end, to leave a flat angled surface from the top outside edge to the bottom of the rabbet (see figure 3, this page). Make the initial cuts with a dovetail saw on the waste side of the lines, stopping short of sawing into the rabbet's base or into the chest's outside surface. Then, chisel out the waste between the sawcuts.

Next, you will notch the back frame piece to mesh with the notches you just cut in the chest. First, measure in 1 in. from the bottom back edge of the frame piece, and mark this point on one end. Draw an angled line on this end from the 1-in. mark to the top, back corner. The angle will be about 39°, the same as you chiseled on the back edge of the chest. Tilt the tablesaw blade to cut this angle. Because most tablesaws don't tilt past 45°, set the tilt angle at 39° from the vertical and run the frame piece edge down and with its surface flat against the fence. Rip this angle the length of the piece, then hold the frame piece against the notched back edge of the chest and mark it for the coinciding notches. Fxtend the marks across the angled surface with a square, and saw out alternate segments. I crosscut to the lines with the tablesaw blade set to cut 1 in. deep by holding the frame piece on edge and running it over the blade using the miter gauge. Then, I bandsaw out the notches and pare them clean with a chisel. After you round the frame piece's notched ends to match the radius of the rabbet's corners, it should drop into the rabbet, flush with the chest's top, its notches meshing with those on the chest back, as shown in figure 3.

To make the barrel of the hinge, begin with 13 1¾-in. by 1¾-in. blocks that are slightly less than 4 in. long. Crosscut two of the blocks 2 in. long for the ends. Make sure all end cuts are square, and use a stop block to ensure uniform length. Mark the center on one end of each block, and after checking your drill-press table to be sure it's square with the bit, bore a ¼-in.-dia. hole through each block. To mount the blocks on the lathe, I replace the point of the spur center with a short piece of ¼-in.-dia. metal rod, which fits into the hole in the blocks, and use a cone-bearing center in the tailstock, which centers itself in the holes. The blocks are turned to 1½-in.-dia. cylinders. Lock your calipers at 1½ in. and make sizing cuts with a parting tool at both ends and at the center of each block. Then remove the waste between these cuts with a large gouge. After turning, the holes in the blocks are reamed out to ⁹⁄₃₂ in. and the cylinders are strung on a ¼-in.-dia. steel rod that is approximately 50 in. long with threaded ends. Arrange the cylinders in the order you want them on the chest, with a 2-in. segment at each end, and clamp them with a washer and nut on each end. I line up the segments as closely as possible and sand the whole hinge barrel smooth. This segmented dowel can now be run across the joiner as if it were one piece of wood until you've got a flat area 1 in. wide. I number the cylinders on this flat side before I remove them from the rod so I can reassemble them on the chest in the same order.

Now you're ready to glue the hinge-barrel segments to the lid frame. To aid in clamping these segments, clamp a 1-in. by 4-in. board to the underside of the frame piece so it extends out over the 39° angle, as shown in the photo this page. Then dry-clamp one of the 2-in. segments at one end. Start at the other end and glue and clamp the numbered hinge segments to the frame piece. Line them up with the frame's back edge, and align them by sighting through their holes. Use the sequentially numbered segments to test for the proper spacing between the segments you are gluing. When you reach the end, unclamp the dry-clamped 2-in. segment and glue it in place. You can test the alignment by running the rod through the segments, but I've found the eyeball method works every time.

After the glue for the hinge segments dries, glue up the frame-and-panel lid. Clamp to the flat, notched areas, not to the hinge segments. When the lid is unclamped, position it on the chest, and once again, sight through the holes as you glue the remaining hinge segments to the chest. Clamp these hinge segments to the back of the chest with pipe clamps. Remove the lid while the glue dries, and chip off any glue squeeze-out between the segments. When the glue has thoroughly dried, replace the lid and slide a 46½-in.-long, ¼-in.-dia. steel rod through the hinge barrel. The first time you operate the assembled hinge, do so cautiously. Minor adjustments to the angled notches are usually necessary. Note anywhere that they don't swing smoothly past each other; remove the hinge pin and file or sand the offending parts. When the hinge operates smoothly, open and close it a few times. If any of the hinge segments are rubbing end to end, you will see a polished area on their endgrain when you take the hinge apart again. Fix these with a sanding block. When these adjustments have been made, trap the metal hinge pin by gluing short sections of doweling in each end.

The base—I laminate the pedestal from 2-in.-thick stock. The long sides are each glued up from two pieces of 2x4x48-in. stock, and the end pieces are glued up between the sides so the endgrain continues across the whole end of the base. One of the ends is

The author aligns the hinge segments by sighting through their holes while gluing them to the lid frame. The 1x4 clamped to the frame piece extends over the notched and angled edge to aid in clamping the hinge segments.

Fig. 4: Pedestal

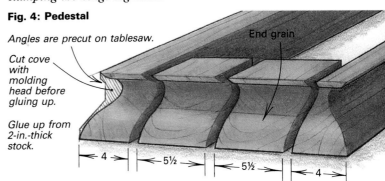

Angles are precut on tablesaw.

Cut cove with molding head before gluing up.

Glue up from 2-in.-thick stock.

End grain

← 4 → | ← 5½ → | ← 5½ → | ← 4 →

Bandsaw end blocks to profile before glue-up.

split horizontally for the front of the hidden drawer. Before laminating the long sides, preshape the profile as much as possible on the tablesaw, as shown in figure 4, above. For the end without the drawer front, glue up two blocks 5½ in. long by 4 in. wide. These two blocks get glued together side to side when the whole base is assembled, but first I mark the profile of the cove on their ends and saw this curve out on the bandsaw. The end with the drawer front is made up of four pieces of 2-in.-thick stock: two 5½ in. wide by 4 in. long for the drawer front and two 5½ in. wide by 5 in. long for the base. These four pieces are bandsawn to the cove's profile, and the drawer-front parts are glued together. Before gluing up the base parts, plow a ⅜-in. by ⅜-in. dado on the inside of the two long pieces, as shown in figure 4, to insert glides for the hidden drawer.

The pedestal can now be glued up and the ⅜-in. by 1-in. drawer glides glued in. To be sure the base is flat, I clamp the long pieces to my tablesaw while gluing the base together. I do as much cleanup as possible on the cove with curved-bottom molding planes, then I scrape and hand-sand to 120 grit. The carcase is secured to the base with screws from the inside of the carcase bottom.

The drawer front is rabbeted so the drawer sides can be glued on flush to its sides (see figure 1 on p. 122). Rabbet or dado the drawer back into the sides, and groove the drawer parts for the ¼-in. plywood bottom. Finally, carve a finger grip in the underside of the curve in the drawer front and slide the drawer into the base. All that's left is to install the pivoting handle in the chest's lid, plug the pivot pin slots and sand the plugs flush.

The chest is now ready for finishing. I use a minimum of three coats of Watco Danish oil, wet-sanding the first coat with 220-grit wet-or-dry sandpaper. I often leave the inside unfinished to avoid trapping the smell of the oil. You could also line the inside of the chest with thin, aromatic cedar paneling—adding one more surprise. □

John Dunham builds custom furniture in Glens Falls, N.Y.

Index